Obama vs. McCain

Voting Records

of

Barack Obama

&

John McCain

for

the 109th and 110th Congress

Obama vs. McCain

Voting Records

of

Barack Obama

&

John McCain

for

the 109th and 110th Congress

MANOR
Rockville, Maryland
2008

324973

ISBN: 978-1-60450-249-7

Information and illustrations (including photographs of Senators Obama and Mc-Cain) contained in this book has been released to the public by various US agencies and departments including the US Congress and the Library of Congress Archives. Arc Manor, LLC is not associated with the any of these US agencies or any other agency of the US Federal Government. Arc Manor has compiled the information contained in this book through many means which include (but are not limited to) US Government documents and web-sites and other information released through the Freedom of Information Act (FOIA) and otherwise made public by relevant federal departments/agencies.

Published by Arc Manor
P. O. Box 10339
Rockville, MD 20849-0339
www.ArcManor.com
Printed in the United States of America/United Kingdom

A Note From the Publisher

Due to the length of many legislative pieces considered by the Senate, this book only gives a brief official summary of each vote considered. However, many readers may be interested in obtaining the details of particular pieces of legislation mentioned in the book. They may do so on the internet by following these directions:

Go to:

http://www.senate.gov

Select *Legislation & Records* (red menu bar near top of page)

Then select *Votes* (blue navigation bar on left of page)

Click on the relevant Session (list near the bottom of page, Sessions listed by year, reverse chronological order).

Click on *'Vote' number* in table to see how all the Senators voted.

Click on *'Issue' number* in table to see details on the legislation (clicking will take you to an expanded menu where you can select, among other items, the complete text of the legislation.

Please note that these instructions are current as of June 2008 and may change. However, even if the Senate makes changes to how it displays this information, the Senate's official web site (www.senate.gov) will give directions on how to retrieve relevant information.

Voting Records of

BARACK OBAMA & JOHN MCCAIN

CONTENTS

The Voting Records

of

BARACK OBAMA

&

JOHN MCCAIN

for

the 109th and 110th Congress

THE 109TH CONGRESS

1ST SESSION

VOTE No.	SES- SION	DATE	VOTE QUESTION Description	RESULT	OBAMA'S POSTION	MCCAIN'S POSTION
1	1	1/06/05	On the Objection (Shall Objection Submitted Be Sustained Re: Electoral Ballot Count)	Objection Not Sustained (1-74)	Nay	Not Voting
2	1	1/26/05	On the Nomination PN8 Condoleezza Rice, of California, to be Secretary of State	Nomination Confirmed (85-13)	Yea	Yea
3	1	2/03/05	On the Nomination PN12 Alberto R. Gonzales, of Texas, to be Attorney General	Nomination Confirmed (60-36)	Nay	Yea
4	1	2/07/05	On the Resolution S.Res. 38 A resolution commending the people of Iraq on the January 30, 2005, national elections.	Resolution Agreed to (93-0)	Yea	Yea

VOTE No.	SES- SION	DATE	VOTE QUESTION *Description*	RESULT	OBAMA'S POSTION	McCAIN'S POSTION
5	1	2/09/05	On the Motion to Table S.Amdt. 5 to S. 5 (Class Action Fairness Act of 2005) To exempt class action lawsuits brought by the attorney general of any State from the modified civil procedures required by this Act.	Motion to Table Agreed to (60-39)	Nay	Yea
6	1	2/09/05	On the Amendment S.Amdt. 2 to S. 5 (Class Action Fairness Act of 2005) To amend the definition of class action in title 28, United States Code, to exclude class actions relating to civil rights or the payment of wages.	Amendment Rejected (40-59)	Yea	Nay
7	1	2/09/05	On the Amendment S.Amdt. 4 to S. 5 (Class Action Fairness Act of 2005) To clarify the application of State law in certain class actions, and for other purposes.	Amendment Rejected (38-61)	Yea	Nay
8	1	2/10/05	On the Amendment S.Amdt. 12 to S. 5 (Class Action Fairness Act of 2005) To establish time limits for action by Federal district courts on motions to remand cases that have been removed to Federal court.	Amendment Rejected (37-61)	Yea	Nay
9	1	2/10/05	On Passage of the Bill S. 5 A bill to amend the procedures that apply to consideration of interstate class actions to assure fairer outcomes for class members and defendants, and for other purposes.	Bill Passed (72-26)	Yea	Yea
10	1	2/15/05	On the Nomination PN122 Michael Chertoff, of New Jersey, to be Secretary of Homeland Security	Nomination Confirmed (98-0)	Yea	Yea
11	1	2/17/05	On Passage of the Bill S. 306 A bill to prohibit discrimination on the basis of genetic information with respect to health insurance and employment.	Bill Passed (98-0)	Yea	Yea

Vote No.	Session	Date	Vote Question *Description*	Result	Obama's Postion	McCain's Postion
12	1	3/01/05	On the Amendment S.Amdt. 23 to S. 256 (Bankruptcy Abuse Prevention and Consumer Protection Act of 2005) To clarify the safe harbor with respect to debtors who have serious medical conditions or who have been called or ordered to active duty in the Armed Forces and low income veterans.	Amendment Agreed to (63-32)	Nay	Yea
13	1	3/01/05	On the Amendment S.Amdt. 16 to S. 256 (Bankruptcy Abuse Prevention and Consumer Protection Act of 2005) To protect servicemembers and veterans from means testing in bankruptcy, to disallow certain claims by lenders charging usurious interest rates to servicemembers, and to allow servicemembers to exempt property based on the law of the State of their premilitary residence.	Amendment Rejected (38-58)	Yea	Nay
14	1	3/02/05	On the Amendment S.Amdt. 17 to S. 256 (Bankruptcy Abuse Prevention and Consumer Protection Act of 2005) To provide a homestead floor for the elderly.	Amendment Rejected (40-59)	Yea	Nay
15	1	3/02/05	On the Amendment S.Amdt. 15 to S. 256 (Bankruptcy Abuse Prevention and Consumer Protection Act of 2005) To require enhanced disclosure to consumers regarding the consequences of making only minimum required payments in the repayment of credit card debt, and for other purposes.	Amendment Rejected (40-59)	Yea	Nay
16	1	3/02/05	On the Amendment S.Amdt. 28 to S. 256 (Bankruptcy Abuse Prevention and Consumer Protection Act of 2005) To exempt debtors whose financial problems were caused by serious medical problems from means testing.	Amendment Rejected (39-58)	Yea	Nay

VOTE No.	SES-SION	DATE	VOTE QUESTION Description	RESULT	OBAMA'S POSTION	MCCAIN'S POSTION
17	1	3/02/05	On the Amendment S.Amdt. 29 to S. 256 (Bankruptcy Abuse Prevention and Consumer Protection Act of 2005) To provide protection for medical debt homeowners.	Amendment Rejected (39-58)	Yea	Nay
18	1	3/02/05	On the Amendment S.Amdt. 32 to S. 256 (Bankruptcy Abuse Prevention and Consumer Protection Act of 2005) To preserve existing bankruptcy protections for individuals experiencing economic distress as caregivers to ill or disabled family members.	Amendment Rejected (37-60)	Yea	Nay
19	1	3/03/05	On the Joint Resolution S.J.Res. 4 A joint resolution providing for congressional disapproval of the rule submitted by the Department of Agriculture under chapter 8 of title 5, United States Code, relating to risk zones for introduction of bovine spongiform encephalopathy.	Joint Resolution Passed (52-46)	Yea	Nay
20	1	3/03/05	On the Amendment S.Amdt. 31 to S. 256 (Bankruptcy Abuse Prevention and Consumer Protection Act of 2005) To limit the amount of interest that can be charged on any extension of credit to 30 percent.	Amendment Rejected (24-74)	Nay	Nay
21	1	3/03/05	On the Amendment S.Amdt. 37 to S. 256 (Bankruptcy Abuse Prevention and Consumer Protection Act of 2005) To exempt debtors from means testing if their financial problems were caused by identity theft.	Amendment Rejected (37-61)	Yea	Nay
22	1	3/03/05	On the Amendment S.Amdt. 38 to S. 256 (Bankruptcy Abuse Prevention and Consumer Protection Act of 2005) To discourage predatory lending practices.	Amendment Rejected (40-58)	Yea	Nay

Vote No.	Ses- sion	Date	Vote Question Description	Result	Obama's Postion	McCain's Postion
23	1	3/03/05	**On the Amendment S.Amdt. 42 to S. 256 (Bankruptcy Abuse Prevention and Consumer Protection Act of 2005)** To limit the exemption for asset protection trusts.	Amendment Rejected (39-56)	Yea	Nay
24	1	3/03/05	**On the Amendment S.Amdt. 24 to S. 256 (Bankruptcy Abuse Prevention and Consumer Protection Act of 2005)** To amend the wage priority provision and to amend the payment of insurance benefits to retirees.	Amendment Rejected (40-54)	Yea	Nay
25	1	3/03/05	**On the Amendment S.Amdt. 49 to S. 256 (Bankruptcy Abuse Prevention and Consumer Protection Act of 2005)** To protect employees and retirees from corporate practices that deprive them of their earnings and retirement savings when a business files for bankruptcy.	Amendment Rejected (40-54)	Yea	Nay
26	1	3/07/05	**On the Amendment S.Amdt. 44 to S. 256 (Bankruptcy Abuse Prevention and Consumer Protection Act of 2005)** To amend the Fair Labor Standards Act of 1938 to provide for an increase in the Federal minimum wage.	Amendment Rejected (46-49)	Yea	Nay
27	1	3/07/05	**On the Amendment S.Amdt. 128 to S. 256 (Bankruptcy Abuse Prevention and Consumer Protection Act of 2005)** To promote job creation, family time, and small business preservation in the adjustment of the Federal minimum wage.	Amendment Rejected (38-61)	Nay	Yea

Vote No.	Session	Date	Vote Question *Description*	Result	Obama's Postion	McCain's Postion
28	1	3/08/05	**On the Amendment S.Amdt. 47 to S. 256 (Bankruptcy Abuse Prevention and Consumer Protection Act of 2005)** To prohibit the discharge, in bankruptcy, of a debt resulting from the debtor's unlawful interference with the provision of lawful goods or services or damage to property used to provide lawful goods or services.	Amendment Rejected (46-53)	Yea	Nay
29	1	3/08/05	**On the Cloture Motion S. 256** A bill to amend title 11 of the United States Code, and for other purposes.	Cloture Motion Agreed to (69-31, 3/5 majority required)	Nay	Yea
30	1	3/08/05	**On the Amendment S.Amdt. 89 to S. 256 (Bankruptcy Abuse Prevention and Consumer Protection Act of 2005)** To strike certain small business related bankruptcy provisions in the bill.	Amendment Rejected (41-59)	Yea	Nay
31	1	3/09/05	**On the Amendment S.Amdt. 110 to S. 256 (Bankruptcy Abuse Prevention and Consumer Protection Act of 2005)** To clarify that the means test does not apply to debtors below median income.	Amendment Rejected (42-58)	Yea	Nay
32	1	3/09/05	**On the Amendment S.Amdt. 66 to S. 256 (Bankruptcy Abuse Prevention and Consumer Protection Act of 2005)** To increase the accrual period for the employee wage priority in bankruptcy.	Amendment Rejected (48-52)	Yea	Nay
33	1	3/09/05	**On the Amendment S.Amdt. 62 to S. 256 (Bankruptcy Abuse Prevention and Consumer Protection Act of 2005)** To provide for the potential disallowance of certain claims.	Amendment Rejected (40-60)	Yea	Nay

Vote No.	Session	Date	Vote Question / Description	Result	Obama's Position	McCain's Position
34	1	3/09/05	On the Amendment S.Amdt. 67 to S. 256 (Bankruptcy Abuse Prevention and Consumer Protection Act of 2005) To modify the bill to protect families, and for other purposes.	Amendment Rejected (42-58)	Yea	Nay
35	1	3/09/05	On the Amendment S.Amdt. 68 to S. 256 (Bankruptcy Abuse Prevention and Consumer Protection Act of 2005) To provide a maximum amount for a homestead exemption under State law.	Amendment Rejected (47-53)	Yea	Nay
36	1	3/10/05	On the Amendment S.Amdt. 70 to S. 256 (Bankruptcy Abuse Prevention and Consumer Protection Act of 2005) To exempt debtors whose financial problems were caused by failure to receive alimony or child support, or both, from means testing.	Amendment Rejected (41-58)	Yea	Nay
37	1	3/10/05	On the Amendment S.Amdt. 69 to S. 256 (Bankruptcy Abuse Prevention and Consumer Protection Act of 2005) To amend the definition of current monthly income.	Amendment Rejected (41-58)	Yea	Nay
38	1	3/10/05	On the Amendment S.Amdt. 105 to S. 256 (Bankruptcy Abuse Prevention and Consumer Protection Act of 2005) To limit claims in bankruptcy by certain unsecured creditors.	Amendment Rejected (38-61)	Yea	Nay
39	1	3/10/05	On the Amendment S.Amdt. 83 to S. 256 (Bankruptcy Abuse Prevention and Consumer Protection Act of 2005) To modify the definition of disinterested person in the Bankruptcy Code.	Amendment Rejected (44-55)	Yea	Nay

Vote No.	Ses-sion	Date	Vote Question Description	Result	Obama's Postion	McCain's Postion
40	1	3/10/05	On the Amendment S.Amdt. 112 to S. 256 (Bankruptcy Abuse Prevention and Consumer Protection Act of 2005) To protect disabled veterans from means testing in bankruptcy under certain circumstances.	Amendment Agreed to (99-0)	Yea	Yea
41	1	3/10/05	On the Amendment S.Amdt. 129 to S.Amdt. 121 to S. 256 (Bankruptcy Abuse Prevention and Consumer Protection Act of 2005) To limit the exemption for asset protection trusts.	Amendment Rejected (43-56)	Yea	Nay
42	1	3/10/05	On the Amendment S.Amdt. 121 to S. 256 (Bankruptcy Abuse Prevention and Consumer Protection Act of 2005) To deter corporate fraud and prevent the abuse of State self-settled trust law.	Amendment Agreed to (73-26)	Nay	Yea
43	1	3/10/05	On Passage of the Bill S. 250 A bill to amend the Carl D. Perkins Vocational and Technical Education Act of 1998 to improve the Act.	Bill Passed (99-0)	Yea	Yea
44	1	3/10/05	On Passage of the Bill S. 256 A bill to amend title 11 of the United States Code, and for other purposes.	Bill Passed (74-25)	Nay	Yea
45	1	3/14/05	On the Amendment S.Amdt. 143 to S.Con.Res. 18 (Appropriations resolution FY2006, Budget) To restore funding for education programs that are cut and reduce debt by closing corporate tax loopholes.	Amendment Rejected (44-49)	Yea	Not Voting
46	1	3/15/05	On the Amendment S.Amdt. 152 to S.Con.Res. 18 (Appropriations resolution FY2006, Budget) To express the sense of the Senate regarding the urgent need for legislation to ensure the long-term viability of the Social Security program.	Amendment Agreed to (100-0)	Yea	Yea

Vote No.	Session	Date	Vote Question Description	Result	Obama's Position	McCain's Position
47	1	3/15/05	On the Amendment S.Amdt. 144 to S.Con.Res. 18 (Appropriations resolution FY2006, Budget) To ensure that 75-year solvency has been restored to Social Security before Congress considers new deficit-financed legislation that would increase mandatory spending or cut taxes.	Amendment Rejected (45-55)	Yea	Nay
48	1	3/15/05	On the Amendment S.Amdt. 150 to S.Con.Res. 18 (Appropriations resolution FY2006, Budget) To express the sense of the Senate that failing to address the financial condition of Social Security will result in massive debt, deep benefit cuts and tax increases.	Amendment Agreed to (56-43)	Nay	Yea
49	1	3/15/05	On the Amendment S.Amdt. 145 to S.Con.Res. 18 (Appropriations resolution FY2006, Budget) To express the sense of the Senate that Congress should reject any Social Security plan that requires deep benefit cuts or a massive increase in debt.	Amendment Rejected (50-50)	Yea	Nay
50	1	3/15/05	On the Amendment S.Amdt. 147 to S.Con.Res. 18 (Appropriations resolution FY2006, Budget) To protect the American people from terrorist attacks by providing the necessary resources to our firefighters, police, EMS workers and other first-responders by restoring $1,626 billion in cuts to first-responder programs.	Amendment Rejected (46-54)	Yea	Nay
51	1	3/16/05	On the Amendment S.Amdt. 158 to S.Con.Res. 18 (Appropriations resolution FY2006, Budget) To provide adequate funding of $1.4 billion in fiscal year 2006 to preserve a national intercity passenger rail system.	Amendment Rejected (46-52)	Yea	Nay

VOTE No.	SESSION	DATE	VOTE QUESTION Description	RESULT	OBAMA'S POSITION	MCCAIN'S POSITION
52	1	3/16/05	On the Amendment S.Amdt. 168 to S.Con.Res. 18 (Appropriations resolution FY2006, Budget) To strike section 201(a)(4) relative to the Arctic National Wildlife Refuge.	Amendment Rejected (49-51)	Yea	Yea
53	1	3/16/05	On the Amendment S.Amdt. 186 to S.Con.Res. 18 (Appropriations resolution FY2006, Budget) To fully reinstate the pay-as-you-go requirement.	Amendment Rejected (50-50)	Yea	Yea
54	1	3/16/05	On the Amendment S.Amdt. 171 to S.Con.Res. 18 (Appropriations resolution FY2006, Budget) To increase veterans medical care by $410,000,000 in fiscal year 2006.	Amendment Agreed to (96-4)	Yea	Yea
55	1	3/16/05	On the Amendment S.Amdt. 149 to S.Con.Res. 18 (Appropriations resolution FY2006, Budget) To increase veterans medical care by $2.8 billion in 2006.	Amendment Rejected (47-53)	Yea	Nay
56	1	3/16/05	On the Amendment S.Amdt. 173 to S.Con.Res. 18 (Appropriations resolution FY2006, Budget) To increase discretionary health and education funding by $2,000,000,000.	Amendment Agreed to (63-37)	Yea	Nay
57	1	3/17/05	On the Amendment S.Amdt. 229 to S.Con.Res. 18 (Appropriations resolution FY2006, Budget) To express the sense of the Senate regarding Medicaid reconciliation legislation consistent with recommendations from the Secretary of Health and Human Services.	Amendment Rejected (49-51)	Nay	Yea

VOTE No.	SES-SION	DATE	VOTE QUESTION *Description*	RESULT	OBAMA'S POSTION	MCCAIN'S POSTION
58	1	3/17/05	**On the Amendment S.Amdt. 204 to S.Con.Res. 18 (Appropriations resolution FY2006, Budget)** To create a reserve fund for the establishment of a Bipartisan Medicaid Commission to consider and recommend appropriate reforms to the Medicaid program, and to strike Medicaid cuts to protect states and vulnerable populations.	Amendment Agreed to (52-48)	Yea	Nay
59	1	3/17/05	**On the Amendment S.Amdt. 207 to S.Con.Res. 18 (Appropriations resolution FY2006, Budget)** To provide for full consideration of tax cuts in the Senate under regular order.	Amendment Rejected (49-51)	Yea	Yea
60	1	3/17/05	**On the Amendment S.Amdt. 214 to S.Con.Res. 18 (Appropriations resolution FY2006, Budget)** To ensure that any savings associated with legislation that provides the Secretary of Health and Human Services with the authority to participate in the negotiation of contracts with manufacturers of covered part D drugs to achieve the best possible prices for such drugs under part D of title XVIII of the Social Security Act, that requires the Secretary to negotiate contracts with manufacturers of such drugs for each fallback prescription drug plan, and that requires the Secretary to participate in the negotiation for a contract for any such drug upon the request of a prescription drug plan or an MA-PD plan, is reserved for reducing expenditures under such part.	Amendment Rejected (49-50)	Yea	Yea

VOTE No.	SES-SION	DATE	VOTE QUESTION *Description*	RESULT	OBAMA'S POSTION	MCCAIN'S POSTION
61	1	3/17/05	On the Amendment S.Amdt. 172 to S.Con.Res. 18 (Appropriations resolution FY2006, Budget) To restore the Perkins Vocational Education program and provide for deficit reduction paid for through the elimination of the phase out of the personal exemption limitation and itemized deduction limitation for high-income taxpayers now scheduled to start in 2006.	Amendment Rejected (44-56)	Yea	Nay
62	1	3/17/05	On the Amendment S.Amdt. 219 to S.Con.Res. 18 (Appropriations resolution FY2006, Budget) To establish a reserve fund in the event that legislation is passed to provide a 50 percent tax credit to employers that continue to pay the salaries of Guard and Reserve employees who have been called to active duty.	Amendment Agreed to (100-0)	Yea	Yea
63	1	3/17/05	On the Amendment S.Amdt. 210 to S.Con.Res. 18 (Appropriations resolution FY2006, Budget) To repeal the tax subsidy for certain domestic companies which move manufacturing operations and American jobs offshore.	Amendment Rejected (40-59)	Yea	Nay
64	1	3/17/05	On the Amendment S.Amdt. 220 to S.Con.Res. 18 (Appropriations resolution FY2006, Budget) To protect the American people from terrorist attacks by restoring $565 million in cuts to vital first-responder programs in the Department of Homeland Security, including the State Homeland Security Grant program, by providing $150 million for port security grants and by providing $140 million for 1,000 new border patrol agents.	Amendment Agreed to (63-37)	Yea	Nay

Vote No.	Session	Date	Vote Question Description	Result	Obama's Position	McCain's Position
65	1	3/17/05	On the Amendment S.Amdt. 156 to S.Con.Res. 18 (Appropriations resolution FY2006, Budget) To restore funding for the Community Development Block Grant (CDBG) program.	Amendment Rejected (49-51)	Yea	Nay
66	1	3/17/05	On the Amendment S.Amdt. 230 to S.Con.Res. 18 (Appropriations resolution FY2006, Budget) To fully fund the Community Development Block Grant (CDBG) program.	Amendment Agreed to (68-31)	Yea	Nay
67	1	3/17/05	On the Amendment S.Amdt. 208 to S.Con.Res. 18 (Appropriations resolution FY2006, Budget) To modify the designation authority for an emergency requirement.	Amendment Agreed to (73-26)	Yea	Nay
68	1	3/17/05	On the Amendment S.Amdt. 177 to S.Con.Res. 18 (Appropriations resolution FY2006, Budget) Relative to education funding.	Amendment Agreed to (51-49)	Yea	Nay
69	1	3/17/05	On the Amendment S.Amdt. 234 to S.Con.Res. 18 (Restore Pay-As-You Go Tax Cuts bill) To ensure that legislation to make cuts in agriculture programs receives full consideration and debate in the Senate under regular order, rather than being fast-tracked under reconciliation procedures.	Amendment Rejected (46-54)	Yea	Nay
70	1	3/17/05	On the Amendment S.Amdt. 239 to S.Con.Res. 18 (Appropriations resolution FY2006, Budget) Relative to funding to the Office of Community Oriented Policing Services.	Amendment Rejected (45-55)	Yea	Nay
71	1	3/17/05	On the Amendment S.Amdt. 240 to S.Con.Res. 18 (Appropriations resolution FY2006, Budget) Relative to transportation funding.	Amendment Rejected (45-54)	Yea	Nay

Vote No.	Session	Date	Vote Question Description	Result	Obama's Position	McCain's Position
72	1	3/17/05	On the Amendment S.Amdt. 225 to S.Con.Res. 18 (Appropriations resolution FY2006, Budget) To provide the flexibility to consider all available transportation funding options.	Amendment Agreed to (81-19)	Yea	Nay
73	1	3/17/05	On the Amendment S.Amdt. 243 to S.Con.Res. 18 (Appropriations resolution FY2006, Budget) To express the sense of the Senate that the tax cuts assumed in the budget resolution should include the repeal of the 1993 increase in the income tax on Social Security benefits.	Amendment Agreed to (94-6)	Yea	Yea
74	1	3/17/05	On the Amendment S.Amdt. 241 to S.Con.Res. 18 (Appropriations resolution FY2006, Budget) To repeal the 1993 tax increase on Social Security benefits.	Amendment Agreed to (55-45)	Nay	Yea
75	1	3/17/05	On the Amendment S.Amdt. 244 to S.Con.Res. 18 (Appropriations resolution FY2006, Budget) To expand access to preventive health care services that reduce unintended pregnancy (including teen pregnancy), reduce the number of abortions, and improve access to women's health care.	Amendment Rejected (47-53)	Yea	Nay
76	1	3/17/05	On the Amendment S.Amdt. 187 to S.Con.Res. 18 (Appropriations resolution FY2006, Budget) To strike the debt ceiling reconciliation instruction.	Amendment Rejected (45-54)	Yea	Yea
77	1	3/17/05	On the Amendment S.Amdt. 257 to S.Con.Res. 18 (Appropriations resolution FY2006, Budget) To establish a point of order.	Amendment Rejected (44-54)	Yea	Nay

Vote No.	Ses-sion	Date	Vote Question Description	Result	Obama's Postion	McCain's Postion
78	1	3/17/05	On the Amendment S.Amdt. 211 to S.Con.Res. 18 (Appropriations resolution FY2006, Budget) To restore funding for tribal programs and provide necessary additional funding based on recommendations from Indian country	Amendment Rejected (45-55)	Yea	Nay
79	1	3/17/05	On the Amendment S.Amdt. 202 to S.Con.Res. 18 (Appropriations resolution FY2006, Budget)	Amendment Rejected (37-63)	Yea	Nay
80	1	3/17/05	On the Amendment S.Amdt. 238 to S.Con.Res. 18 (Appropriations resolution FY2006, Budget) To promote innovation and U.S. competitiveness by expressing the sense of the Senate urging the Senate Committee on Appropriations to make efforts to fund the Advanced Technology Program, which supports industry-led research and development of cutting-edge technologies with broad commercial potential and societal benefits.	Amendment Agreed to (53-46)	Yea	Nay
81	1	3/17/05	On the Concurrent Resolution S.Con. Res. 18 An original concurrent resolution setting forth the congressional budget for the United States Government for fiscal year 2006 and including the appropriate budgetary levels for fiscal years 2005 and 2007 through 2010.	Concurrent Resolution Agreed to (51-49)	Nay	Yea
82	1	4/05/05	On the Resolution S.Res. 95 A resolution relating to the death of the Holy Father, Pope John Paul II.	Resolution Agreed to (98-0)	Yea	Yea

VOTE No.	SESSION	DATE	VOTE QUESTION *Description*	RESULT	OBAMA'S POSTION	MCCAIN'S POSTION
83	1	4/05/05	**On the Amendment S.Amdt. 278 to S. 600 (Foreign Affairs Authorization Act, Fiscal Years 2006 and 2007)** To prohibit the application of certain restrictive eligibility requirements to foreign nongovernmental organizations with respect to the provision of assistance under part I of the Foreign Assistance Act of 1961.	Amendment Agreed to (52-46)	Yea	Nay
84	1	4/06/05	**On the Amendment S.Amdt. 286 to S. 600 (Foreign Affairs Authorization Act, Fiscal Years 2006 and 2007)** To provide a second degree amendment related to the United States share of assessment for United Nations Peacekeeping operations.	Amendment Rejected (40-57)	Yea	Nay
85	1	4/06/05	**On the Motion to Table S.Amdt. 284 to S. 600 (Foreign Affairs Authorization Act, Fiscal Years 2006 and 2007)** To prohibit funds from being used for television broadcasting to Cuba.	Motion to Table Agreed to (65-35)	Nay	Yea
86	1	4/06/05	**On the Motion to Table S.Amdt. 309 to S. 600 (Foreign Affairs Authorization Act, Fiscal Years 2006 and 2007)** To authorize appropriate action if the negotiations with the People's Republic of China regarding China's undervalued currency are not successful.	Motion to Table Failed (33-67)	Nay	Yea
87	1	4/11/05	**On the Nomination PN211** Paul A. Crotty, of New York, to be United States District Judge for the Southern District of New York	Nomination Confirmed (95-0)	Yea	Yea
88	1	4/11/05	**On the Resolution S.Con.Res. 25** A concurrent resolution expressing the sense of Congress regarding the application of Airbus for launch aid.	Resolution Agreed to (96-0)	Yea	Yea

Vote No.	Session	Date	Vote Question / Description	Result	Obama's Position	McCain's Position
89	1	4/12/05	On the Motion (Motion to Waive Sec. 402, S. Con. Res. 95 (108th) "Emergency designation" Re: Murray Amdt. No. 344, As Modified) To provide $1,975,183,000 for medical care for veterans.	Motion Rejected (46-54, 3/5 majority required)	Yea	Nay
90	1	4/12/05	On the Motion (Motion to Waive C.B.A. Re: Murray Amdt. No. 344, As Modified) To provide $1,975,183,000 for medical care for veterans.	Motion Rejected (46-54, 3/5 majority required)	Yea	Nay
91	1	4/13/05	On the Motion to Table S.Amdt. 356 to H.R. 1268 (Emergency Supplemental Appropriations Act for Defense, the Global War on Terror, and Tsunami Relief, 2005) To ensure that a Federal employee who takes leave without pay in order to perform service as a member of the uniformed services or member of the National Guard shall continue to receive pay in an amount which when taken together with the pay and allowances such individual is receiving for such service, will be no less than the basic pay such individual would then be receiving if no interruption in employment had occurred.	Motion to Table Failed (39-61)	Nay	Yea
92	1	4/13/05	On the Motion (Motion to Table Kerry Amdt. No. 334) To increase the military death gratuity to $100,000, effective with respect to any deaths of members of the Armed Forces on active duty after October 7, 2001.	Motion Rejected (25-75)	Nay	Nay

Vote No.	Session	Date	Vote Question / Description	Result	Obama's Postion	McCain's Postion
93	1	4/13/05	On the Amendment S.Amdt. 367 to H.R. 1268 (Emergency Supplemental Appropriations Act for Defense, the Global War on Terror, and Tsunami Relief, 2005) To reduce by $36,000,000 the amount appropriated for "Military Construction, Army", with the amount of the reduction to be allocated to funds available under that heading for the Camp 6 Detention Facility at Guantanamo Bay, Cuba.	Amendment Rejected (27-71)	Nay	Nay
94	1	4/13/05	On the Amendment S.Amdt. 372 to H.R. 1268 (Emergency Supplemental Appropriations Act for Defense, the Global War on Terror, and Tsunami Relief, 2005) To express the sense of the Senate that Congress should not delay enactment of critical appropriations necessary to ensure the well-being of the men and women of the United States Armed Forces fighting in Iraq and elsewhere around the world, by attempting to conduct a debate about immigration reform while the supplemental appropriations bill is pending on the floor of the United States Senate.	Amendment Agreed to (61-38)	Nay	Yea
95	1	4/14/05	On the Amendment S.Amdt. 430 to H.R. 1268 (Emergency Supplemental Appropriations Act for Defense, the Global War on Terror, and Tsunami Relief, 2005) To prohibit the use of funds by any Federal agency to produce a prepackaged news story without including in such story a clear notification for the audience that the story was prepared or funded by a Federal agency.	Amendment Agreed to (98-0)	Yea	Yea

VOTE No.	SESSION	DATE	VOTE QUESTION Description	RESULT	OBAMA'S POSTION	McCAIN'S POSTION
96	1	4/18/05	On the Amendment S.Amdt. 464 to H.R. 1268 (Emergency Supplemental Appropriations Act for Defense, the Global War on Terror, and Tsunami Relief, 2005) To express the sense of the Senate on future requests for funding for military operations in Afghanistan and Iraq.	Amendment Agreed to (61-31)	Not Voting	Yea
97	1	4/19/05	On the Cloture Motion S.Amdt. 432 to H.R. 1268 (Emergency Supplemental Appropriations Act for Defense, the Global War on Terror, and Tsunami Relief, 2005) To simplify the process for admitting temporary alien agricultural workers under section 101(a)(15)(H)(ii)(a) of the Immigration and Nationality Act, to increase access to such workers, and for other purposes.	Cloture Motion Rejected (21-77, 3/5 majority required)	Not Voting	Nay
98	1	4/19/05	On the Cloture Motion S.Amdt. 375 to H.R. 1268 (Emergency Supplemental Appropriations Act for Defense, the Global War on Terror, and Tsunami Relief, 2005) To provide for the adjustment of status of certain foreign agricultural workers, to amend the Immigration and Nationality Act to reform the H-2A worker program under that Act, to provide a stable, legal agricultural workforce, to extend basic legal protections and better working conditions to more workers, and for other purposes.	Cloture Motion Rejected (53-45, 3/5 majority required)	Not Voting	Yea

VOTE No.	SESSION	DATE	VOTE QUESTION / Description	RESULT	OBAMA'S POSITION	MCCAIN'S POSITION
99	1	4/19/05	On the Motion (Motion to Instruct the Sgt. At Arms) Making emergency supplemental appropriations for the fiscal year ending September 30, 2005, to establish and rapidly implement regulations for State driver's license and identification document security standards, to prevent terrorists from abusing the asylum laws of the United States, to unify terrorism-related grounds for inadmissibility and removal, to ensure expeditious construction of the San Diego border fence, and for other purposes.	Motion Agreed to (91-7)	Not Voting	Yea
100	1	4/19/05	On the Motion (Motion to Recess, As Modified) Making emergency supplemental appropriations for the fiscal year ending September 30, 2005, to establish and rapidly implement regulations for State driver's license and identification document security standards, to prevent terrorists from abusing the asylum laws of the United States, to unify terrorism-related grounds for inadmissibility and removal, to ensure expeditious construction of the San Diego border fence, and for other purposes.	Motion Agreed to (56-42)	Not Voting	Yea
101	1	4/19/05	On the Cloture Motion S.Amdt. 387 to H.R. 1268 (Emergency Supplemental Appropriations Act for Defense, the Global War on Terror, and Tsunami Relief, 2005) To revise certain requirements for H-2B employers and require submission of information regarding H-2B non-immigrants.	Cloture Motion Agreed to (83-17, 3/5 majority required)	Yea	Yea

Vote No.	Session	Date	Vote Question / Description	Result	Obama's Position	McCain's Position
102	1	4/19/05	**On the Amendment S.Amdt. 387 to H.R. 1268 (Emergency Supplemental Appropriations Act for Defense, the Global War on Terror, and Tsunami Relief, 2005)** To revise certain requirements for H-2B employers and require submission of information regarding H-2B non-immigrants.	Amendment Agreed to (94-6)	Yea	Yea
103	1	4/19/05	**On the Cloture Motion H.R. 1268** Making emergency supplemental appropriations for the fiscal year ending September 30, 2005, to establish and rapidly implement regulations for State driver's license and identification document security standards, to prevent terrorists from abusing the asylum laws of the United States, to unify terrorism-related grounds for inadmissibility and removal, to ensure expeditious construction of the San Diego border fence, and for other purposes.	Cloture Motion Agreed to (100-0, 3/5 majority required)	Yea	Yea
104	1	4/20/05	**On the Motion to Table S.Amdt. 471 to H.R. 1268 (Emergency Supplemental Appropriations Act for Defense, the Global War on Terror, and Tsunami Relief, 2005)** To reduce appropriations for the Iraqi embassy to reduce outlays expected to occur in fiscal year 2007 or later.	Motion to Table Agreed to (54-45)	Nay	Yea
105	1	4/20/05	**On the Amendment S.Amdt. 516 to H.R. 1268 (Emergency Supplemental Appropriations Act for Defense, the Global War on Terror, and Tsunami Relief, 2005)** To increase funding for border security.	Amendment Agreed to (65-34)	Yea	Nay

Vote No.	Ses-sion	Date	Vote Question *Description*	Result	Obama's Postion	McCain's Postion
106	1	4/20/05	**On the Amendment S.Amdt. 498 to H.R. 1268 (Emergency Supplemental Appropriations Act for Defense, the Global War on Terror, and Tsunami Relief, 2005)** Relating to the aircraft carriers of the Navy.	Amend-ment Agreed to (58-38)	Yea	Nay
107	1	4/21/05	**On the Nomination PN329** John D. Negroponte, of New York, to be Director of National Intelligence	Nomina-tion Confirmed (98-2)	Yea	Yea
108	1	4/21/05	**On the Amendment S.Amdt. 520 to H.R. 1268 (Emergency Supplemental Appropriations Act for Defense, the Global War on Terror, and Tsunami Relief, 2005)** To appropriate an additional $213,000,000 for Other Procurement, Army, for the procurement of Up-Ar-mored High Mobility Multipurpose Wheeled Vehicles (UAHMMWVS).	Amend-ment Agreed to (61-39)	Yea	Yea
109	1	4/21/05	**On Passage of the Bill H.R. 1268** An act making Emergency Supple-mental Appropriations for Defense, the Global War on Terror, and Tsunami Re-lief, for the fiscal year ending September 30, 2005, and for other purposes.	Bill Passed (99-0)	Yea	Yea
110	1	4/26/05	**On the Cloture Motion H.R. 3** A bill Reserved.	Cloture Motion Agreed to (94-6, 3/5 majority required)	Yea	Nay
111	1	4/27/05	**On the Nomination PN204** J. Michael Seabright, of Hawaii, to be United States District Judge for the District of Hawaii	Nomina-tion Confirmed (98-0)	Yea	Yea
112	1	4/28/05	**On the Motion (Motion to Recess Until 2:00 p.m. Today)** A bill Reserved.	Motion Agreed to (98-1)	Yea	Yea

Vote No.	Session	Date	Vote Question *Description*	Result	Obama's Position	McCain's Position
113	1	4/28/05	On the Motion to Table S.Amdt. 592 to S.Amdt. 567 to H.R. 3 (Transportation Equity Act: A Legacy for Users) To strike the highway stormwater discharge mitigation program.	Motion to Table Agreed to (51-49)	Yea	Yea
114	1	4/28/05	On the Conference Report H.Con. Res. 95 A concurrent resolution establishing the congressional budget for the United States Government for fiscal year 2006, revising appropriate budgetary levels for fiscal year 2005, and setting forth appropriate budgetary levels for fiscal years 2007 through 2010.	Conference Report Agreed to (52-47)	Nay	Yea
115	1	4/29/05	On the Cloture Motion PN328 Stephen L. Johnson, of Maryland, to be Administrator of the Environmental Protection Agency	Cloture Motion Agreed to (61-37, 3/5 majority required)	Nay	Yea
116	1	5/09/05	On the Amendment S.Amdt. 600 to S.Amdt. 567 to H.R. 3 (Transportation Equity Act: A Legacy for Users) To require notice regarding the criteria for small business concerns to participate in Federally-funded projects.	Amendment Agreed to (89-0)	Yea	Not Voting
117	1	5/10/05	On the Conference Report H.R. 1268 An act making Emergency Supplemental Appropriations for Defense, the Global War on Terror, and Tsunami Relief, for the fiscal year ending September 30, 2005, and for other purposes.	Conference Report Agreed to (100-0)	Yea	Yea
118	1	5/11/05	On the Motion (Motion to Waive CBA Re: Amdt. No. 605 and H.R. 3) A bill to authorize funds for Federal-aid highways, highway safety programs, and transit programs, and for other purposes.	Motion Agreed to (76-22, 3/5 majority required)	Yea	Nay

Vote No.	Session	Date	Vote Question Description	Result	Obama's Position	McCain's Position
119	1	5/11/05	On the Motion to Table S.Amdt. 606 to S.Amdt. 605 to H.R. 3 (Transportation Equity Act: A Legacy for Users) To establish the effect of a section of the United States Code relating to the letting of contracts on individual contributions to political campaigns, and to require the Secretary of Transportation to consider State laws that limit political contributions to be in accordance with competitive procurement requirements.	Motion to Table Agreed to (57-40)	Nay	Nay
120	1	5/11/05	On the Amendment S.Amdt. 625 to S.Amdt. 605 to H.R. 3 (Transportation Equity Act: A Legacy for Users) To provide funding for motorcycle safety programs in States without universal helmet laws.	Amendment Rejected (28-69)	Nay	Nay
121	1	5/11/05	On the Amendment S.Amdt. 618 to S.Amdt. 605 to H.R. 3 (Transportation Equity Act: A Legacy for Users) To improve the safety of nonmotorized transportation, including bicycle and pedestrian safety.	Amendment Rejected (44-53)	Yea	Nay
122	1	5/12/05	On the Cloture Motion S.Amdt. 605 to H.R. 3 (Transportation Equity Act: A Legacy for Users) To provide a complete substitute.	Cloture Motion Agreed to (92-7, 3/5 majority required)	Yea	Nay
123	1	5/17/05	On the Amendment S.Amdt. 611 to S.Amdt. 605 to H.R. 3 (Transportation Equity Act: A Legacy for Users) To modify the eligibility requirements for States to receive a grant under section 405 of title 49, United States Code.	Amendment Rejected (14-86)	Nay	Nay
124	1	5/17/05	On the Amendment S.Amdt. 646 to S.Amdt. 605 to H.R. 3 (Transportation Equity Act: A Legacy for Users) To reduce funding for certain programs.	Amendment Rejected (16-84)	Nay	Yea

VOTE No.	SES-SION	DATE	VOTE QUESTION *Description*	RESULT	OBAMA'S POSTION	MCCAIN'S POSTION
125	1	5/17/05	**On Passage of the Bill H.R. 3** A bill to authorize funds for Federal-aid highways, highway safety programs, and transit programs, and for other purposes.	Bill Passed (89-11)	Yea	Nay
126	1	5/23/05	**On the Motion (Motion To Instruct Sgt. At Arms)** Priscilla Richman Owen, of Texas, to be United States Circuit Judge for the Fifth Circuit	Motion Agreed to (90-1)	Yea	Yea
127	1	5/24/05	**On the Cloture Motion PN194** Priscilla Richman Owen, of Texas, to be United States Circuit Judge for the Fifth Circuit	Cloture Motion Agreed to (81-18, 3/5 majority required)	Yea	Yea
128	1	5/25/05	**On the Nomination PN194** Priscilla Richman Owen, of Texas, to be United States Circuit Judge for the Fifth Circuit	Nomination Confirmed (55-43)	Nay	Yea
129	1	5/26/05	**On the Cloture Motion PN326** John Robert Bolton, of Maryland, to be the Representative of the United States of America to the United Nations, with the rank and status of Ambassador, and the Representative of the United States of America in the Security Council of the United Nations	Cloture Motion Rejected (56-42, 3/5 majority required)	Nay	Yea
130	1	6/07/05	**On the Cloture Motion PN201** Janice R. Brown, of California, to be United States Circuit Judge for the District of Columbia Circuit	Cloture Motion Agreed to (65-32, 3/5 majority required)	Nay	Yea
131	1	6/08/05	**On the Nomination PN201** Janice R. Brown, of California, to be United States Circuit Judge for the District of Columbia Circuit	Nomination Confirmed (56-43)	Nay	Yea

Vote No.	Session	Date	Vote Question Description	Result	Obama's Position	McCain's Position
132	1	6/08/05	**On the Cloture Motion PN200** William H. Pryor, Jr., of Alabama, to be United States Circuit Judge for the Eleventh Circuit	Cloture Motion Agreed to (67-32, 3/5 majority required)	Nay	Yea
133	1	6/09/05	**On the Nomination PN200** William H. Pryor, Jr., of Alabama, to be United States Circuit Judge for the Eleventh Circuit	Nomination Confirmed (53-45)	Nay	Yea
134	1	6/09/05	**On the Nomination PN195** Richard A. Griffin, of Michigan, to be United States Circuit Judge for the Sixth Circuit	Nomination Confirmed (95-0)	Not Voting	Yea
135	1	6/09/05	**On the Nomination PN196** David W. McKeague, of Michigan, to be United States Circuit Judge for the Sixth Circuit	Nomination Confirmed (96-0)	Yea	Yea
136	1	6/14/05	**On the Nomination PN202** Thomas B. Griffith, of Utah, to be United States Circuit Judge for the District of Columbia Circuit	Nomination Confirmed (73-24)	Yea	Yea
137	1	6/14/05	**On the Motion to Table S.Amdt. 781 to S.Amdt. 779 to H.R. 6 (Energy Policy Act of 2005)** To ensure that ethanol is treated like all other motor vehicle fuels and that taxpayers and local governments do not have to pay for environmental damage caused by ethanol.	Motion to Table Agreed to (59-38)	Nay	Nay
138	1	6/15/05	**On the Motion to Table S.Amdt. 782 to S.Amdt. 779 to H.R. 6 (Energy Policy Act of 2005)** To strike the reliable fuels subtitle of the amendment.	Motion to Table Agreed to (69-28)	Yea	Nay

Vote No.	Ses-sion	Date	Vote Question Description	Result	Obama's Postion	McCain's Postion
139	1	6/15/05	On the Amendment S.Amdt. 779 to H.R. 6 (Energy Policy Act of 2005) To eliminate methyl tertiary butyl ether from the United States fuel supply, to increase production and use of renewable fuel, and to increase the Nation's energy independence.	Amendment Agreed to (70-26)	Yea	Nay
140	1	6/16/05	On the Amendment S.Amdt. 784 to H.R. 6 (Energy Policy Act of 2005) To improve the energy security of the United States and reduce United States dependence on foreign oil imports by 40 percent by 2025.	Amendment Rejected (47-53)	Yea	Nay
141	1	6/16/05	On the Amendment S.Amdt. 791 to H.R. 6 (Energy Policy Act of 2005) To establish a renewable portfolio standard.	Amendment Agreed to (52-48)	Yea	Nay
142	1	6/20/05	On the Cloture Motion PN326 John Robert Bolton, of Maryland, to be the Representative of the United States of America to the United Nations, with the rank and status of Ambassador, and the Representative of the United States of America in the Security Council of the United Nations	Cloture Motion Rejected (54-38, 3/5 majority required)	Nay	Yea
143	1	6/21/05	On the Amendment S.Amdt. 783 to H.R. 6 (Energy Policy Act of 2005) To strike the section providing for a comprehensive inventory of Outer Continental Shelf oil and natural gas resources.	Amendment Rejected (44-52)	Yea	Yea

Vote No.	Session	Date	Vote Question *Description*	Result	Obama's Postion	McCain's Postion
144	1	6/21/05	**On the Amendment S.Amdt. 817 to H.R. 6 (Energy Policy Act of 2005)** To provide for the conduct of activities that promote the adoption of technologies that reduce greenhouse gas intensity in the United States and in developing countries and to provide credit-based financial assistance and investment protection for projects that employ advanced climate technologies or systems in the United States.	Amendment Agreed to (66-29)	Nay	Nay
145	1	6/21/05	**On the Amendment S.Amdt. 799 to H.R. 6 (Energy Policy Act of 2005)** To make grants and loans to States and other organizations to strengthen the economy, public health and environment of the United States by reducing emissions from diesel engines.	Amendment Agreed to (92-1)	Yea	Yea
146	1	6/22/05	**On the Motion to Table S.Amdt. 841 to H.R. 6 (Energy Policy Act of 2005)** To prohibit the Commission from approving an application for the authorization of the siting, construction, expansion, or operation of facilities located onshore or in State waters for the import of natural gas from a foreign country or the export of natural gas to a foreign country without the approval of the Governor of the State in which the facility would be located.	Motion to Table Agreed to (52-45)	Nay	Yea
147	1	6/22/05	**On the Motion to Table S.Amdt. 805 to H.R. 6 (Energy Policy Act of 2005)** To express the sense of the Senate regarding management of the Strategic Petroleum Reserve to lower the burden of gasoline prices on the economy of the United States and circumvent the efforts of OPEC to reap windfall profits.	Motion to Table Agreed to (57-39)	Nay	Yea

Vote No.	Ses-sion	Date	Vote Question *Description*	Result	Obama's Postion	McCain's Postion
148	1	6/22/05	On the Amendment S.Amdt. 826 to H.R. 6 (Energy Policy Act of 2005) To provide for a program to accelerate the reduction of greenhouse gas emissions in the United States.	Amendment Rejected (38-60)	Yea	Yea
149	1	6/22/05	On the Motion to Table S.Amdt. 866 to H.R. 6 (Energy Policy Act of 2005) To express the sense of the Senate on climate change legislation.	Motion to Table Failed (44-53)	Nay	Nay
150	1	6/22/05	On the Amendment S.Amdt. 961 to H.R. 6 (Energy Policy Act of 2005) To provide for local control for the sitting of windmills.	Amendment Rejected (32-63)	Nay	Yea
151	1	6/22/05	On the Amendment S.Amdt. 844 to H.R. 6 (Energy Policy Act of 2005) To express the sense of the Senate regarding the need for the United States to address global climate change through comprehensive and cost-effective national measures and through the negotiation of fair and binding international commitments under the United Nations Framework Convention on Climate Change.	Amendment Rejected (46-49)	Yea	Yea
152	1	6/23/05	On the Cloture Motion H.R. 6 To ensure jobs for our future with secure, affordable, and reliable energy.	Cloture Motion Agreed to (92-4, 3/5 majority required)	Yea	Nay
153	1	6/23/05	On the Motion (Motion to Waive CBA Re: Domenici Amdt. No. 891)	Motion Agreed to (69-26, 3/5 majority required)	Yea	Nay
154	1	6/23/05	On the Amendment S.Amdt. 810 to H.R. 6 (Energy Policy Act of 2005) To strike a provision relating to medical isotope production.	Amendment Agreed to (52-46)	Yea	Yea

VOTE No.	SES-SION	DATE	VOTE QUESTION Description	RESULT	OBAMA'S POSTION	MCCAIN'S POSTION
155	1	6/23/05	**On the Amendment S.Amdt. 873 to** H.R. 6 (Energy Policy Act of 2005) To strike the title relating to incentives for innovative technologies.	Amend-ment Rejected (21-76)	Nay	Yea
156	1	6/23/05	**On the Amendment S.Amdt. 925 to** H.R. 6 (Energy Policy Act of 2005) To impose additional require-ments for improving automobile fuel economy and reducing vehicle emissions.	Amend-ment Agreed to (64-31)	Nay	Nay
157	1	6/23/05	**On the Amendment S.Amdt. 902 to** H.R. 6 (Energy Policy Act of 2005) To amend title 49, United States Code, to improve the system for en-hancing automobile fuel efficiency, and for other purposes.	Amend-ment Rejected (28-67)	Yea	Nay
158	1	6/28/05	**On Passage of the Bill H.R. 6** To ensure jobs for our future with se-cure, affordable, and reliable energy.	Bill Passed (85-12)	Yea	Nay
159	1	6/28/05	**On the Motion (Motion to Waive C.B.A. re: Coburn Amdt. No. 1019)** To transfer funding to the Special Diabetes Program for Indians and the Alcohol and Substance Abuse Program within the Indian Health Service from funding for federal land acquisition.	Motion Rejected (17-75, 3/5 majority required)	Nay	Yea
160	1	6/28/05	**On the Amendment S.Amdt. 1003 to H.R. 2361 (Department of the Interior, Environment, and Re-lated Agencies Appropriations Act, 2006)** To require conference report inclu-sion of limitations, directives, and earmarks.	Amend-ment Rejected (33-59)	Nay	Yea

Vote No.	Ses-sion	Date	Vote Question Description	Result	Obama's Postion	McCain's Postion
161	1	6/29/05	**On the Amendment S.Amdt. 1068 to H.R. 2361 (Department of the Interior, Environment, and Related Agencies Appropriations Act, 2006)** To direct the Administrator of the Environmental Protection Agency to conduct a review of all third party intentional human dosing studies to identify or quantify toxic effects.	Amendment Agreed to (57-40)	Nay	Yea
162	1	6/29/05	**On the Amendment S.Amdt. 1023 to H.R. 2361 (Department of the Interior, Environment, and Related Agencies Appropriations Act, 2006)** To prohibit the use of funds by the Administrator of the Environmental Protection Agency to accept, consider, or rely on third-party intentional dosing human studies for pesticides or to conduct intentional dosing human studies for pesticides.	Amendment Agreed to (60-37)	Yea	Yea
163	1	6/29/05	**On the Motion (Motion to Waive C.B.A. Re: Dorgan Amdt. No. 1025)** To require Federal reserve banks to transfer certain surplus funds to the general fund of the Treasury, to be used for the provision of Indian health care services.	Motion Rejected (47-51, 3/5 majority required)	Yea	Nay
164	1	6/29/05	**On the Amendment S.Amdt. 1026 to H.R. 2361 (Department of the Interior, Environment, and Related Agencies Appropriations Act, 2006)** To prohibit the use of funds to plan, design, study, or construct certain forest development roads in the Tongass National Forest.	Amendment Rejected (39-59)	Yea	Yea

VOTE No.	SES-SION	DATE	VOTE QUESTION *Description*	RESULT	OBAMA'S POSITION	MCCAIN'S POSITION
165	1	6/29/05	On the Amendment S.Amdt. 1071 to S.Amdt. 1052 to H.R. 2361 (Department of the Interior, Environment, and Related Agencies Appropriations Act, 2006) To provide additional funding for medical services provided by the Veterans Health Administration.	Amendment Agreed to (96-0)	Yea	Not Voting
166	1	6/29/05	On the Amendment S.Amdt. 1052 to H.R. 2361 (Department of the Interior, Environment, and Related Agencies Appropriations Act, 2006) Making emergency supplemental appropriations for the fiscal year ending September 30, 2005, for the Veterans Health Administration.	Amendment Agreed to (96-0)	Yea	Not Voting
167	1	6/29/05	On the Motion (Motion to Suspend the Rules Relative to the Dorgan Amdt. No. 1059) To facilitate family travel to Cuba in humanitarian circumstances.	Motion Rejected (60-35, 2/3 majority required)	Yea	Not Voting
168	1	6/29/05	On Passage of the Bill H.R. 2361 A bill making appropriations for the Department of the Interior, environment, and related agencies for the fiscal year ending September 30, 2006, and for other purposes.	Bill Passed (94-0)	Yea	Not Voting
169	1	6/29/05	On the Motion to Proceed S. 1307 A bill to implement the Dominican Republic-Central America-United States Free Trade Agreement.	Motion to Proceed Agreed to (61-34)	Nay	Yea
170	1	6/30/05	On Passage of the Bill S. 1307 A bill to implement the Dominican Republic-Central America-United States Free Trade Agreement.	Bill Passed (54-45)	Nay	Yea

Vote No.	Session	Date	Vote Question Description	Result	Obama's Position	McCain's Position
171	1	7/01/05	On the Amendment S.Amdt. 1085 to H.R. 2419 (Energy and Water Development Appropriations Act, 2006) To prohibit the use of funds for the Robust Nuclear Earth Penetrator and utilize the amount of otherwise available to reduce the National debt.	Amendment Rejected (43-53)	Yea	Nay
172	1	7/01/05	On Passage of the Bill H.R. 2419 A bill making appropriations for energy and water development for the fiscal year ending September 30, 2006, and for other purposes.	Bill Passed (92-3)	Yea	Nay
173	1	7/11/05	On the Resolution S.Res. 193 A resolution expressing sympathy for the people of the United Kingdom in the aftermath of the deadly terrorist attacks on London on July 7, 2005.	Resolution Agreed to (76-0)	Not Voting	Not Voting
174	1	7/12/05	On the Amendment S.Amdt. 1129 to H.R. 2360 (Department of Homeland Security Appropriations Act) To provide emergency supplemental funds for medical services provided by the Veterans Health Administration for the fiscal year ending September 30, 2005.	Amendment Agreed to (95-0)	Yea	Yea
175	1	7/12/05	On the Amendment S.Amdt. 1142 to H.R. 2360 (Department of Homeland Security Appropriations Act) To provide for homeland security grant coordination and simplification, and for other purposes.	Amendment Agreed to (71-26)	Nay	Yea
176	1	7/12/05	On the Amendment S.Amdt. 1215 to H.R. 2360 (Department of Homeland Security Appropriations Act) To improve the allocation of grants through the Department of Homeland Security, and for other purposes.	Amendment Rejected (32-65)	Yea	Yea

Vote No.	Session	Date	Vote Question Description	Result	Obama's Position	McCain's Position
177	1	7/13/05	On the Motion (Motion To Waive CBA Re: Dodd Amdt. No. 1202, As Modified) To fund urgent priorities for our Nation's firefighters, law enforcement personnel, emergency medical personnel, and all Americans by reducing the tax breaks for individuals with annual incomes in excess of $1 million.	Motion Rejected (36-60, 3/5 majority required)	Yea	Nay
178	1	7/13/05	On the Motion (Motion To Waive CBA RE: Akaka Amdt. No. 1112, As Modified) To increase funding for State and local grant programs.	Motion Rejected (42-55, 3/5 majority required)	Yea	Nay
179	1	7/14/05	On the Amendment S.Amdt. 1219 to S.Amdt. 1124 to H.R. 2360 (Department of Homeland Security Appropriations Act) Of a perfecting nature.	Amendment Rejected (38-60)	Nay	Yea
180	1	7/14/05	On the Motion (Motion To Waive CBA RE: Schumer Amdt. No. 1189) To provide that certain air cargo security programs are implemented, and for other purposes.	Motion Rejected (45-53, 3/5 majority required)	Yea	Nay
181	1	7/14/05	On the Motion (Motion To Waive CBA RE: Schumer Amdt. No. 1190) To appropriate $70,000,000 to identify and track hazardous materials shipments.	Motion Rejected (36-62, 3/5 majority required)	Yea	Nay
182	1	7/14/05	On the Amendment S.Amdt. 1171 to H.R. 2360 (Department of Homeland Security Appropriations Act) To increase the number of detention beds and positions or FTEs in the United States consistent with the number authorized in the Intelligence Reform and Terrorism Prevention Act of 2004 (Public Law 108-458), and for other purposes.	Amendment Rejected (42-56)	Nay	Yea

Vote No.	Ses-sion	Date	Vote Question *Description*	Result	Obama's Postion	McCain's Postion
183	1	7/14/05	On the Motion (Motion To Waive CBA RE: Stabenow Amdt. No. 1217) To provide funding for interoperable communications equipment grants.	Motion Rejected (35-63, 3/5 majority required)	Yea	Nay
184	1	7/14/05	On the Motion (Motion To Waive CBA Byrd Amdt. No. 1218) To provide additional funding for intercity passenger rail transportation, freight rail, and mass transit.	Motion Rejected (43-55, 3/5 majority required)	Yea	Nay
185	1	7/14/05	On the Amendment S.Amdt. 1220 to H.R. 2360 (Department of Homeland Security Appropriations Act) To allocate funds for certain terrorism prevention activities, including rail and transit security.	Amend-ment Rejected (46-52)	Nay	Yea
186	1	7/14/05	On the Motion (Motion To Waive CBA Shelby Amdt. No. 1205 As Modified) To allocate funds for certain terrorism prevention activities, including rail and transit security.	Motion Rejected (53-45, 3/5 majority required)	Yea	Nay
187	1	7/14/05	On the Amendment S.Amdt. 1223 to H.R. 2360 (Department of Homeland Security Appropriations Act) To protect classified information and to protect our servicemen and women.	Amend-ment Rejected (32-65)	Nay	Nay
188	1	7/14/05	On the Amendment S.Amdt. 1222 to H.R. 2360 (Department of Homeland Security Appropriations Act) To prohibit Federal employees who disclose classified information to persons not authorized to receive such information from holding a security clearance.	Amend-ment Rejected (44-53)	Yea	Nay
189	1	7/14/05	On Passage of the Bill H.R. 2360 A bill making appropriations for the Department of Homeland Security for the fiscal year ending September 30, 2006, and for other purposes.	Bill Passed (96-1)	Yea	Yea

Vote No.	Ses-sion	Date	Vote Question *Description*	Result	Obama's Postion	McCain's Postion
190	1	7/18/05	**On the Nomination PN214** Lester M. Crawford, of Maryland, to be Commissioner of Food and Drugs, Department of Health and Human Services	Nomination Confirmed (78-16)	Nay	Not Voting
191	1	7/19/05	**On the Joint Resolution H.J.Res. 52** A joint resolution approving the renewal of import restrictions contained in the Burmese Freedom and Democracy Act of 2003.	Joint Resolution Passed (97-1)	Yea	Yea
192	1	7/19/05	**On the Amendment S.Amdt. 1242 to H.R. 3057 (Foreign Operations, Export Financial and Related Programs Appropriations Act, 2006)** To prohibit any funds from being used by the Export-Import Bank of the United States to approve a loan or a loan guarantee related to a nuclear project in China.	Amendment Rejected (37-62)	Yea	Nay
193	1	7/19/05	**On the Amendment S.Amdt. 1241 to H.R. 3057 (Foreign Operations, Export Financial and Related Programs Appropriations Act, 2006)** To prohibit funds from being made available to the United States Agency for International Development for entertainment expenses.	Amendment Agreed to (59-40)	Nay	Yea
194	1	7/19/05	**On the Amendment S.Amdt. 1294 to H.R. 3057 (Foreign Operations, Export Financial and Related Programs Appropriations Act, 2006)** To provide that no funds may be made available to provide television broadcasting to Cuba, to increase by $21,100,000 the amount appropriated to the Peace Corps, and to reduce by the same amount the amount appropriated under title I to the Broadcasting Board of Governors for broadcasting to Cuba.	Amendment Rejected (33-66)	Yea	Nay

Vote No.	Ses-sion	Date	Vote Question Description	Result	Obama's Postion	McCain's Postion
195	1	7/20/05	On the Amendment S.Amdt. 1245 to H.R. 3057 (Foreign Operations, Export Financial and Related Programs Appropriations Act, 2006) To express the sense of the Senate regarding the use of funds for orphans, and displaced and abandoned children.	Amendment Agreed to (98-0)	Yea	Yea
196	1	7/20/05	On the Amendment S.Amdt. 1271 to H.R. 3057 (Foreign Operations, Export Financial and Related Programs Appropriations Act, 2006) To prevent funds from being made available to provide assistance to a country which has refused to extradite certain individuals to the United States.	Amendment Agreed to (86-12)	Yea	Yea
197	1	7/20/05	On Passage of the Bill H.R. 3057 An act making appropriations for the Department of State, foreign operations, and related programs for the fiscal year ending September 30, 2006, and for other purposes.	Bill Passed (98-1)	Yea	Yea
198	1	7/21/05	On the Nomination PN68 Thomas C. Dorr, of Iowa, to be Under Secretary of Agriculture for Rural Development	Nomination Confirmed (62-38)	Nay	Yea
199	1	7/21/05	On the Amendment S.Amdt. 1314 to S. 1042 (National Defense Authorization Act for Fiscal Year 2006) To increase, with an offset, amounts available for the procurement of wheeled vehicles for the Army and the Marine Corps and for armor for such vehicles.	Amendment Agreed to (100-0)	Yea	Yea
200	1	7/21/05	On the Amendment S.Amdt. 1380 to S. 1042 (National Defense Authorization Act for Fiscal Year 2006) To improve authorities to address urgent nonproliferation crises and United States nonproliferation operations.	Amendment Agreed to (78-19)	Yea	Yea

Vote No.	Ses- sion	Date	Vote Question Description	Result	Obama's Postion	McCain's Postion
201	1	7/25/05	On the Resolution S.Res. 207 A resolution recognizing and honoring the 15th anniversary of the enactment of the Americans with Disabilities Act of 1990.	Resolution Agreed to (87-0)	Yea	Yea
202	1	7/26/05	On the Amendment S.Amdt. 1377 to S. 1042 (National Defense Authorization Act for Fiscal Year 2006) To ensure that certain persons do not evade or avoid the prohibitions imposed under the International Emergency Powers Act, and for other purposes.	Amendment Agreed to (98-0)	Yea	Yea
203	1	7/26/05	On the Amendment S.Amdt. 1351 to S. 1042 (National Defense Authorization Act for Fiscal Year 2006) To stop corporations from financing terrorism.	Amendment Rejected (47-51)	Yea	Nay
204	1	7/26/05	On the Amendment S.Amdt. 1342 to S. 1042 (National Defense Authorization Act for Fiscal Year 2006) To support certain youth organizations, including the Boy Scouts of America and Girl Scouts of America, and for other purposes.	Amendment Agreed to (98-0)	Yea	Yea
205	1	7/26/05	On the Cloture Motion S. 1042 An original bill to authorize appropriations for fiscal year 2006 for military activities of the Department of Defense, for military construction, and for defense activities of the Department of Energy, to prescribe personnel strengths for such fiscal year for the Armed Forces, and for other purposes.	Cloture Motion Rejected (50-48, 3/5 majority required)	Nay	Nay

Vote No.	Session	Date	Vote Question Description	Result	Obama's Position	McCain's Position
206	1	7/26/05	On the Cloture Motion S. 397 A bill to prohibit civil liability actions from being brought or continued against manufacturers, distributors, dealers, or importers of firearms or ammunition for damages, injunctive or other relief resulting from the misuse of their products by others.	Cloture Motion Agreed to (66-32, 3/5 majority required)	Nay	Yea
207	1	7/28/05	On the Amendment S.Amdt. 1626 to S. 397 (Protection of Lawful Commerce in Arms Act) To amend chapter 44 of title 18, United States Code, to require the provision of a child safety lock in connection with the transfer of a handgun.	Amendment Agreed to (70-30)	Yea	Yea
208	1	7/28/05	On the Motion to Table S.Amdt. 1623 to S. 397 (Protection of Lawful Commerce in Arms Act) To clarify the prohibition on certain civil liability actions.	Motion to Table Agreed to (62-37)	Nay	Yea
209	1	7/28/05	On Passage of the Bill H.R. 3045 A bill to implement the Dominican Republic-Central America-United States Free Trade Agreement.	Bill Passed (55-45)	Nay	Yea
210	1	7/29/05	On the Conference Report H.R. 2361 A bill making appropriations for the Department of the Interior, environment, and related agencies for the fiscal year ending September 30, 2006, and for other purposes.	Conference Report Agreed to (99-1)	Yea	Yea
211	1	7/29/05	On the Conference Report H.R. 2985 A bill making appropriations for the Legislative Branch for the fiscal year ending September 30, 2006, and for other purposes.	Conference Report Agreed to (96-4)	Yea	Yea

Vote No.	Session	Date	Vote Question / Description	Result	Obama's Postion	McCain's Postion
212	1	7/29/05	On the Motion (Motion To Waive CBA Re: Conference Report To Accompany H. R. 6) To ensure jobs for our future with secure, affordable, and reliable energy.	Motion Agreed to (71-29, 3/5 majority required)	Yea	Nay
213	1	7/29/05	On the Conference Report H.R. 6 To ensure jobs for our future with secure, affordable, and reliable energy.	Conference Report Agreed to (74-26)	Yea	Nay
214	1	7/29/05	On the Amendment S.Amdt. 1644 to S. 397 (Protection of Lawful Commerce in Arms Act) To protect the rights of children who are victimized by crime to secure compensation from those who participate in the arming of criminals.	Amendment Agreed to (72-26)	Nay	Yea
215	1	7/29/05	On the Amendment S.Amdt. 1620 to S. 397 (Protection of Lawful Commerce in Arms Act) To exempt lawsuits involving injuries to children from the definition of qualified civil liability action.	Amendment Rejected (35-64)	Yea	Nay
216	1	7/29/05	On the Amendment S.Amdt. 1645 to S. 397 (Protection of Lawful Commerce in Arms Act) To regulate the sale and possession of armor piercing ammunition, and for other purposes.	Amendment Agreed to (87-11)	Yea	Yea
217	1	7/29/05	On the Amendment S.Amdt. 1615 to S. 397 (Protection of Lawful Commerce in Arms Act) To expand the definition of armor piercing ammunition and for other purposes.	Amendment Rejected (31-64)	Yea	Nay
218	1	7/29/05	On the Amendment S.Amdt. 1642 to S. 397 (Protection of Lawful Commerce in Arms Act) To provide a complete substitute.	Amendment Rejected (33-63)	Yea	Nay

Vote No.	Session	Date	Vote Question / Description	Result	Obama's Position	McCain's Position
219	1	7/29/05	**On Passage of the Bill S. 397** A bill to prohibit civil liability actions from being brought or continued against manufacturers, distributors, dealers, or importers of firearms or ammunition for damages, injunctive or other relief resulting from the misuse of their products by others.	Bill Passed (65-31)	Nay	Yea
220	1	7/29/05	**On the Conference Report H.R. 3** A bill to authorize funds for Federal-aid highways, highway safety programs, and transit programs, and for other purposes.	Conference Report Agreed to (91-4)	Yea	Nay
221	1	9/06/05	**On the Resolution S.Res. 233** A resolution expressing the condolences of the Nation to the victims of Hurricane Katrina, commending the resiliency of the people of the States of Louisiana, Mississippi, and Alabama, and committing to stand by them in the relief and recovery efforts.	Resolution Agreed to (94-0)	Yea	Yea
222	1	9/07/05	**On the Resolution S.Res. 234** A resolution relative to the death of William H. Rehnquist, Chief Justice of the United States.	Resolution Agreed to (95-0)	Yea	Yea
223	1	9/08/05	**On Passage of the Bill H.R. 3673** A bill making further emergency supplemental appropriations to meet immediate needs arising from the consequences of Hurricane Katrina, for the fiscal year ending September 30, 2005, and for other purposes.	Bill Passed (97-0)	Yea	Yea
224	1	9/12/05	**On the Motion (Motion To Proceed To Consider S. J. Res. 20)** A joint resolution disapproving a rule promulgated by the Adminstrator of the Environmental Protection Agency to delist coal and oil-direct utility units from the source category list under the Clean Air Act.	Motion Agreed to (92-0)	Yea	Yea

VOTE No.	SES-SION	DATE	VOTE QUESTION Description	RESULT	OBAMA'S POSTION	MCCAIN'S POSTION
225	1	9/13/05	On the Joint Resolution S.J.Res. 20 A joint resolution disapproving a rule promulgated by the Adminstrator of the Environmental Protection Agency to delist coal and oil-direct utility units from the source category list under the Clean Air Act.	Joint Resolution Defeated (47-51)	Yea	Yea
226	1	9/13/05	On the Amendment S.Amdt. 1661 to H.R. 2862 (Departments of Commerce and Justice, Science, and Related Agencies Appropriations Act, 2006) To provide emergency funding for victims of Hurricane Katrina.	Amend-ment Rejected (41-56)	Yea	Nay
227	1	9/14/05	On the Motion (Motion To Waive CBA Stabenow Amdt. No. 1687, As Modified) To provide funding for interoperable communications equipment grants.	Motion Rejected (40-58, 3/5 majority required)	Yea	Nay
228	1	9/14/05	On the Motion (Motion To Suspend Paragraph 4, Rule XVI RE: Dorgan Amdt. No. 1670) To establish a special committee of the Senate to investigate the awarding and carrying out of contracts to conduct activities in Afghanistan and Iraq and to fight the war on terrorism.	Motion Rejected (44-53, 3/5 majority required)	Yea	Nay
229	1	9/14/05	On the Motion (Motion To Suspend Paragraph 4, Rule XVI RE: Clinton Amdt. NO. 1660) To establish a congressional commission to examine the Federal, State, and local response to the devastation wrought by Hurricane Katrina in the Gulf Region of the United States especially in the States of Louisiana, Mississippi, Alabama, and other areas impacted in the aftermath and make immediate corrective measures to improve such responses in the future.	Motion Rejected (44-54, 3/5 majority required)	Yea	Nay

VOTE No.	SES- SION	DATE	VOTE QUESTION Description	RESULT	OBAMA'S POSTION	MCCAIN'S POSTION
230	1	9/14/05	On the Motion (Motion To Table Coburn Amdt. No. 1648) To eliminate the funding for the Advanced Technology Program and increase the funding available for the National Oceanic and Atmospheric Administration, community oriented policing service, and State and local law enforcement assistance.	Motion Agreed to (68-29)	Yea	Nay
231	1	9/15/05	On the Amendment S.Amdt. 1713 to H.R. 2862 (Departments of Commerce and Justice, Science, and Related Agencies Appropriations Act, 2006) To provide that funds must be used in a manner consistent with the Bipartisan Trade Promotion Authority Act of 2002.	Amendment Agreed to (99-0)	Yea	Yea
232	1	9/15/05	On the Amendment S.Amdt. 1665 to H.R. 2862 (Departments of Commerce and Justice, Science, and Related Agencies Appropriations Act, 2006) To prohibit weakening any law that provides safeguards from unfair foreign trade practices.	Amendment Rejected (39-60)	Nay	Nay
233	1	9/15/05	On the Amendment S.Amdt. 1717 to H.R. 2862 (Departments of Commerce and Justice, Science, and Related Agencies Appropriations Act, 2006) To provide assistance for small businesses damaged by Hurricane Katrina.	Amendment Agreed to (96-0)	Yea	Yea
234	1	9/15/05	On the Motion (Motion To Suspend Paragraph 4, Rule XVI RE: Lieberman Amdt. No. 1678) To provide financial relief for individuals and entities affected by Hurricane Katrina.	Motion Rejected (43-52, 3/5 majority required)	Yea	Nay

Vote No.	Ses-sion	Date	Vote Question *Description*	Result	Obama's Postion	McCain's Postion
235	1	9/15/05	On Passage of the Bill H.R. 2862 An Act making appropriations for the Departments of Commerce and Justice, Science, and related agencies, for the fiscal year ending September 30, 2006, and for other purposes.	Bill Passed (91-4)	Yea	Yea
236	1	9/20/05	On the Amendment S.Amdt. 1732 to H.R. 2744 (Agriculture, Rural Development, Food and Drug Administration, and Related Agencies Appropriations Act, 2006) To prohibit the use of funds for developing a final rule with respect to the importation of beef from Japan.	Amend-ment Agreed to (72-26)	Yea	Nay
237	1	9/20/05	On the Amendment S.Amdt. 1753 to H.R. 2744 (Agriculture, Rural Development, Food and Drug Administration, and Related Agencies Appropriations Act, 2006) To prohibit the use of appropriated funds to pay the salaries or expenses of personnel to inspect horses under certain authority or guidelines.	Amend-ment Agreed to (69-28)	Yea	Yea
238	1	9/21/05	On the Amendment S.Amdt. 1775 to H.R. 2744 (Agriculture, Rural Development, Food and Drug Administration, and Related Agencies Appropriations Act, 2006) To require that any limitation, directive, or earmarking contained in either the House of Representatives or Senate report accompanying this bill be included in the conference report or joint statement accompanying the bill in order to be considered as having been approved by both House of Congress.	Amend-ment Agreed to (55-39)	Yea	Yea

Vote No.	Session	Date	Vote Question / Description	Result	Obama's Position	McCain's Position
239	1	9/21/05	On the Amendment S.Amdt. 1797 to H.R. 2744 (Agriculture, Rural Development, Food and Drug Administration, and Related Agencies Appropriations Act, 2006) To increase funds to implement and administer Team Nutrition programs, with an offset.	Amendment Agreed to (66-29)	Yea	Nay
240	1	9/22/05	On the Amendment S.Amdt. 1844 to H.R. 2744 (Agriculture, Rural Development, Food and Drug Administration, and Related Agencies Appropriations Act, 2006) To condition the use of funds for carrying out a provision relating to prevented planting payments, with an offset.	Amendment Rejected (47-52)	Yea	Nay
241	1	9/22/05	On Passage of the Bill H.R. 2744 A bill making appropriations for Agriculture, Rural Development, Food and Drug Administration, and Related Agencies for the fiscal year ending September 30, 2006, and for other purposes.	Bill Passed (97-2)	Yea	Yea
242	1	9/22/05	On the Amendment S.Amdt. 1852 to H.R. 2528 (Military Construction and Veterans Affairs, and Related Agencies Appropriations Act, 2006) To provide an additional $10,000,000 for the Readjustment Counseling Service, with a corresponding offset from the Healthe-Vet account.	Amendment Rejected (48-50)	Yea	Nay
243	1	9/22/05	On Passage of the Bill H.R. 2528 An Act making appropriations for Military Construction and Veterans Affairs, and Related Agencies for the fiscal year ending September 30, 2006, and for other purposes.	Bill Passed (98-0)	Yea	Yea

VOTE No.	SESSION	DATE	VOTE QUESTION Description	RESULT	OBAMA'S POSTION	MCCAIN'S POSTION
244	1	9/26/05	On the Resolution of Ratification Treaty Doc. 108-6 Protocol of Amendment to the International Convention on the Simplification and Harmonization of Customs Procedures done at Brussels on June 26, 1999	Resolution of Ratification Agreed to (87-0, 2/3 majority required)	Yea	Yea
245	1	9/29/05	On the Nomination PN801 John G. Roberts, Jr., of Maryland, to be Chief Justice of the United States	Nomination Confirmed (78-22)	Nay	Yea
246	1	9/30/05	On the Amendment S.Amdt. 1921 to H.J.Res. 68 To continue funding for the Community Services Block Grant at no less than last year's level.	Amendment Rejected (39-53)	Yea	Nay
247	1	10/05/05	Whether the Amendment is Germane S.Amdt. 1955 to H.R. 2863 (Department of Defense Appropriations Act, 2006) To authorize appropriations for fiscal year 2006 for military activities of the Department of Defense, for military construction, and for defense activities of the Department of Energy, to prescribe personnel strengths for such fiscal year for the Armed Forces, and for other purposes.	Amendment Not Germane (49-50)	Yea	Yea
248	1	10/05/05	On the Motion (Motion to Waive C.B.A. re: Bayh Amdt. No. 1933) To increase by $360,800,000 amounts appropriated by title IX for Other Procurement, Army, for the procurement of armored Tactical Wheeled Vehicles for units deployed in Iraq and Afghanistan, and to increase by $5,000,000 amounts appropriated by title IX for Research, Development, Test and Evaluation, Defense-Wide, for industrial preparedness for the implementation of a ballistics engineering research center.	Motion Rejected (56-43, 3/5 majority required)	Yea	Nay

Vote No.	Session	Date	Vote Question / Description	Result	Obama's Position	McCain's Position
249	1	10/05/05	On the Amendment S.Amdt. 1977 to H.R. 2863 (Department of Defense Appropriations Act, 2006) Relating to persons under the detention, custody, or control of the United States Government.	Amendment Agreed to (90-9)	Yea	Yea
250	1	10/05/05	On the Motion (Motion to Waive CBA re: Emergency Designation on Kerry Amdt. No. 2033) To provide for appropriations for the Low-Income Home Energy Assistance Program.	Motion Rejected (50-49, 3/5 majority required)	Yea	Nay
251	1	10/05/05	On the Motion (Motion to Waive CBA Stabenow Amdt. No. 1937) To ensure that future funding for health care for former members of the Armed Forces takes into account changes in population and inflation.	Motion Rejected (48-51, 3/5 majority required)	Yea	Nay
252	1	10/05/05	On the Motion (Motion to Invoke Cloture on H.R. 2863) A bill making appropriations for the Department of Defense for the fiscal year ending September 30, 2006, and for other purposes.	Motion Agreed to (95-4, 3/5 majority required)	Yea	Yea
253	1	10/06/05	On the Motion to Table S.Amdt. 2005 to H.R. 2863 (Department of Defense Appropriations Act, 2006) To curtail waste under the Department of Defense web-based travel system.	Motion to Table Agreed to (65-32)	Nay	Nay
254	1	10/07/05	On Passage of the Bill H.R. 2863 A bill making appropriations for the Department of Defense for the fiscal year ending September 30, 2006, and for other purposes.	Bill Passed (97-0)	Yea	Yea

VOTE No.	SES-SION	DATE	VOTE QUESTION _Description_	RESULT	OBAMA'S POSTION	MCCAIN'S POSTION
255	1	10/17/05	On the Amendment S.Amdt. 2061 to H.R. 3058 (Transportation, Treasury, Housing and Urban Development, the Judiciary, the District of Columbia, and Independent Agencies Appropriations Act, 2006) To clarify the ability of HUD to recover assets used in violation of a regulatory agreement.	Amendment Agreed to (93-0)	Yea	Not Voting
256	1	10/18/05	On the Amendment S.Amdt. 2062 to H.R. 3058 (Transportation, Treasury, Housing and Urban Development, the Judiciary, the District of Columbia, and Independent Agencies Appropriations Act, 2006) To provide that Members of Congress shall not receive a cost-of-living adjustment in pay during fiscal year 2006.	Amendment Agreed to (92-6)	Yea	Yea
257	1	10/19/05	On the Motion (Motion to Waive CBA Kenedy Amdt. No. 2063 As Modified Further) To provide for an increase in the Federal minimum wage.	Motion Rejected (47-51, 3/5 majority required)	Yea	Nay
258	1	10/19/05	On the Motion (Motion to Waive CBA Enzi Amdt. No. 2115) To promote job creation, and small business preservation in the adjustment of the Federal minimum wage.	Motion Rejected (42-57, 3/5 majority required)	Nay	Yea
259	1	10/19/05	On the Motion (Motion to Suspend Rule XVI, Paragraph 4 Re: Dorgan Amdt. No. 2078) To establish a special committee of the Senate on war and reconstruction contracting.	Motion Rejected (44-54, 2/3 majority required)	Yea	Nay

VOTE No.	SES-SION	DATE	VOTE QUESTION *Description*	RESULT	OBAMA'S POSTION	MCCAIN'S POSTION
260	1	10/20/05	On the Motion to Table S.Amdt. 2093 to H.R. 3058 (Transportation, Treasury, Housing and Urban Development, the Judiciary, the District of Columbia, and Independent Agencies Appropriations Act, 2006) To prohibit any funds under the Act from being used for a parking facility as part of the Joslyn Art Museum Master Plan, in Omaha, Nebraska.	Motion to Table Agreed to (86-13)	Yea	Nay
261	1	10/20/05	On the Motion (Motion To Waive CBA Re: Reed Amdt. No. 2077 "Emergency Designation") To provide for appropriations for the Low-Income Home Energy Assistance Program.	Motion Rejected (53-46, 3/5 majority required)	Yea	Nay
262	1	10/20/05	On the Amendment S.Amdt. 2165 to H.R. 3058 (Transportation, Treasury, Housing and Urban Development, the Judiciary, the District of Columbia, and Independent Agencies Appropriations Act, 2006) To make a perfecting amendment.	Amendment Rejected (15-82)	Nay	Not Voting
263	1	10/20/05	On the Amendment S.Amdt. 2181 to H.R. 3058 (Transportation, Treasury, Housing and Urban Development, the Judiciary, the District of Columbia, and Independent Agencies Appropriations Act, 2006) To ensure reconstruction of the Twin Spans Bridge.	Amendment Rejected (33-61)	Nay	Not Voting
264	1	10/20/05	On Passage of the Bill H.R. 3058 A bill making appropriations for the Departments of Transportation, Treasury, and Housing and Urban Development, the Judiciary, District of Columbia, and independent agencies for the fiscal year ending September 30, 2006, and for other purposes.	Bill Passed (93-1)	Yea	Not Voting

VOTE No.	SES-SION	DATE	VOTE QUESTION Description	RESULT	OBAMA'S POSTION	MCCAINS POSTION
265	1	10/24/05	On the Nomination PN258 Brian Edward Sandoval, of Nevada, to be United States District Judge for the District of Nevada	Nomination Confirmed (89-0)	Not Voting	Not Voting
266	1	10/24/05	On the Nomination PN781 Harry Sandlin Mattice, Jr., of Tennessee, to be United States District Judge for the Eastern District of Tennessee	Nomination Confirmed (91-0)	Yea	Not Voting
267	1	10/25/05	On the Amendment S.Amdt. 2196 to H.R. 3010 (Departments of Labor, Health and Human Services, and Education, and Related Agencies Appropriations Act, 2006) To require the Secretary of Health and Human Services to submit to Congress a plan for changing the numerical identifier used to identify Medicare beneficiaries under the Medicare program.	Amendment Agreed to (98-0)	Yea	Yea
268	1	10/25/05	On the Motion (Motion to Waive CBA Re: Kennedy Amdt. No. 2213) To increase the maximum Federal Pell Grant award by $200 to $4,250.	Motion Rejected (48-51, 3/5 majority required)	Yea	Nay
269	1	10/26/05	On the Motion (Motion to Waive CBA Re: Byrd Amdt. No. 2275) To provide additional funding for title I of the Elementary and Secondary Education Act of 1965.	Motion Rejected (44-51, 3/5 majority required)	Yea	Nay
270	1	10/26/05	On the Motion (Motion to Waive CBA Reed Amdt. No. 2194, As Further Modified) To provide for appropriations for the Low-Income Home Energy Assistance Program.	Motion Rejected (54-43, 3/5 majority required)	Yea	Nay

Vote No.	Session	Date	Vote Question Description	Result	Obama's Position	McCain's Position
271	1	10/26/05	On the Amendment S.Amdt. 2253 to H.R. 3010 (Departments of Labor, Health and Human Services, and Education, and Related Agencies Appropriations Act, 2006) To increase appropriations for the Low-Income Home Energy Assistance Program by $1,276,000,000, with an across-the-board reduction.	Amendment Rejected (46-53)	Nay	Yea
272	1	10/26/05	On the Motion (Motion to Waive CBA Re: Dodd Amdt. No. 2254) To increase appropriations for Head Start programs.	Motion Rejected (47-52, 3/5 majority required)	Yea	Nay
273	1	10/26/05	On the Motion (Motion to Waive CBA Re: Clinton Amdt. No. 2292) To provide additional funding for part B of the Individuals with Disabilities Education Act.	Motion Rejected (46-53, 3/5 majority required)	Yea	Nay
274	1	10/26/05	On the Amendment S.Amdt. 2232 to H.R. 3010 (Departments of Labor, Health and Human Services, and Education, and Related Agencies Appropriations Act, 2006) To increase funding for the AIDS drug assistance program.	Amendment Rejected (14-85)	Nay	Yea
275	1	10/27/05	On the Cloture Motion H.R. 3010 A bill making appropriations for the Departments of Labor, Health and Human Services, and Education, and Related Agencies for the fiscal year ending September 30, 2006, and for other purposes.	Cloture Motion Agreed to (97-0, 3/5 majority required)	Yea	Yea
276	1	10/27/05	On the Nomination PN600 John Richard Smoak, of Florida, to be United States District Judge for the Northern District of Florida	Nomination Confirmed (97-0)	Yea	Yea

VOTE No.	SES-SION	DATE	VOTE QUESTION Description	RESULT	OBAMA'S POSTION	MCCAIN'S POSTION
277	1	10/27/05	On the Nomination PN197 Susan Bieke Neilson, of Michigan, to be United States Circuit Judge for the Sixth Circuit	Nomination Confirmed (97-0)	Yea	Yea
278	1	10/27/05	On the Motion (Motion to Waive CBA Re: Smith Amdt. No. 2259) To provide funding for the AIDS Drug Assistance Program within the Health Resources and Services Administration.	Motion Rejected (46-50, 3/5 majority required)	Yea	Nay
279	1	10/27/05	On the Motion (Motion to Waive CBA Re: Boxer Amdt. No. 2287, As Modified) To increase appropriations for after-school programs through 21st century community learning centers.	Motion Rejected (41-56, 3/5 majority required)	Yea	Nay
280	1	10/27/05	On the Amendment S.Amdt. 2300 to H.R. 3010 (Departments of Labor, Health and Human Services, and Education, and Related Agencies Appropriations Act, 2006) To prohibit funding for the support, development, or distribution of the Department of Education's e-Language Learning System (ELLS).	Amendment Rejected (41-56)	Nay	Nay
281	1	10/27/05	On Passage of the Bill H.R. 3010 A bill making appropriations for the Departments of Labor, Health and Human Services, and Education, and Related Agencies for the fiscal year ending September 30, 2006, and for other purposes.	Bill Passed (94-3)	Yea	Yea
282	1	11/03/05	On the Conference Report H.R. 2744 A bill making appropriations for Agriculture, Rural Development, Food and Drug Administration, and Related Agencies for the fiscal year ending September 30, 2006, and for other purposes.	Conference Report Agreed to (81-18)	Yea	Nay

Vote No.	Ses-sion	Date	Vote Question Description	Result	Obama's Postion	McCain's Postion
283	1	11/03/05	On the Motion (Motion to Waive CBA Re: Conrad Amdt. No. 2351) To fully reinstate the pay-as-you-go requirement through 2010.	Motion Rejected (50-49, 3/5 majority required)	Yea	Yea
284	1	11/03/05	On the Motion (Motion To Waive CBA Re: Ensign Amdt. No. 2404) To provide assistance for elementary and secondary schools and students, and institutions of higher education, affected by Hurricane Katrina.	Motion Rejected (31-68, 3/5 majority required)	Nay	Yea
285	1	11/03/05	On the Motion (Motion To Waive CBA Re: Lincoln Amdt. No. 2356) To provide emergency health care and other relief for survivors of Hurricane Katrina.	Motion Rejected (48-51, 3/5 majority required)	Yea	Nay
286	1	11/03/05	On the Motion (Motion To Waive CBA Re: Inhofe Amdt. No. 2355) To cap non-defense, non-trust-fund, discretionary spending at the previous fiscal year's level, beginning with fiscal year 2007.	Motion Rejected (32-67, 3/5 majority required)	Nay	Yea
287	1	11/03/05	On the Amendment S.Amdt. 2357 to S. 1932 (Deficit Reduction Omnibus Reconciliation Act of 2005) To hold Medicare beneficiaries harmless for the increase in the 2007 Medicare monthly part B premium that would otherwise occur because of the 2006 increase in payments under the physician fee schedule.	Amendment Rejected (49-50)	Yea	Nay
288	1	11/03/05	On the Amendment S.Amdt. 2358 to S. 1932 (Deficit Reduction Omnibus Reconciliation Act of 2005) To strike the title relating to the establishment of an oil and gas leasing program in the Coastal Plain.	Amendment Rejected (48-51)	Yea	Yea

Vote No.	Ses- sion	Date	Vote Question Description	Result	Obama's Postion	McCain's Postion
289	1	11/03/05	On the Amendment S.Amdt. 2362 to S. 1932 (Deficit Reduction Omnibus Reconciliation Act of 2005) To enhance the energy security of the United States by prohibiting the exportation of oil and gas produced under leases in the Arctic National Wildlife Refuge.	Amend- ment Agreed to (83-16)	Yea	Nay
290	1	11/03/05	On the Motion (Motion To Waive CBA Re: Grassley Amdt. No. 2359) To clarify certain payment limita- tions applicable to certain payments under title I of the Farm Security and Rural Investment Act of 2002 and section 1101 of the Agricultural Reconciliation Act of 2005 and to partially restore funding to programs reduced by section 1101, 1201, and 1202 of the Agricultural Reconcilia- tion Act of 2005.	Motion Rejected (46-53, 3/5 majority required)	Yea	Nay
291	1	11/03/05	On the Amendment S.Amdt. 2365 to S. 1932 (Deficit Reduction Omnibus Reconciliation Act of 2005) To prevent a severe reduction in the Federal medical assistance percentage determined for a State for fiscal year 2006 and to extend rebates for pre- scription drugs to enrollees in Medic- aid managed care organizations.	Amend- ment Agreed to (54-45)	Yea	Nay
292	1	11/03/05	On the Amendment S.Amdt. 2360 to S. 1932 (Deficit Reduction Omnibus Reconciliation Act of 2005) To reauthorize Amtrak, and for other purposes.	Amend- ment Agreed to (93-6)	Yea	Yea
293	1	11/03/05	On the Amendment S.Amdt. 2370 to S. 1932 (Deficit Reduction Omnibus Reconciliation Act of 2005) To move forward the date on which the transition to digital television is to occur.	Amend- ment Rejected (30-69)	Nay	Yea

VOTE No.	SES-SION	DATE	VOTE QUESTION *Description*	RESULT	OBAMA'S POSTION	MCCAIN'S POSTION
294	1	11/03/05	On the Motion (Motion to Waive CBA Re: Murray Amdt. No. 2372) To provide a 6-month transition period for coverage of prescription drugs under Medicaid for individuals whose drug coverage is to be moved to the Medicare prescription drug program.	Motion Rejected (43-56, 3/5 majority required)	Yea	Nay
295	1	11/03/05	On the Amendment S.Amdt. 2367 to S. 1932 (Deficit Reduction Omnibus Reconciliation Act of 2005) To replace title VIII of the bill with an amendment to section 214(c) of the Immigration and Nationality Act to impose a fee on employers who hire certain non-immigrants.	Amend-ment Rejected (14-85)	Nay	Nay
296	1	11/03/05	On the Motion (Motion to Waive CBA Re: Byrd Amdt. No. 2414) To provide for the suspension of the debate limitation on reconciliation legislation that causes a deficit or in-creases the deficit.	Motion Rejected (44-55, 3/5 majority required)	Yea	Nay
297	1	11/03/05	On the Motion (Motion To Waive CBA Re: Lautenberg Amdt. No. 2381) To require certification prior to ben-eficiary enrollment in a prescription drug plan or an MA-PD plan that has a gap in the coverage of prescription drugs under part D of title XVIII of the Social Security Act.	Motion Rejected (43-56, 3/5 majority required)	Yea	Nay
298	1	11/03/05	On the Amendment S.Amdt. 2400 to S. 1932 (Deficit Reduction Omnibus Reconciliation Act of 2005) To ensure the payment to the Trea-sury of the United States of 50 percent of revenues from oil and gas leasing and production on the Coastal Plain.	Amend-ment Rejected (48-51)	Yea	Yea

Vote No.	Ses-sion	Date	Vote Question Description	Result	Obama's Position	McCain's Postion
299	1	11/03/05	On the Amendment S.Amdt. 2348 to S. 1932 (Deficit Reduction Omnibus Reconciliation Act of 2005) To strike the provisions increasing the Medicaid rebate for generic drugs.	Amend-ment Rejected (49-50)	Yea	Yea
300	1	11/03/05	On the Amendment S.Amdt. 2409 to S. 1932 (Deficit Reduction Omnibus Reconciliation Act of 2005) To strike provisions relating to reforms of targeted case management.	Amend-ment Rejected (46-52)	Yea	Nay
301	1	11/03/05	On the Amendment S.Amdt. 2396 to S. 1932 (Deficit Reduction Omnibus Reconciliation Act of 2005) To strike subtitle C of title II relating to FHA asset disposition.	Amend-ment Rejected (48-51)	Yea	Nay
302	1	11/03/05	On the Motion (Motion To Waive CBA Re: Snowe Amdt. No. 2371) To amend title XVIII of the Social Se-curity Act to provide the authority for negotiating fair prices for medicare prescription drugs.	Motion Rejected (51-48, 3/5 majority required)	Yea	Yea
303	1	11/03/05	On Passage of the Bill S. 1932 An original bill to provide for recon-ciliation pursuant to section 202(a) of the concurrent resolution on the budget for fiscal year 2006 (H. Con. Res. 95).	Bill Passed (52-47)	Nay	Yea
304	1	11/07/05	On the Amendment S.Amdt. 2423 to S. 1042 (National Defense Authori-zation Act for Fiscal Year 2006) To authorize a program to provide health, medical, and life insurance benefits to workers at the Rocky Flats Environmental Technology Site, Colorado, who would other-wise fail to qualify for such benefits because of an early physical comple-tion date.	Amend-ment Rejected (38-53)	Yea	Not Voting

VOTE No.	SES-SION	DATE	VOTE QUESTION Description	RESULT	OBAMA'S POSTION	MCCAIN'S POSTION
305	1	11/08/05	On the Amendment S.Amdt. 2439 to S. 1042 (National Defense Authorization Act for Fiscal Year 2006) Relating to the American Forces Network.	Amendment Agreed to (55-43)	Nay	Not Voting
306	1	11/08/05	On the Amendment S.Amdt. 2438 to S. 1042 (National Defense Authorization Act for Fiscal Year 2006) Relating to the American Forces Network.	Amendment Rejected (44-54)	Yea	Not Voting
307	1	11/08/05	On the Amendment S.Amdt. 2424 to S. 1042 (National Defense Authorization Act for Fiscal Year 2006) To repeal the requirement for the reduction of certain Survivor Benefit Plan annuities by the amount of dependency and indemnity compensation and to modify the effective date for paid-up coverage under the Survivor Benefit Plan.	Amendment Agreed to (92-6)	Yea	Not Voting
308	1	11/08/05	On the Amendment S.Amdt. 2436 to S. 1042 (National Defense Authorization Act for Fiscal Year 2006) To require the Secretary of Defense, subject to a national security exception, to offer to transfer to local redevelopment authorities for no consideration real property and personal property located at military installations that are closed or realigned as part of the 2005 round of defense base closure and realignment, and to clarify that the requirement does not affect certain property interests.	Amendment Rejected (36-62)	Yea	Not Voting
309	1	11/08/05	On the Amendment S.Amdt. 2430 to S. 1042 (National Defense Authorization Act for Fiscal Year 2006) To establish a national commission on policies and practices on the treatment of detainees since September 11, 2001.	Amendment Rejected (43-55)	Yea	Not Voting

VOTE No.	SESSION	DATE	VOTE QUESTION Description	RESULT	OBAMA'S POSTION	MCCAIN'S POSTION
310	1	11/08/05	On the Amendment S.Amdt. 2442 to S. 1042 (National Defense Authorization Act for Fiscal Year 2006) To provide for a report on the establishment of a Deputy Secretary of Defense for Management.	Amendment Agreed to (97-0)	Yea	Not Voting
311	1	11/08/05	On the Amendment S.Amdt. 2427 to S. 1042 (National Defense Authorization Act for Fiscal Year 2006) To make available, with an offset, an additional $50,000,000 for Operation and Maintenance for Cooperative Threat Reduction.	Amendment Rejected (37-60)	Yea	Not Voting
312	1	11/09/05	On the Amendment S.Amdt. 2440 to S. 1042 (National Defense Authorization Act for Fiscal Year 2006) To ensure by law the ability of the military service academies to include the offering of a voluntary, nondenominational prayer as an element of their activities.	Amendment Agreed to (99-0)	Yea	Yea
313	1	11/09/05	On the Amendment S.Amdt. 2443 to S. 1042 (National Defense Authorization Act for Fiscal Year 2006) To restate United States policy on the use of riot control agents by members of the Armed Forces, and for other purposes.	Amendment Agreed to (98-1)	Yea	Yea
314	1	11/09/05	On the Amendment S.Amdt. 2433 to S. 1042 (National Defense Authorization Act for Fiscal Year 2006) To reduce the eligibility age for receipt of non-regular military service retired pay for members of the Ready Reserve in active federal status or on active duty for significant periods.	Amendment Agreed to (99-0)	Yea	Yea

Vote No.	Session	Date	Vote Question / Description	Result	Obama's Position	McCain's Position
315	1	11/09/05	**On the Amendment S.Amdt. 2473 to S. 1042 (National Defense Authorization Act for Fiscal Year 2006)** To provide for eligibility for retired pay for non-regular service.	Amendment Rejected (40-59)	Yea	Nay
316	1	11/10/05	**On the Amendment S.Amdt. 2476 to S. 1042 (National Defense Authorization Act for Fiscal Year 2006)** To establish a special committee of the Senate to investigate the awarding and carrying out of contracts to conduct activities in Afghanistan and Iraq and to fight the war on terrorism.	Amendment Rejected (44-53)	Yea	Nay
317	1	11/10/05	**On the Amendment S.Amdt. 2477 to S. 1042 (National Defense Authorization Act for Fiscal Year 2006)** To modify the multiyear procurement authority for C-17 aircraft.	Amendment Agreed to (89-8)	Yea	Nay
318	1	11/10/05	**On the Amendment S.Amdt. 2507 to S. 1042 (National Defense Authorization Act for Fiscal Year 2006)** To require reports on clandestine facilities for the detention of individuals captured in the global war on terrorism.	Amendment Agreed to (82-9)	Yea	Yea
319	1	11/10/05	**On the Amendment S.Amdt. 2516 to S.Amdt. 2515 to S. 1042 (National Defense Authorization Act for Fiscal Year 2006)** Relating to the review of the status of detainees of the United States Government.	Amendment Agreed to (49-42)	Nay	Yea
320	1	11/10/05	**On the Conference Report H.R. 3057** An act making appropriations for the Department of State, foreign operations, and related programs for the fiscal year ending September 30, 2006, and for other purposes.	Conference Report Agreed to (91-0)	Yea	Yea

VOTE No.	SES- SION	DATE	VOTE QUESTION Description	RESULT	OBAMA'S POSTION	MCCAIN'S POSTION
321	1	11/14/05	On the Conference Report H.R. 2419 A bill making appropriations for energy and water development for the fiscal year ending September 30, 2006, and for other purposes.	Conference Report Agreed to (84-4)	Yea	Not Voting
322	1	11/15/05	On the Amendment S.Amdt. 2519 to S. 1042 (National Defense Authorization Act for Fiscal Year 2006) To clarify and recommend changes to the policy of the United States on Iraq and to require reports on certain matters relating to Iraq.	Amendment Rejected (40-58)	Yea	Nay
323	1	11/15/05	On the Amendment S.Amdt. 2518 to S. 1042 (National Defense Authorization Act for Fiscal Year 2006) To clarify and recommend changes to the policy of the United States on Iraq and to require reports on certain matters relating to Iraq.	Amendment Agreed to (79-19)	Yea	Nay
324	1	11/15/05	On the Amendment S.Amdt. 2523 to S.Amdt. 2515 to S. 1042 (National Defense Authorization Act for Fiscal Year 2006) To provide for judicial review of detention of enemy combatants.	Amendment Rejected (44-54)	Yea	Nay
325	1	11/15/05	On the Amendment S.Amdt. 2524 to S.Amdt. 2515 to S. 1042 (National Defense Authorization Act for Fiscal Year 2006) In the nature of a substitute.	Amendment Agreed to (84-14)	Yea	Yea
326	1	11/15/05	On Passage of the Bill S. 1042 An original bill to authorize appropriations for fiscal year 2006 for military activities of the Department of Defense, for military construction, and for defense activities of the Department of Energy, to prescribe personnel strengths for such fiscal year for the Armed Forces, and for other purposes.	Bill Passed (98-0)	Yea	Yea

Vote No.	Ses-sion	Date	Vote Question Description	Result	Obama's Postion	McCain's Postion
327	1	11/16/05	On the Amendment S.Amdt. 2583 to S. 1783 (Pension Security and Transparency Act of 2005) To compute the actuarial value of monthly benefits in the form of a life annuity commencing at age 60 for certain airline pilots.	Amendment Agreed to (58-41)	Yea	Nay
328	1	11/16/05	On Passage of the Bill S. 1783 A bill to amend the Employee Retirement Income Security Act of 1974 and the Internal Revenue Code of 1986 to reform the pension funding rules, and for other purposes.	Bill Passed (97-2)	Yea	Yea
329	1	11/16/05	On the Conference Report H.R. 2862 An Act making appropriations for the Departments of Commerce and Justice, Science, and related agencies, for the fiscal year ending September 30, 2006, and for other purposes.	Conference Report Agreed to (94-5)	Yea	Yea
330	1	11/17/05	On the Motion (Motion to Waive CBA Re: Conrad Amdt. No. 2602) To amend the Internal Revenue Code of 1986 to provide tax benefits for areas affected by Hurricanes Katrina, Rita, and Wilma and to extend certain expiring provisions, and for other purposes.	Motion Rejected (44-55, 3/5 majority required)	Yea	Nay
331	1	11/17/05	On the Motion (Motion to Waive CBA Re: Dorgan Amdt. No. 2587) To amend the Internal Revenue Code of 1986 to impose a temporary windfall profit tax on crude oil and to rebate the tax collected back to the American consumer, and for other purposes.	Motion Rejected (35-64, 3/5 majority required)	Yea	Nay
332	1	11/17/05	On the Motion (Motion to Waive CBA Re: Feinstein Amdt. No. 2609) To repeal certain tax benefits relating to oil and gas wells intangible drilling and development costs.	Motion Rejected (48-51, 3/5 majority required)	Yea	Yea

Vote No.	Ses-sion	Date	Vote Question Description	Result	Obama's Postion	McCain's Postion
333	1	11/17/05	On the Motion (Motion to Waive CBA Re: Feinstein Amdt. No. 2610) To reinstate for millionaires a top individual income tax rate of 39.6 percent, the pre-May 2003 rates of tax on capital gains and divi-dends, and to repeal the reduction and termination of the phase out of personal exemptions and overall limitation on itemized deductions, until the Federal budget deficit is eliminated.	Motion Rejected (40-59, 3/5 majority required)	Yea	Nay
334	1	11/17/05	On the Motion (Motion to Waive CBA Re: Cantwell Amdt. No. 2612) To improve the Federal Trade Com-mission's ability to protect con-sumers from price-gouging during energy emergencies, and for other purposes.	Motion Rejected (57-42, 3/5 majority required)	Yea	Nay
335	1	11/17/05	On the Motion (Motion to Waive CBA Lott Amdt. No. 2633) To clarify treatment of outside income and expenses in the Senate.	Motion Rejected (51-47, 3/5 majority required)	Yea	Yea
336	1	11/17/05	On the Motion (Motion to Waive CBA Grassley Amdt. No. 2654) To express the sense of the Senate.	Motion Rejected (53-45, 3/5 majority required)	Nay	Yea
337	1	11/17/05	On the Motion (Motion to Waive CBA Durbin Amdt. No. 2596) To express the sense of the Senate con-cerning the provision of health care for children before providing tax cuts for the wealthy.	Motion Rejected (43-55, 3/5 majority required)	Yea	Nay
338	1	11/17/05	On the Motion (Motion to Waive CBA Kennedy Amdt. No. 2588) To eliminate child poverty.	Motion Rejected (36-62, 3/5 majority required)	Yea	Nay

Vote No.	Ses-sion	Date	Vote Question Description	Result	Obama's Postion	McCain's Postion
339	1	11/17/05	On the Motion (Motion to Waive CBA Re: Reed Amdt. No. 2626) To impose a temporary windfall profits tax on crude oil and to use the proceeds of the tax collected to fund programs under the Low-Income Energy Assistance Act of 1981 through a trust fund.	Motion Rejected (50-48, 3/5 majority required)	Yea	Nay
340	1	11/17/05	On the Motion (Motion to Waive CBA Feingold Amdt. No. 2650) To fully reinstate the pay-as-you-go requirement through 2010.	Motion Rejected (50-48, 3/5 majority required)	Yea	Yea
341	1	11/17/05	On the Motion (Motion to Waive CBA Re: Schumer Amdt. No. 2635) To amend the Internal Revenue Code of 1986 to impose a temporary windfall profit tax on crude oil and to use the proceeds of the tax collected to provide a nonrefundable tax credit of $100 for every personal exemption claimed for taxable years beginning in 2005.	Motion Rejected (33-65, 3/5 majority required)	Yea	Nay
342	1	11/17/05	On the Motion (Motion to Waive CBA Nelson Amdt. No. 2601) To amend title XVIII of the Social Security Act to provide extended and additional protection to Medicare beneficiaries who enroll for the Medicare prescription drug benefit during 2006.	Motion Rejected (51-47, 3/5 majority required)	Yea	Nay
343	1	11/17/05	On the Motion (Motion to Waive CBA Boxer Amdt. No. 2634) To provide an additional $500,000,000 for each of fiscal years 2006 through 2010, to be used for readjustment counseling, related mental health services, and treatment and rehabilitative services for veterans with mental illness, post-traumatic stress disorder, or substance use disorder.	Motion Rejected (43-55, 3/5 majority required)	Yea	Nay

VOTE No.	SES-SION	DATE	VOTE QUESTION Description	RESULT	OBAMA'S POSTION	MCCAIN'S POSTION
344	1	11/17/05	On the Motion (Motion to Waive CBA Kerry Amdt. No. 2616) To accelerate marriage penalty relief for the earned income tax credit, to extend the election to include combat pay in earned income, and to make modifications of effective dates of leasing provisions of the American Jobs Creation Act of 2004.	Motion Rejected (55-43, 3/5 majority required)	Yea	Yea
345	1	11/17/05	On the Motion (Motion to Waive CBA Dayton Amdt. No. 2629) To allow a refundable tax credit for the energy costs of farmers and ranchers, and to modify the foreign tax credit rules applicable to dual capacity taxpayers.	Motion Rejected (47-51, 3/5 majority required)	Yea	Nay
346	1	11/17/05	On the Motion (Motion to Waive CBA Harkin Amdt. No. 2665) To amend the Internal Revenue Code of 1986 to restore the phaseout of personal exemptions and the overall limitation on itemized deductions and to modify the income threshold used to calculate the refundable portion of the child tax credit.	Motion Rejected (42-56, 3/5 majority required)	Yea	Nay
347	1	11/18/05	On Passage of the Bill S. 2020 An original bill to provide for reconciliation pursuant to section 202(b) of the concurrent resolution on the budget for fiscal year 2006.	Bill Passed (64-33)	Nay	Yea
348	1	11/18/05	On the Amendment S.Amdt. 2672 to H.J.Res. 72 To increase the amount appropriated to carry out under the Community Services Block Grant Act.	Amendment Rejected (46-50)	Yea	Nay

VOTE No.	SES-SION	DATE	VOTE QUESTION Description	RESULT	OBAMA'S POSTION	McCAIN'S POSTION
349	1	11/18/05	On the Motion (Specter Motion to Instruct Conferees Re: H.R. 3010) A bill making appropriations for the Departments of Labor, Health and Human Services, and Education, and Related Agencies for the fiscal year ending September 30, 2006, and for other purposes.	Motion Agreed to (66-28)	Yea	Nay
350	1	11/18/05	On the Motion (Durbin Motion to Instruct Conferees Re: H.R. 3010) A bill making appropriations for the Departments of Labor, Health and Human Services, and Education, and Related Agencies for the fiscal year ending September 30, 2006, and for other purposes.	Motion Agreed to (58-36)	Yea	Nay
351	1	12/14/05	On the Motion (Carper Motion to Instruct Conferees on S. 1932) An original bill to provide for reconciliation pursuant to section 202(a) of the concurrent resolution on the budget for fiscal year 2006 (H. Con. Res. 95).	Motion Agreed to (64-27)	Yea	Not Voting
352	1	12/14/05	On the Motion (Baucus Motion to Instruct Conferees on S. 1932) An original bill to provide for reconciliation pursuant to section 202(a) of the concurrent resolution on the budget for fiscal year 2006 (H. Con. Res. 95).	Motion Agreed to (75-16)	Yea	Not Voting
353	1	12/14/05	On the Motion (Harkin Motion To Instruct Conferees on S. 1932) An original bill to provide for reconciliation pursuant to section 202(a) of the concurrent resolution on the budget for fiscal year 2006 (H. Con. Res. 95).	Motion Agreed to (66-26)	Yea	Not Voting
354	1	12/15/05	On the Motion (Dewine Motion to Instruct Conferees on S. 1932) An original bill to provide for reconciliation pursuant to section 202(a) of the concurrent resolution on the budget for fiscal year 2006 (H. Con. Res. 95).	Motion Agreed to (71-20)	Yea	Nay

Vote No.	Ses-sion	Date	Vote Question Description	Result	Obama's Postion	McCain's Postion
355	1	12/15/05	On the Motion (Kohl Motion to In-struct Conferees on S. 1932) An original bill to provide for reconcili-ation pursuant to section 202(a) of the concurrent resolution on the budget for fiscal year 2006 (H. Con. Res. 95).	Motion Agreed to (75-16)	Yea	Yea
356	1	12/15/05	On the Motion (Kennedy Motion to Instruct Conferees on S. 1932) An original bill to provide for recon-ciliation pursuant to section 202(a) of the concurrent resolution on the budget for fiscal year 2006 (H. Con. Res. 95).	Motion Agreed to (83-8)	Yea	Yea
357	1	12/15/05	On the Motion (Reed Motion to In-struct Conferees on S. 1932) An original bill to provide for recon-ciliation pursuant to section 202(a) of the concurrent resolution on the budget for fiscal year 2006 (H. Con. Res. 95).	Motion Agreed to (63-28)	Yea	Yea
358	1	12/16/05	On the Cloture Motion H.R. 3199 A bill to extend and modify authori-ties needed to combat terrorism, and for other purposes.	Cloture Motion Rejected (52-47, 3/5 majority required)	Nay	Yea
359	1	12/19/05	On the Motion to Proceed H.R. 2863 A bill making appropriations for the Department of Defense for the fiscal year ending September 30, 2006, and for other purposes.	Motion to Proceed Agreed to (94-1)	Yea	Not Voting
360	1	12/19/05	On the Motion to Proceed H.R. 1815 To authorize appropriations for fiscal year 2006 for military activities of the Department of Defense, for military construction, and for defense activities of the Department of Energy, to pre-scribe military personnel strengths for such fiscal year.	Motion to Proceed Agreed to (95-0)	Yea	Not Voting

VOTE No.	SES-SION	DATE	VOTE QUESTION *Description*	RESULT	OBAMA'S POSTION	MCCAIN'S POSTION
361	1	12/19/05	On the Motion to Proceed S. 1932 An original bill to provide for reconciliation pursuant to section 202(a) of the concurrent resolution on the budget for fiscal year 2006 (H. Con. Res. 95).	Motion to Proceed Agreed to (86-9)	Nay	Not Voting
362	1	12/21/05	On the Motion (Motion to Waive CBA (Sects. 313(b)(1)(A) and 313(b)(1)(D)) Re: Conference Report to Accompany S. 1932) An original bill to provide for reconciliation pursuant to section 202(a) of the concurrent resolution on the budget for fiscal year 2006 (H. Con. Res. 95).	Motion Rejected (52-48, 3/5 majority required)	Nay	Yea
363	1	12/21/05	On the Motion (Motion to Concur in House Amdt. To S. 1932, With an Amdt.) An original bill to provide for reconciliation pursuant to section 202(a) of the concurrent resolution on the budget for fiscal year 2006 (H. Con. Res. 95).	Motion Agreed to (50-50, Vice President voted Yea)	Nay	Yea
364	1	12/21/05	On the Cloture Motion H.R. 2863 A bill making appropriations for the Department of Defense for the fiscal year ending September 30, 2006, and for other purposes.	Cloture Motion Rejected (56-44, 3/5 majority required)	Nay	Yea
365	1	12/21/05	On the Concurrent Resolution S.Con.Res. 74 A concurrent resolution correcting the enrollment of H.R. 2863.	Concurrent Resolution Agreed to (48-45)	Yea	Not Voting
366	1	12/21/05	On the Conference Report H.R. 2863 A bill making appropriations for the Department of Defense for the fiscal year ending September 30, 2006, and for other purposes.	Conference Report Agreed to (93-0)	Yea	Not Voting

2ND SESSION

VOTE No.	SES-SION	DATE	VOTE QUESTION *Description*	RESULT	OBAMA'S POSTION	MCCAIN'S POSTION
1	2	1/30/06	On the Cloture Motion PN1059 Samuel A. Alito, Jr., of New Jersey, to be an Associate Justice of the Supreme Court of the United States	Cloture Motion Agreed to (72-25, 3/5 majority required)	Nay	Yea

Vote No.	Session	Date	Vote Question Description	Result	Obama's Postion	McCain's Postion
2	2	1/31/06	On the Nomination PN1059 Samuel A. Alito, Jr., of New Jersey, to be an Associate Justice of the Supreme Court of the United States	Nomination Confirmed (58-42)	Nay	Yea
3	2	2/02/06	On the Motion (Motion to Waive CBA Conrad Amdt. No. 2729) To provide revenue provisions.	Motion Rejected (44-52, 3/5 majority required)	Yea	Not Available
4	2	2/02/06	On the Amendment S.Amdt. 2731 to S.Amdt. 2707 to H.R. 4297 (Tax Relief Extension Reconciliation Act of 2005) To express the sense of the Senate regarding the Medicare part D prescription drug program.	Amendment Rejected (42-54)	Nay	Yea
5	2	2/02/06	On the Motion (Motion to Waive CBA Re: Nelson (FL) Amdt. No. 2730) To provide for necessary beneficiary protections in order to ensure access to coverage under the Medicare part D prescription drug program.	Motion Rejected (52-45, 3/5 majority required)	Yea	Nay
6	2	2/02/06	On the Motion (Motion to Waive CBA Clinton Amdt. No. 2716) To establish a congressional commission to examine the Federal, State, and local response to the devastation wrought by Hurricane Katrina in the Gulf Region of the United States especially in the States of Louisiana, Mississippi, Alabama, and other areas impacted in the aftermath and make immediate corrective measures to improve such responses in the future.	Motion Rejected (44-53, 3/5 majority required)	Yea	Nay
7	2	2/02/06	On the Motion (Motion to Waive CBA Dodd Amdt. No. 2735) To support the health needs of our veterans and military personnel and reduce the deficit by making tax rates fairer for all Americans.	Motion Rejected (44-53, 3/5 majority required)	Yea	Nay

Vote No.	Ses- sion	Date	Vote Question Description	Result	Obama's Postion	McCain's Postion
8	2	2/02/06	On the Motion (Motion to Waive CBA Reed Amdt. No. 2737) To strengthen America's military, to repeal the extension of tax rates for capital gains and dividends, to reduce the deficit, and for other purposes.	Motion Rejected (44-53, 3/5 majority required)	Yea	Nay
9	2	2/02/06	On the Amendment S.Amdt. 2705 to S.Amdt. 2707 to H.R. 4297 (Tax Relief Extension Reconciliation Act of 2005) To express the sense of the Senate that protecting middle-class families from the alternative minimum tax should be a higher priority for Congress in 2006 than extending a tax cut that does not expire until the end of 2008.	Amend- ment Agreed to (73-24)	Yea	Nay
10	2	2/02/06	On Passage of the Bill H.R. 4297 A bill to provide for reconciliation pursuant to section 201(b) of the concurrent resolution on the budget for fiscal year 2006.	Bill Passed (66-31)	Nay	Yea
11	2	2/02/06	On Passage of the Bill H.R. 4659 A bill to amend the USA PATRIOT ACT to extend the sunset of certain provisions of such Act.	Bill Passed (95-1)	Yea	Yea
12	2	2/07/06	On Cloture on the Motion to Proceed S. 852 A bill to create a fair and efficient system to resolve claims of victims for bodily injury caused by asbestos exposure, and for other purposes.	Cloture on the Motion to Proceed Agreed to (98-1, 3/5 majority required)	Yea	Yea
13	2	2/09/06	On the Motion to Table S.Amdt. 2748 to S. 852 (Fairness in Asbestos Injury Resolution Act of 2005) To provide a new system by which to resolve claims for bodily injury caused by asbestos exposure, and for other purposes.	Motion to Table Agreed to (70-27)	Yea	Not Voting

Vote No.	Ses- sion	Date	Vote Question Description	Result	Obama's Postion	McCain's Postion
14	2	2/13/06	On the Motion (Grassley Motion to Instruct Conferees on H.R. 4297 Re: Veterans) A bill to provide for reconciliation pursuant to section 201(b) of the concurrent resolution on the budget for fiscal year 2006.	Motion Agreed to (92-0)	Yea	Not Voting
15	2	2/13/06	On the Motion (Dodd Motion to Instruct Conferees on H.R. 4297 Re: Veterans) A bill to provide for reconciliation pursuant to section 201(b) of the concurrent resolution on the budget for fiscal year 2006.	Motion Rejected (40-53)	Yea	Not Voting
16	2	2/14/06	On the Motion (Grassley Motion to Instruct Conferees on H.R. 4297 Re: AMT/Capital Gains) A bill to provide for reconciliation pursuant to section 201(b) of the concurrent resolution on the budget for fiscal year 2006.	Motion Agreed to (53-47)	Nay	Yea
17	2	2/14/06	On the Motion (Kennedy Motion to Instruct Conference on H.R. 4297 Re: Capital Gains) A bill to provide for reconciliation pursuant to section 201(b) of the concurrent resolution on the budget for fiscal year 2006.	Motion Rejected (47-53)	Yea	Nay
18	2	2/14/06	On the Motion (Reed Motion to Instruct Conferees on H.R. 4297 Re: Military) A bill to provide for reconciliation pursuant to section 201(b) of the concurrent resolution on the budget for fiscal year 2006.	Motion Rejected (45-55)	Yea	Nay
19	2	2/14/06	On the Motion (Hutchison Motion to Instruct Conferees on H.R. 4297 Re: States Sales Taxes) A bill to provide for reconciliation pursuant to section 201(b) of the concurrent resolution on the budget for fiscal year 2006.	Motion Agreed to (75-25)	Yea	Yea

Vote No.	Ses- sion	Date	Vote Question *Description*	Result	Obama's Postion	McCain's Postion
20	2	2/14/06	On the Motion (Lautenberg Motion to Instruct Conferees on H.R. 4297 Re: National Debt) A bill to provide for reconciliation pursuant to section 201(b) of the concurrent resolution on the budget for fiscal year 2006.	Motion Rejected (46-54)	Yea	Nay
21	2	2/14/06	On the Motion (Motion to Waive CBA Re: S. 852) A bill to create a fair and efficient system to resolve claims of victims for bodily injury caused by asbestos exposure, and for other purposes.	Motion Rejected (58-41, 3/5 majority required)	Nay	Nay
22	2	2/16/06	On the Cloture Motion S. 2271 A bill to clarify that individuals who receive FISA orders can challenge nondisclosure requirements, that individuals who receive national security letters are not required to disclose the name of their attorney, that libraries are not wire or electronic communication service providers unless they provide specific services, and for other purposes.	Cloture Motion Agreed to (96-3, 3/5 majority required)	Yea	Yea
23	2	2/28/06	On the Cloture Motion S. 2271 A bill to clarify that individuals who receive FISA orders can challenge nondisclosure requirements, that individuals who receive national security letters are not required to disclose the name of their attorney, that libraries are not wire or electronic communication service providers unless they provide specific services, and for other purposes.	Cloture Motion Agreed to (69-30, 3/5 majority required)	Nay	Yea
24	2	3/01/06	On the Amendment S.Amdt. 2895 to S. 2271 (USA PATRIOT Act Additional Reauthorizing Amendments Act of 2006) To establish the enactment date of the Act.	Amendment Agreed to (81-18)	Nay	Yea

VOTE No.	SES-SION	DATE	VOTE QUESTION Description	RESULT	OBAMA'S POSTION	MCCAIN'S POSTION
25	2	3/01/06	**On Passage of the Bill S. 2271** A bill to clarify that individuals who receive FISA orders can challenge non-disclosure requirements, that individuals who receive national security letters are not required to disclose the name of their attorney, that libraries are not wire or electronic communication service providers unless they provide specific services, and for other purposes.	Bill Passed (95-4)	Yea	Yea
26	2	3/01/06	**On the Motion to Proceed H.R. 3199** A bill to extend and modify authorities needed to combat terrorism, and for other purposes.	Motion to Proceed Agreed to (86-13)	Yea	Yea
27	2	3/01/06	**On the Motion to Reconsider H.R. 3199** A bill to extend and modify authorities needed to combat terrorism, and for other purposes.	Motion to Reconsider Agreed to (85-14)	Yea	Yea
28	2	3/01/06	**On the Cloture Motion H.R. 3199** A bill to extend and modify authorities needed to combat terrorism, and for other purposes.	Cloture Motion Agreed to (84-15, 3/5 majority required)	Yea	Yea
29	2	3/02/06	**On the Conference Report H.R. 3199** A bill to extend and modify authorities needed to combat terrorism, and for other purposes.	Conference Report Agreed to (89-10)	Yea	Yea
30	2	3/02/06	**On the Motion (Motion to Waive CBA Re: S. 2320)** A bill to make available funds included in the Deficit Reduction Act of 2005 for the Low-Income Home Energy Assistance Program for fiscal year 2006, and for other purposes.	Motion Agreed to (66-31, 3/5 majority required)	Yea	Nay
31	2	3/06/06	**On the Nomination PN938** Timothy C. Batten, Sr., of Georgia, to be United States District Judge for the Northern District of Georgia	Nomination Confirmed (88-0)	Yea	Not Voting

Vote No.	Session	Date	Vote Question / Description	Result	Obama's Position	McCain's Position
32	2	3/06/06	On the Nomination PN940 Thomas E. Johnston, of West Virginia, to be United States District Judge for the Southern District of West Virginia	Nomination Confirmed (89-0)	Yea	Not Voting
33	2	3/07/06	On the Cloture Motion S. 2320 A bill to make available funds included in the Deficit Reduction Act of 2005 for the Low-Income Home Energy Assistance Program for fiscal year 2006, and for other purposes.	Cloture Motion Agreed to (75-25, 3/5 majority required)	Yea	Nay
34	2	3/07/06	On the Amendment S.Amdt. 2913 to S.Amdt. 2899 to S. 2320 To improve the distribution of funds to States under there Low-Income Home Energy Assistance Program.	Amendment Agreed to (68-31)	Yea	Nay
35	2	3/08/06	On the Amendment S.Amdt. 2932 to S. 2349 (Legislative Transparency and Accountability Act of 2006) To provide additional transparency in the legislative process.	Amendment Rejected (44-55)	Yea	Nay
36	2	3/09/06	On the Cloture Motion S. 2349 An original bill to provide greater transparency in the legislative process.	Cloture Motion Rejected (51-47, 2/3 majority required)	Nay	Yea
37	2	3/13/06	On the Nomination PN1060 Leo Maury Gordon, of New Jersey, to be a Judge of the United States Court of International Trade	Nomination Confirmed (82-0)	Yea	Yea
38	2	3/14/06	On the Amendment S.Amdt. 3013 to S.Con.Res. 83 To fully reinstate the pay-as-you-go requirement through 2011.	Amendment Rejected (50-50)	Yea	Yea

VOTE No.	SES-SION	DATE	VOTE QUESTION Description	RESULT	OBAMA'S POSTION	MCCAIN'S POSTION
39	2	3/14/06	On the Amendment S.Amdt. 3028 to S.Con.Res. 83 To support college access and job training by: (1) restoring program cuts slated for vocational education, TRIO, GEAR UP, Perkins Loans, and other student aid programs; (2) increasing investment in student aid programs, including increasing the maximum Pell Grant to $4,500; and (3) restoring cuts slated for job training programs; paid for by closing $6.3 billion in corporate tax loopholes.	Amendment Rejected (50-50)	Yea	Nay
40	2	3/14/06	On the Amendment S.Amdt. 2999 to S.Con.Res. 83 To provide increased funding for veterans health programs, and to negate the need for enrollment fees and increase in pharmacy co-payments.	Amendment Agreed to (100-0)	Yea	Yea
41	2	3/14/06	On the Amendment S.Amdt. 3007 to S.Con.Res. 83 To increase Veterans medical services funding by $1.5 billion in FY 2007 to be paid for by closing corporate tax loopholes.	Amendment Rejected (46-54)	Yea	Nay
42	2	3/14/06	On the Amendment S.Amdt. 3039 to S.Con.Res. 83 To make energy more affordable and sustainable, to increase our national security through foreign oil replacement with biofuels and alternative fuels and advanced/hybrid vehicle use, to accelerate production and market penetration of clean and renewable energy technologies and generation, and to more fully utilize energy efficiency and conservation technologies and practices.	Amendment Rejected (46-54)	Yea	Nay

Vote No.	Session	Date	Vote Question Description	Result	Obama's Postion	McCain's Postion
43	2	3/15/06	**On the Amendment S.Amdt. 3063 to S.Con.Res. 83** To restore funding for the Community Development Block Grant Program to the fiscal 2004 level by closing tax loopholes previously slated for elimination in Senate-passed legislation.	Amendment Rejected (45-53)	Yea	Nay
44	2	3/15/06	**On the Amendment S.Amdt. 3050 to S.Con.Res. 83** To increase funding for the Community Deveeopment Block Grant Program.	Amendment Agreed to (60-38)	Nay	Yea
45	2	3/15/06	**On the Amendment S.Amdt. 3056 to S.Con.Res. 83** To provide $5 billion for our emergency responders so that they can field effective and reliable interoperable communications equipment to respond to natural disasters, terrorist attacks and the public safety needs of America's communities and fully offset this by closing tax loopholes and collecting more from the tax gap.	Amendment Rejected (43-55)	Yea	Nay
46	2	3/15/06	**On the Amendment S.Amdt. 3061 to S.Con.Res. 83** To provide funding for maritime security, including the Container Security Initiative, improved data for targeted cargo searches, and full background checks and security threat assessments of personnel at our nation's seaports.	Amendment Agreed to (90-8)	Yea	Yea
47	2	3/15/06	**On the Amendment S.Amdt. 3054 to S.Con.Res. 83** To provide an additional $965 million to make our ports more secure by increasing port security grants, increasing inspections, improving existing programs, and increasing research and development, and to fully offset this additional funding by closing tax loopholes.	Amendment Rejected (43-53)	Yea	Nay

Vote No.	Session	Date	Vote Question Description	Result	Obama's Position	McCain's Position
48	2	3/15/06	**On the Amendment S.Amdt. 3073 to S.Con.Res. 83** To establish a reserve fund to allow for deficit-neutral legislation that would provide for an extension of the Medicare part D enrollment period.	Amendment Agreed to (76-22)	Nay	Nay
49	2	3/15/06	**On the Amendment S.Amdt. 3009 to S.Con.Res. 83** To establish a deficit-neutral reserve fund to protect medicare beneficiaries who enroll in the prescription drug benefit during 2006.	Amendment Rejected (49-49)	Yea	Nay
50	2	3/15/06	**On the Amendment S.Amdt. 3004 to S.Con.Res. 83** To ensure that any savings associated with legislation that authorizes the Secretary of Health and Human Services to use the collective purchasing power of 40,000,000 Medicare beneficiaries to negotiate the best possible prices for prescription drugs provided through part D of title XVIII of the Social Security Act in fallback plans, by private drug plans (if asked) and in other circumstances, but not permitting a uniform formulary or price setting, is reserved for deficit reduction of to improve the Medicare drug benefit.	Amendment Agreed to (54-44)	Yea	Yea
51	2	3/15/06	**On the Amendment S.Amdt. 3086 to S.Con.Res. 83** To preserve a national intercity passenger rail system by providing adequate funding of $1.45 billion for Amtrak in Fiscal Year 2007 and to fully offset this additional funding by closing corporate tax loopholes.	Amendment Rejected (44-53)	Yea	Nay
52	2	3/15/06	**On the Amendment S.Amdt. 3015 to S.Con.Res. 83** To provide an additional $550,000,000 for Amtrak for fiscal year 2007.	Amendment Rejected (39-59)	Nay	Nay

Vote No.	Session	Date	Vote Question *Description*	Result	Obama's Position	McCain's Position
53	2	3/16/06	On the Amendment S.Amdt. 3131 to H.J.Res. 47 (Increased Public Debt resolution) To require a study of debt held by foreigners.	Amendment Rejected (44-55)	Yea	Nay
54	2	3/16/06	On the Joint Resolution H.J.Res. 47 A joint resolution increasing the statutory limit on the public debt.	Joint Resolution Passed (52-48)	Nay	Yea
55	2	3/16/06	On the Amendment S.Amdt. 3133 to S.Con.Res. 83 To increase funding to combat avian flu, increase local preparedness, and create a Manhattan Project-like effort to develop a vaccine to inoculate the U.S. Population against a pandemic by $5 billion in FY 2007 paid for by requiring tax withholding on government payments to contractors like Halliburton.	Amendment Rejected (44-55)	Yea	Nay
56	2	3/16/06	On the Amendment S.Amdt. 3114 to S.Con.Res. 83 To provide for the establishment of a reserve fund concerning pandemic influenza preparedness planning.	Amendment Agreed to (99-1)	Yea	Yea
57	2	3/16/06	On the Amendment S.Amdt. 3074 to S.Con.Res. 83 To increase funding for the Low-Income Home Energy Assistance Program by $3,318,000,000 for fiscal year 2007, increasing the funds available to carry out that program to the fully authorized level of $5,100,000,000, to be paid for by closing corporate tax loopholes.	Amendment Agreed to (51-49)	Yea	Nay
58	2	3/16/06	On the Amendment S.Amdt. 3048 to S.Con.Res. 83 To increase the advance appropriations allowance in order to fund health, education and training, and low-income programs.	Amendment Agreed to (73-27)	Yea	Nay

VOTE No.	SES- SION	DATE	VOTE QUESTION Description	RESULT	OBAMA'S POSTION	MCCAIN'S POSTION
59	2	3/16/06	On the Amendment S.Amdt. 3034 to S.Con.Res. 83 To protect the American people from terrorist attacks by providing $8 billion in additional funds for homeland security government-wide, by restoring cuts to vital first responder programs in the Departments of Homeland Security and Justice, by providing an additional $1.2 billion for first responders, $1.7 billion for the Coast Guard and port security, $150 million for chemical security, $1 billion for rail and transit security, $456 million for FEMA, $1 billion for health preparedness programs, and $752 million for aviation security.	Amend- ment Rejected (43-53)	Yea	Nay
60	2	3/16/06	On the Amendment S.Amdt. 3103 to S.Con.Res. 83 To restore funding for the civil works programs of the Corps of Engineers, the Federal Water Pollution Control State Revolving Fund, the National Park Service, the Forest Service, the National Oceanic and Atmospheric Administration, Federal conservation programs, and other natural resource needs, through an offset achieved by closing corporate tax loopholes.	Amend- ment Rejected (48-49)	Yea	Nay
61	2	3/16/06	On the Amendment S.Amdt. 3102 to S.Con.Res. 83 To increase funding by $1 billion for various tribal programs and provide necessary additional funding based on recommendations from Indian country, by closing corporate tax loopholes.	Amend- ment Rejected (42-56)	Yea	Nay
62	2	3/16/06	On the Amendment S.Amdt. 3100 to S.Con.Res. 83 To provide for reconciliation instructions to the Committee on Finance to reduce mandatory spending.	Amend- ment Rejected (43-57)	Nay	Yea

Vote No.	Ses- sion	Date	Vote Question Description	Result	Obama's Postion	McCain's Postion
63	2	3/16/06	On the Amendment S.Amdt. 3141 to S.Con.Res. 83 To provide an assured stream of funding for veteran's health care that will take into account the annual changes in the veteran's population and inflation to be paid for by restoring the pre-2001 top rate for income over $1 million, closing corporate tax loopholes and delaying tax cuts for the wealthy.	Amendment Rejected (46-54)	Yea	Nay
64	2	3/16/06	On the Amendment S.Amdt. 3071 to S.Con.Res. 83 To increase funding for Title I grants and reduce debt by closing corporate tax loopholes.	Amendment Rejected (49-51)	Yea	Nay
65	2	3/16/06	On the Amendment S.Amdt. 3093 to S.Con.Res. 83 To provide for discretionary spending control.	Amendment Rejected (35-62)	Nay	Yea
66	2	3/16/06	On the Amendment S.Amdt. 3106 to S.Con.Res. 83 To restore the discretionary budget for the Department of Agriculture with an offset achieved by closing corporate tax loopholes.	Amendment Rejected (48-52)	Yea	Nay
67	2	3/16/06	On the Amendment S.Amdt. 3143 to S.Con.Res. 83 To prevent the imposition of excessive TRICARE fees and co-pays on military retirees.	Amendment Rejected (46-53)	Yea	Nay
68	2	3/16/06	On the Amendment S.Amdt. 3087 to S.Con.Res. 83 To establish a reserve fund for Social Security reform.	Amendment Rejected (46-53)	Nay	Yea
69	2	3/16/06	On the Amendment S.Amdt. 3105 to S.Con.Res. 83 No Statement of Purpose on File.	Amendment Rejected (43-57)	Yea	Nay

VOTE No.	SES-SION	DATE	VOTE QUESTION Description	RESULT	OBAMA'S POSTION	MCCAIN'S POSTION
70	2	3/16/06	On the Amendment S.Amdt. 3121 to S.Con.Res. 83 To strike the direct spending limitation.	Amendment Rejected (50-50)	Yea	Nay
71	2	3/16/06	On the Amendment S.Amdt. 3164 to S.Con.Res. 83 To establish a reserve fund to allow for deficit-neutral legislation that would provide seniors with a prescription drug benefit option that is affordable, user-friendly, and administered directly by the Secretary of Health and Human Services.	Amendment Rejected (39-60)	Yea	Nay
72	2	3/16/06	On the Amendment S.Amdt. 3128 to S.Con.Res. 83 To provide funding for implementing the Energy Policy Act of 2005 from ANWR.	Amendment Agreed to (51-49)	Nay	Yea
73	2	3/16/06	On the Amendment S.Amdt. 3166 to S.Con.Res. 83 To deny funds in FY2007 for the United Nations Human Rights Council, which the United States just voted against because countries found complicit in sustained human rights abuses are eligible for Council membership. Savings redirected to border security.	Amendment Rejected (50-50)	Nay	Yea
74	2	3/16/06	On Passage of the Bill S.Con.Res. 83 An original concurrent resolution setting forth the congressional budget for the United States Government for fiscal year 2007 and including the appropriate budgetary levels for fiscal years 2006 and 2008 through 2011.	Bill Passed (51-49)	Nay	Yea
75	2	3/16/06	On the Nomination PN1117 Jack Zouhary, of Ohio, to be United States District Judge for the Northern District of Ohio	Nomination Confirmed (96-0)	Yea	Yea

VOTE No.	SES-SION	DATE	VOTE QUESTION Description	RESULT	OBAMA'S POSTION	MCCAIN'S POSTION
76	2	3/27/06	On the Nomination PN1322 Dennis R. Spurgeon, of Florida, to be an Assistant Secretary of Energy (Nuclear Energy)	Nomination Confirmed (88-0)	Yea	Yea
77	2	3/28/06	On the Amendment S.Amdt. 3176 to S.Amdt. 2944 to S. 2349 (Legislative Transparency and Accountability Act of 2006) To establish the Senate Office of Public Integrity.	Amendment Rejected (30-67)	Yea	Yea
78	2	3/28/06	On the Amendment S.Amdt. 2944 to S. 2349 (Legislative Transparency and Accountability Act of 2006) To establish as a standing order of the Senate a requirement that a Senator publicly disclose a notice of intent to object to proceeding to any measure or matter.	Amendment Agreed to (84-13)	Yea	Yea
79	2	3/28/06	On the Cloture Motion S. 2349 An original bill to provide greater transparency in the legislative process.	Cloture Motion Agreed to (81-16, 2/3 majority required)	Nay	Nay
80	2	3/29/06	On the Motion to Table S.Amdt. 2962 to S. 2349 (Legislative Transparency and Accountability Act of 2006) To clarify the application of the gift rule to lobbyists.	Motion to Table Agreed to (68-30)	Nay	Yea
81	2	3/29/06	On the Motion to Table S.Amdt. 2980 to S. 2349 (Legislative Transparency and Accountability Act of 2006) To include Federal entities in the definition of earmarks.	Motion to Table Agreed to (57-41)	Nay	Nay
82	2	3/29/06	On Passage of the Bill S. 2349 An original bill to provide greater transparency in the legislative process.	Bill Passed (90-8)	Nay	Nay

VOTE No.	SES-SION	DATE	VOTE QUESTION Description	RESULT	OBAMA'S POSTION	MCCAIN'S POSTION
83	2	3/30/06	On the Amendment S.Amdt. 3191 to S.Amdt. 3192 to S. 2454 (Securing America's Borders Act) To require the Commissioner of the Bureau of Customs and Border Protection to collect statistics, and prepare reports describing the statistics, relating to deaths occurring at the border between the United States and Mexico.	Amendment Agreed to (94-0)	Yea	Yea
84	2	4/03/06	On the Amendment S.Amdt. 3210 to S.Amdt. 3192 to S. 2454 (Securing America's Borders Act) To provide financial aid to local law enforcement officials along the Nation's borders, and for other purposes.	Amendment Agreed to (84-6)	Yea	Not Voting
85	2	4/03/06	On the Amendment S.Amdt. 3193 to S.Amdt. 3192 to S. 2454 (Securing America's Borders Act) To prescribe the binding oath or affirmation of renunciation and allegiance required to be naturalized as a citizen of the United States, to encourage and support the efforts of prospective citizens of the United States to become citizens, and for other purposes.	Amendment Agreed to (91-1)	Yea	Not Voting
86	2	4/04/06	On the Nomination PN1180 Michael A. Chagares, of New Jersey, to be United States Circuit Judge for the Third Circuit	Nomination Confirmed (98-0)	Yea	Yea
87	2	4/04/06	On the Motion to Table S.Amdt. 3206 to S.Amdt. 3192 to S. 2454 (Securing America's Borders Act) To make certain aliens ineligible for conditional nonimmigrant work authorization and status.	Motion to Table Failed (0-99)	Nay	Nay

Vote No.	Session	Date	Vote Question *Description*	Result	Obama's Position	McCain's Position
88	2	4/06/06	On the Cloture Motion S.Amdt. 3192 to S. 2454 (Securing America's Borders Act) To amend the Immigration and Nationality Act to provide for comprehensive reform and to provide conditional nonimmigrant authorization for employment to undocumented aliens, and for other purposes.	Cloture Motion Rejected (39-60, 3/5 majority required)	Yea	Nay
89	2	4/07/06	On the Cloture Motion S. 2454 A bill to amend the Immigration and Nationality Act to provide for comprehensive reform and for other purposes.	Cloture Motion Rejected (38-60, 3/5 majority required)	Yea	Nay
90	2	4/07/06	On the Cloture Motion S. 2454 A bill to amend the Immigration and Nationality Act to provide for comprehensive reform and for other purposes.	Cloture Motion Rejected (36-62, 3/5 majority required)	Nay	Nay
91	2	4/07/06	On the Nomination PN922 Dorrance Smith, of Virginia, to be an Assistant Secretary of Defense	Nomination Confirmed (59-34)	Nay	Yea
92	2	4/07/06	On the Cloture Motion PN70 Peter Cyril Wyche Flory, of Virginia, to be an Assistant Secretary of Defense	Cloture Motion Rejected (52-41, 3/5 majority required)	Nay	Yea
93	2	4/25/06	On the Nomination PN1187 Gray Hampton Miller, of Texas, to be United States District Judge for the Southern District of Texas	Nomination Confirmed (93-0)	Not Voting	Yea
94	2	4/26/06	On the Amendment S.Amdt. 3594 to H.R. 4939 (Emergency Supplemental Appropriations Act for Defense, the Global War on Terror, and Hurricane Recovery, 2006) To provide, with an offset, emergency funding for border security efforts.	Amendment Agreed to (59-39)	Nay	Yea

Vote No.	Ses-sion	Date	Vote Question *Description*	Result	Obama's Postion	McCain's Postion
95	2	4/26/06	On the Amendment S.Amdt. 3604 to H.R. 4939 (Emergency Supplemental Appropriations Act for Defense, the Global War on Terror, and Hurricane Recovery, 2006) To provide, with an offset, emergency funding for border security efforts.	Amendment Rejected (44-54)	Yea	Nay
96	2	4/26/06	On the Motion to Table S.Amdt. 3615 to H.R. 4939 (Emergency Supplemental Appropriations Act for Defense, the Global War on Terror, and Hurricane Recovery, 2006) To return the bill to the President's proposal.	Motion to Table Agreed to (72-26)	Yea	Nay
97	2	4/26/06	On the Motion to Table H.R. 4939 A bill making emergency supplemental appropriations for the fiscal year ending September 30, 2006, and for other purposes.	Motion to Table Agreed to (68-28)	Yea	Nay
98	2	4/26/06	On the Amendment S.Amdt. 3642 to H.R. 4939 (Emergency Supplemental Appropriations Act for Defense, the Global War on Terror, and Hurricane Recovery, 2006) To provide an additional $430,000,000 for the Department of Veteran Affairs for Medical Services for outpatient care and treatment for veterans.	Amendment Agreed to (84-13)	Yea	Nay
99	2	4/26/06	On the Motion to Table S.Amdt. 3641 to H.R. 4939 (Emergency Supplemental Appropriations Act for Defense, the Global War on Terror, and Hurricane Recovery, 2006) To perfect the bill.	Motion to Table Agreed to (50-47)	Nay	Nay

Vote No.	Session	Date	Vote Question Description	Result	Obama's Postion	McCain's Postion
100	2	4/27/06	On the Motion to Table S.Amdt. 3641 to H.R. 4939 (Emergency Supplemental Appropriations Act for Defense, the Global War on Terror, and Hurricane Recovery, 2006) To perfect the bill.	Motion to Table Failed (44-51)	Nay	Nay
101	2	4/27/06	On the Amendment S.Amdt. 3709 to H.R. 4939 (Emergency Supplemental Appropriations Act for Defense, the Global War on Terror, and Hurricane Recovery, 2006) To express the sense of the Senate on requests for funds for military operations in Iraq and Afghanistan for fiscal years after fiscal year 2007.	Amendment Agreed to (94-0)	Yea	Yea
102	2	5/01/06	On the Nomination PN1136 Michael Ryan Barrett, of Ohio, to be United States District Judge for the Southern District of Ohio	Nomination Confirmed (90-0)	Yea	Yea
103	2	5/02/06	On the Cloture Motion H.R. 4939 A bill making emergency supplemental appropriations for the fiscal year ending September 30, 2006, and for other purposes.	Cloture Motion Agreed to (92-4, 3/5 majority required)	Yea	Yea
104	2	5/02/06	On the Amendment S.Amdt. 3617 to H.R. 4939 (Emergency Supplemental Appropriations Act for Defense, the Global War on Terror, and Hurricane Recovery, 2006) To strike a provision providing $6 million to sugarcane growers in Hawaii, which was not included in the Administration's emergency supplemental request.	Amendment Rejected (40-59)	Nay	Yea

Vote No.	Ses- sion	Date	Vote Question Description	Result	Obama's Postion	McCain's Postion
105	2	5/02/06	On the Amendment S.Amdt. 3641 to H.R. 4939 (Emergency Supplemental Appropriations Act for Defense, the Global War on Terror, and Hurricane Recovery, 2006) To perfect the bill.	Amendment Rejected (48-51)	Yea	Yea
106	2	5/02/06	On the Amendment S.Amdt. 3810 to H.R. 4939 (Emergency Supplemental Appropriations Act for Defense, the Global War on Terror, and Hurricane Recovery, 2006) To provide that none of the funds appropriated by this Act may be made available for hurricane relief and recovery contracts exceeding $500,000 that are awarded using procedures other than competitive procedures.	Amendment Agreed to (98-0)	Yea	Yea
107	2	5/03/06	On the Amendment S.Amdt. 3688 to H.R. 4939 (Emergency Supplemental Appropriations Act for Defense, the Global War on Terror, and Hurricane Recovery, 2006) To provide funding to compensate individuals harmed by pandemic influenza vaccine.	Amendment Agreed to (53-46)	Yea	Nay
108	2	5/03/06	On the Amendment S.Amdt. 3616 to H.R. 4939 (Emergency Supplemental Appropriations Act for Defense, the Global War on Terror, and Hurricane Recovery, 2006) To strike a provision that provides $74.5 million to states based on their production of certain types of crops, livestock and or diary products, which was not included in the Administration's emergency supplemental request.	Amendment Rejected (37-61)	Nay	Yea

Vote No.	Session	Date	Vote Question Description	Result	Obama's Postion	McCain's Postion
109	2	5/03/06	On the Amendment S.Amdt. 3673 to H.R. 4939 (Emergency Supplemental Appropriations Act for Defense, the Global War on Terror, and Hurricane Recovery, 2006) To increase funds made available for assessments of critical reservoirs and dams in the State of Hawaii.	Amendment Rejected (43-53)	Yea	Nay
110	2	5/03/06	On the Amendment S.Amdt. 3601 to H.R. 4939 (Emergency Supplemental Appropriations Act for Defense, the Global War on Terror, and Hurricane Recovery, 2006) To provide assistance relating to assessments and monitoring of waters in the State of Hawaii.	Amendment Agreed to (51-45)	Yea	Nay
111	2	5/04/06	On the Amendment S.Amdt. 3704 to H.R. 4939 (Emergency Supplemental Appropriations Act for Defense, the Global War on Terror, and Hurricane Recovery, 2006) To provide, with an offset, $20,000,000 for the Department of Veterans Affairs for Medical Facilities.	Amendment Rejected (39-59)	Nay	Nay
112	2	5/04/06	On Passage of the Bill H.R. 4939 A bill making emergency supplemental appropriations for the fiscal year ending September 30, 2006, and for other purposes.	Bill Passed (77-21)	Yea	Nay
113	2	5/04/06	On the Nomination PN1183 Brian M. Cogan, of New York, to be United States District Judge for the Eastern District of New York	Nomination Confirmed (95-0)	Yea	Yea
114	2	5/04/06	On the Nomination PN1184 Thomas M. Golden, of Pennsylvania, to be United States District Judge for the Eastern District of Pennsylvania	Nomination Confirmed (96-0)	Yea	Yea

Vote No.	Session	Date	Vote Question / Description	Result	Obama's Position	McCain's Position
115	2	5/08/06	**On Cloture on the Motion to Proceed S. 22** A bill to improve patient access to health care services and provide improved medical care by reducing the excessive burden the liability system places on the health care delivery system.	Cloture on the Motion to Proceed Rejected (48-42, 3/5 majority required)	Not Voting	Not Voting
116	2	5/08/06	**On Cloture on the Motion to Proceed S. 23** A bill to improve women's access to health care services and provide improved medical care by reducing the excessive burden the liability system places on the delivery of obstetrical and gynecological services.	Cloture on the Motion to Proceed Rejected (49-44, 3/5 majority required)	Nay	Not Voting
117	2	5/09/06	**On the Cloture Motion S. 1955** A bill to amend title I of the Employee Retirement Security Act of 1974 and the Public Health Service Act to expand health care access and reduce costs through the creation of small business health plans and through modernization of the health insurance marketplace.	Cloture Motion Agreed to (96-2, 3/5 majority required)	Yea	Yea
118	2	5/11/06	**On the Conference Report H.R. 4297** A bill to provide for reconciliation pursuant to section 201(b) of the concurrent resolution on the budget for fiscal year 2006.	Conference Report Agreed to (54-44)	Nay	Yea
119	2	5/11/06	**On the Cloture Motion S. 1955** A bill to amend title I of the Employee Retirement Security Act of 1974 and the Public Health Service Act to expand health care access and reduce costs through the creation of small business health plans and through modernization of the health insurance marketplace.	Cloture Motion Rejected (55-43, 3/5 majority required)	Nay	Yea

Vote No.	Session	Date	Vote Question Description	Result	Obama's Postion	McCain's Postion
120	2	5/16/06	On the Nomination PN1327 Milan D. Smith, Jr., of California, to be United States Circuit Judge for the Ninth Circuit	Nomination Confirmed (93-0)	Yea	Not Voting
121	2	5/16/06	On the Amendment S.Amdt. 3961 to S. 2611 (Comprehensive Immigration Reform Act of 2006) To prohibit the granting of legal status, or adjustment of current status, to any individual who enters or entered the United States in violation of Federal law unless the border security measures authorized under Title I and section 233 are fully completed and fully operational.	Amendment Rejected (40-55)	Nay	Not Voting
122	2	5/16/06	On the Amendment S.Amdt. 3994 to S. 2611 (Comprehensive Immigration Reform Act of 2006) To prohibit implementation of title IV and title VI until the President determines that implementation of such titles will strengthen the national security of the United States.	Amendment Agreed to (79-16)	Yea	Not Voting
123	2	5/16/06	On the Motion to Table S.Amdt. 4017 to S. 2611 (Comprehensive Immigration Reform Act of 2006) To prohibit aliens who are currently outside the United States from participating in the H-2C guestworker visa program.	Motion to Table Agreed to (69-28)	Nay	Yea
124	2	5/16/06	On the Motion to Table S.Amdt. 3981 to S. 2611 (Comprehensive Immigration Reform Act of 2006) To reduce the number of H-2C nonimmigrants to 200,000 during any fiscal year.	Motion to Table Failed (18-79)	Nay	Yea

VOTE No.	SES-SION	DATE	VOTE QUESTION Description	RESULT	OBAMA'S POSTION	MCCAIN'S POSTION
125	2	5/17/06	On the Amendment S.Amdt. 4027 to S. 2611 (Comprehensive Immigration Reform Act of 2006) To make certain aliens ineligible for adjustment to lawful permanent resident status or Deferred Mandatory Departure status.	Amendment Agreed to (99-0)	Yea	Yea
126	2	5/17/06	On the Amendment S.Amdt. 3979 to S. 2611 (Comprehensive Immigration Reform Act of 2006) To increase the amount of fencing and improve vehicle barriers installed along the southwest border of the United States.	Amendment Agreed to (83-16)	Nay	Yea
127	2	5/17/06	On the Amendment S.Amdt. 3963 to S. 2611 (Comprehensive Immigration Reform Act of 2006) To strike the provisions related to certain undocumented individuals.	Amendment Rejected (33-66)	Nay	Nay
128	2	5/17/06	On the Amendment S.Amdt. 3965 to S. 2611 (Comprehensive Immigration Reform Act of 2006) To modify the conditions under which an H-2C nonimmigrant may apply for an employment-based immigrant visa.	Amendment Agreed to (50-48)	Nay	Nay
129	2	5/18/06	On the Amendment S.Amdt. 4066 to S. 2611 (Comprehensive Immigration Reform Act of 2006) To modify the conditions under which an H-2C nonimmigrant may apply for adjustment of status.	Amendment Agreed to (56-43)	Yea	Yea

Vote No.	Ses-sion	Date	Vote Question *Description*	Result	Obama's Postion	McCain's Postion
130	2	5/18/06	On the Motion to Table S.Amdt. 3985 to S. 2611 (Comprehensive Immigration Reform Act of 2006) To reduce document fraud, prevent identity theft, and preserve the integrity of the Social Security system, by ensuring that persons who receive an adjustment of status under this bill are not able to receive Social Security benefits as a result of unlawful activity.	Motion to Table Agreed to (50-49)	Yea	Yea
131	2	5/18/06	On the Amendment S.Amdt. 4064 to S. 2611 (Comprehensive Immigration Reform Act of 2006) To amend title 4 United States Code, to declare English as the national language of the United States and to promote the patriotic integration of prospective US citizens.	Amendment Agreed to (62-35)	Nay	Yea
132	2	5/18/06	On the Amendment S.Amdt. 4073 to S. 2611 (Comprehensive Immigration Reform Act of 2006) To declare that English is the common and unifying language of the United States, and to preserve and enhance the role of the English language.	Amendment Agreed to (58-39)	Yea	Yea
133	2	5/18/06	On the Amendment S.Amdt. 4072 to S. 2611 (Comprehensive Immigration Reform Act of 2006) To establish a grant program to provide financial assistance to States and local governments for the costs of providing health care and educational services to noncitizens, and to provide additional funding for the State Criminal Alien Assistance Program.	Amendment Rejected (43-52)	Yea	Nay

Vote No.	Ses-sion	Date	Vote Question Description	Result	Obama's Postion	McCain's Postion
134	2	5/18/06	On the Amendment S.Amdt. 4038 to S. 2611 (Comprehensive Immigration Reform Act of 2006) To require aliens seeking adjustment of status under section 245B of the Immigration and Nationality Act or Deferred Mandatory Departure status under section 245C of such Act to pay a supplemental application fee, which shall be used to provide financial assistance to States for health and educational services for noncitizens.	Amendment Agreed to (64-32)	Nay	Nay
135	2	5/18/06	On the Motion to Table S.Amdt. 3969 to S. 2611 (Comprehensive Immigration Reform Act of 2006) To prohibit H-2C nonimmigrants from adjusting to lawful permanent resident status.	Motion to Table Agreed to (58-35)	Yea	Yea
136	2	5/22/06	On the Motion to Table S.Amdt. 4009 to S. 2611 (Comprehensive Immigration Reform Act of 2006) To modify the wage requirements for employers seeking to hire H-2A and blue card agricultural workers.	Motion to Table Agreed to (50-43)	Yea	Not Voting
137	2	5/22/06	On the Amendment S.Amdt. 4076 to S. 2611 (Comprehensive Immigration Reform Act of 2006) To authorize the use of the National Guard to secure the southern border of the United States.	Amendment Agreed to (83-10)	Yea	Not Voting
138	2	5/23/06	On the Amendment S.Amdt. 4087 to S. 2611 (Comprehensive Immigration Reform Act of 2006) To modify the conditions under which aliens who are unlawfully present in the United States are granted legal status.	Amendment Rejected (37-61)	Yea	Nay

Vote No.	Ses- sion	Date	Vote Question *Description*	Result	Obama's Position	McCain's Postion
139	2	5/23/06	On the Motion to Table S.Amdt. 4117 to S. 2611 (Comprehensive Immigration Reform Act of 2006) To amend section 212 of the Immigration and Nationality Act regarding restrictions on the admission of aliens.	Motion to Table Agreed to (79-19)	Nay	Yea
140	2	5/23/06	On the Amendment S.Amdt. 4177 to S. 2611 (Comprehensive Immigration Reform Act of 2006) To provide a substitute to title III.	Amend- ment Agreed to (59-39)	Yea	Yea
141	2	5/23/06	On the Motion to Table S.Amdt. 4106 to S. 2611 (Comprehensive Immigration Reform Act of 2006) To enhance the enforcement of labor protections for United States workers and guest workers.	Motion to Table Agreed to (57-40)	Nay	Yea
142	2	5/23/06	On the Motion to Table S.Amdt. 4142 to S. 2611 (Comprehensive Immigration Reform Act of 2006) To authorize the waiver of certain grounds of inadmissibility or removal where denial of admission or removal would result in hardship for a spouse, parent, or child who is a citizen or permanent resident alien.	Motion to Table Agreed to (63-34)	Nay	Yea
143	2	5/24/06	On the Motion to Table S.Amdt. 4085 to S. 2611 (Comprehensive Immigration Reform Act of 2006) To implement the recommendation of the Carter-Baker Commission on Federal Election Reform to protect and secure the franchise of all United States citizens from ballots being cast illegally by non-United States citizens.	Motion to Table Failed (48-49)	Yea	Nay
144	2	5/24/06	On the Cloture Motion S. 2611 A bill to provide for comprehensive immigration reform and for other purposes.	Cloture Motion Agreed to (73-25, 3/5 majority required)	Yea	Yea

VOTE No.	SES-SION	DATE	VOTE QUESTION Description	RESULT	OBAMA'S POSTION	MCCAIN'S POSTION
145	2	5/24/06	On the Motion (Motion to Waive CBA Re: S. 2611) A bill to provide for comprehensive immigration reform and for other purposes.	Motion Agreed to (67-31, 3/5 majority required)	Yea	Yea
146	2	5/24/06	On the Amendment S.Amdt. 4127 to S. 2611 (Comprehensive Immigration Reform Act of 2006) To fund improvements in border and interior security by assessing a $500 supplemental fee under title VI.	Amendment Agreed to (73-25)	Yea	Nay
147	2	5/24/06	On the Amendment S.Amdt. 4114 to S. 2611 (Comprehensive Immigration Reform Act of 2006) To amend title II of the Immigration and Nationality Act to reform the diversity visa program and create a program that awards visas to aliens with an advanced degree in science mathematics, technology, or engineering.	Amendment Agreed to (56-42)	Nay	Nay
148	2	5/24/06	On the Amendment S.Amdt. 4101 to S. 2611 (Comprehensive Immigration Reform Act of 2006) To enhance border security by creating a pilot SAFE Visa Program to grant visas to authorized nationals of a NAFTA or CAFTA-DR country who receive employment offers in job areas in the United States that have been certified by the Secretary of Labor as having a shortage of workers.	Amendment Rejected (31-67)	Nay	Nay
149	2	5/24/06	On the Motion to Table S.Amdt. 4084 to S. 2611 (Comprehensive Immigration Reform Act of 2006) To modify the eligible requirements for blue card status and to increase the fines to be paid by aliens granted such status or legal permanent resident status.	Motion to Table Agreed to (62-35)	Yea	Yea

VOTE No.	SES- SION	DATE	VOTE QUESTION Description	RESULT	OBAMA'S POSTION	MCCAIN'S POSTION
150	2	5/24/06	On the Amendment S.Amdt. 4095 to S. 2611 (Comprehensive Immigration Reform Act of 2006) To sunset the H-2C visa program after the date that is 5 years after the date of enactment of this Act.	Amendment Rejected (48-49)	Yea	Nay
151	2	5/25/06	On the Amendment S.Amdt. 4097 to S. 2611 (Comprehensive Immigration Reform Act of 2006) To modify the requirements for confidentiality certain information submitted by an alien seeking an adjustment of status under section 245B.	Amendment Rejected (49-49)	Nay	Nay
152	2	5/25/06	On the Amendment S.Amdt. 4131 to S. 2611 (Comprehensive Immigration Reform Act of 2006) To limit the total number of aliens, including spouses and children, granted employment-based legal permanent resident status to 650,000 during any fiscal year.	Amendment Agreed to (51-47)	Nay	Nay
153	2	5/25/06	On the Amendment S.Amdt. 4083 to S. 2611 (Comprehensive Immigration Reform Act of 2006) To strike the provision prohibiting a court from staying the removal of an alien in certain circumstances.	Amendment Agreed to (52-45)	Yea	Yea
154	2	5/25/06	On the Amendment S.Amdt. 4108 to S. 2611 (Comprehensive Immigration Reform Act of 2006) To limit the application of the Earned Income Tax Credit.	Amendment Rejected (37-60)	Nay	Nay

VOTE No.	SES-SION	DATE	VOTE QUESTION Description	RESULT	OBAMA'S POSTION	McCAIN'S POSTION
155	2	5/25/06	On the Amendment S.Amdt. 4136 to S. 2611 (Comprehensive Immigration Reform Act of 2006) To ensure the integrity of the Earned Income Tax Credit program by reducing the potential for fraud and to ensure that aliens who receive an adjustment of this status under this bill meet their obligation to pay back taxes without creating a burden on the American public.	Amendment Agreed to (50-47)	Nay	Nay
156	2	5/25/06	On the Amendment S.Amdt. 4188 to S. 2611 (Comprehensive Immigration Reform Act of 2006) To improve the bill.	Amendment Agreed to (56-41)	Yea	Yea
157	2	5/25/06	On Passage of the Bill S. 2611 A bill to provide for comprehensive immigration reform and for other purposes.	Bill Passed (62-36)	Yea	Yea
158	2	5/25/06	On the Cloture Motion PN1179 Brett M. Kavanaugh, of Maryland, to be United States Circuit Judge for the District of Columbia Circuit	Cloture Motion Agreed to (67-30, 3/5 majority required)	Yea	Yea
159	2	5/26/06	On the Nomination PN1179 Brett M. Kavanaugh, of Maryland, to be United States Circuit Judge for the District of Columbia Circuit	Nomination Confirmed (57-36)	Nay	Yea
160	2	5/26/06	On the Nomination PN1552 General Michael V. Hayden, United States Air Force, to be Director of the Central Intelligence Agency	Nomination Confirmed (78-15)	Nay	Yea
161	2	5/26/06	On the Cloture Motion PN1446 Dirk Kempthorne, of Idaho, to be Secretary of the Interior	Cloture Motion Agreed to (85-8)	Yea	Yea
162	2	6/06/06	On the Nomination PN1182 Renee Marie Bumb, of New Jersey, to be United States District Judge for the District of New Jersey	Nomination Confirmed (89-0)	Yea	Yea

VOTE No.	SES-SION	DATE	VOTE QUESTION Description	RESULT	OBAMA'S POSTION	MCCAIN'S POSTION
163	2	6/07/06	On the Cloture Motion S.J.Res. 1 A joint resolution proposing an amendment to the Constitution of the United States relating to marriage.	Cloture Motion Rejected (49-48, 3/5 majority required)	Nay	Nay
164	2	6/08/06	On the Cloture Motion H.R. 8 A bill to make the repeal of the estate tax permanent.	Cloture Motion Rejected (57-41, 3/5 majority required)	Nay	Yea
165	2	6/08/06	On the Cloture Motion S. 147 A bill to express the policy of the United States regarding the United States relationship with Native Hawaiians and to provide a process for the recognition by the United States of the Native Hawaiian governing entity.	Cloture Motion Rejected (56-41, 3/5 majority required)	Yea	Yea
166	2	6/08/06	On the Nomination PN1186 Noel Lawrence Hillman, of New Jersey, to be United States District Judge for the District of New Jersey	Nomination Confirmed (98-0)	Yea	Yea
167	2	6/08/06	On the Nomination PN210 Peter G. Sheridan, of New Jersey, to be United States District Judge for the District of New Jersey	Nomination Confirmed (98-0)	Yea	Yea
168	2	6/13/06	On the Amendment S.Amdt. 4208 to S. 2766 (National Defense Authorization Act for Fiscal Year 2007) To express the sense of Congress that the United States Armed Forces, the intelligence community, and other agencies, as well as the coalition partners of the United States and the Iraqi Security Forces should be commended for their actions that resulted in the death of Abu Musab al-Zarqawi, the leader of the al-Qaeda in Iraq terrorist organization and the most wanted terrorist in Iraq.	Amendment Agreed to (97-0)	Yea	Yea

Vote No.	Ses-sion	Date	Vote Question *Description*	Result	Obama's Postion	McCain's Postion
169	2	6/14/06	On the Motion to Table S.Amdt. 4230 to S. 2766 (National Defense Authorization Act for Fiscal Year 2007) To improve Federal contracting and procurement by eliminating fraud and abuse and improving competition in contracting and procurement and by enhancing administration of Federal contracting personnel.	Motion to Table Agreed to (55-43)	Nay	Yea
170	2	6/14/06	On the Amendment S.Amdt. 4242 to S. 2766 (National Defense Authorization Act for Fiscal Year 2007) To require regular budgeting for ongoing military operations.	Amend-ment Agreed to (98-0)	Yea	Yea
171	2	6/15/06	On the Conference Report H.R. 4939 A bill making emergency supplemental appropriations for the fiscal year ending September 30, 2006, and for other purposes.	Conference Report Agreed to (98-1)	Yea	Yea
172	2	6/15/06	On the Amendment S.Amdt. 4234 to S. 2766 (National Defense Authorization Act for Fiscal Year 2007) To authorize, with an offset, assistance for prodemocracy programs and activities inside and outside Iran, to make clear that the United States supports the ability of the people of Iran to exercise self-determination over their form of government, and to make enhancements to the Iran-Libya Sanctions Act of 1996.	Amend-ment Rejected (46-53)	Nay	Nay
173	2	6/15/06	On the Amendment S.Amdt. 4257 to S. 2766 (National Defense Authorization Act for Fiscal Year 2007) To state the policy of the United States on the nuclear programs of Iran.	Amend-ment Agreed to (99-0)	Yea	Yea

VOTE No.	SES- SION	DATE	VOTE QUESTION Description	RESULT	OBAMA'S POSTION	McCAIN'S POSTION
174	2	6/15/06	On the Motion to Table S.Amdt. 4269 to S.Amdt. 4265 to S. 2766 (National Defense Authorization Act for Fiscal Year 2007) To require the withdrawal of the United States Armed Forces from Iraq and urge the convening of an Iraq summit.	Motion to Table Agreed to (93-6)	Yea	Yea
175	2	6/19/06	On the Nomination PN1296 Sandra Segal Ikuta, of California, to be United States Circuit Judge for the Ninth Circuit	Nomination Confirmed (81-0)	Yea	Not Voting
176	2	6/20/06	On the Amendment S.Amdt. 4292 to S. 2766 (National Defense Authorization Act for Fiscal Year 2007) To establish a special committee of the Senate to investigate the awarding and carrying out of contracts to conduct activities in Afghanistan and Iraq and to fight the war on terrorism.	Amendment Rejected (44-52)	Yea	Nay
177	2	6/20/06	On the Amendment S.Amdt. 4272 to S. 2766 (National Defense Authorization Act for Fiscal Year 2007) To affirm the Iraqi Government position of no amnesty for terrorists who have attacked U.S. forces.	Amendment Agreed to (64-34)	Nay	Yea
178	2	6/20/06	On the Amendment S.Amdt. 4265 to S. 2766 (National Defense Authorization Act for Fiscal Year 2007) To express the sense of Congress that the Government of Iraq should not grant amnesty to persons known to have attacked, killed, or wounded members of the Armed Forces of the United States.	Amendment Agreed to (79-19)	Yea	Nay

Vote No.	Session	Date	Vote Question Description	Result	Obama's Postion	McCain's Postion
179	2	6/21/06	**On the Amendment S.Amdt. 4322 to S. 2766 (National Defense Authorization Act for Fiscal Year 2007)** To amend the Fair Labor Standards Act of 1938 to provide for an increase in the Federal minimum wage.	Amendment Agreed to (52-46)	Yea	Nay
180	2	6/21/06	**On the Amendment S.Amdt. 4376 to S. 2766 (National Defense Authorization Act for Fiscal Year 2007)** To promote job creation and small business preservation in the adjustment of the Federal minimum wage.	Amendment Rejected (45-53)	Nay	Yea
181	2	6/22/06	**On the Amendment S.Amdt. 4442 to S. 2766 (National Defense Authorization Act for Fiscal Year 2007)** To require the redeployment of United States Armed Forces from Iraq in order to further a political solution in Iraq, encourage the people of Iraq to provide for their own security, and achieve victory in the war on terror.	Amendment Rejected (13-86)	Nay	Nay
182	2	6/22/06	**On the Amendment S.Amdt. 4320 to S. 2766 (National Defense Authorization Act for Fiscal Year 2007)** To state the sense of Congress on United States policy on Iraq.	Amendment Rejected (39-60)	Yea	Nay
183	2	6/22/06	**On the Cloture Motion S. 2766** An original bill to authorize appropriations for fiscal year 2007 for military activities of the Department of Defense, for military construction, and for defense activities of the Department of Energy, to prescribe personnel strengths for such fiscal year for the Armed Forces, and for other purposes.	Cloture Motion Agreed to (98-1, 3/5 majority required)	Yea	Yea

Vote No.	Ses-sion	Date	Vote Question *Description*	Result	Obama's Postion	McCain's Postion
184	2	6/22/06	**On the Amendment S.Amdt. 4261 to S. 2766 (National Defense Authorization Act for Fiscal Year 2007)** To authorize multiyear procurement of F-22A fighter aircraft and F-119 engines.	Amend-ment Agreed to (70-28)	Nay	Nay
185	2	6/22/06	**On the Amendment S.Amdt. 4471 to S. 2766 (National Defense Authorization Act for Fiscal Year 2007)** To provide, with an offset, additional funding for missile defense testing and operations.	Amend-ment Agreed to (98-0)	Yea	Yea
186	2	6/22/06	**On Passage of the Bill S. 2766** An original bill to authorize appropriations for fiscal year 2007 for military activities of the Department of Defense, for military construction, and for defense activities of the Department of Energy, to prescribe personnel strengths for such fiscal year for the Armed Forces, and for other purposes.	Bill Passed (96-0)	Yea	Yea
187	2	6/22/06	**On the Nomination PN1185** Andrew J. Guilford, of California, to be United States District Judge for the Central District of California	Nomina-tion Confirmed (93-0)	Yea	Yea
188	2	6/27/06	**On the Amendment S.Amdt. 4543 to S.J.Res. 12 (No short title on file)** To provide a complete substitute.	Amend-ment Rejected (36-64)	Yea	Nay
189	2	6/27/06	**On the Joint Resolution S.J.Res. 12** A joint resolution proposing an amendment to the Constitution of the United States authorizing Congress to prohibit the physical desecration of the flag of the United States.	Joint Resolution Defeated (66-34, 2/3 majority required)	Nay	Yea
190	2	6/29/06	**On Passage of the Bill S. 3569** A bill to implement the United States-Oman Free Trade Agreement.	Bill Passed (60-34)	Yea	Yea

Vote No.	Ses-sion	Date	Vote Question Description	Result	Obama's Postion	McCain's Postion
191	2	7/11/06	On the Amendment S.Amdt. 4548 to H.R. 5441 (Department of Homeland Security Appropriations Act, 2007) To prohibit the United States Customs and Border Protection from preventing an individual not in the business of importing a prescription drug from importing an FDA-approved prescription drug.	Amend-ment Agreed to (68-32)	Yea	Yea
192	2	7/11/06	On the Amendment S.Amdt. 4560 to H.R. 5441 (Department of Homeland Security Appropriations Act, 2007) To amend the Homeland Security Act of 2002 to establish the United States Emergency Management Authority.	Amend-ment Agreed to (87-11)	Yea	Yea
193	2	7/11/06	On the Amendment S.Amdt. 4563 to H.R. 5441 (Department of Homeland Security Appropriations Act, 2007) To establish the Federal Emergency Management Agency as an independent agency, and for other purposes.	Amend-ment Rejected (32-66)	Yea	Nay
194	2	7/12/06	On the Motion (Motion to Waive CBA Re: Biden Amdt. No. 4553) To increase amounts for the rail and transit security programs, and for other purposes.	Motion Rejected (50-50, 3/5 majority required)	Yea	Nay
195	2	7/12/06	On the Motion (Motion to Waive the Emergency Designation Re: Clinton Amdt. No. 4576) To restore funding to States and local governments for terrorism prevention activities in the Homeland Security Grant Program to fiscal year 2005 levels.	Motion Rejected (47-53, 3/5 majority required)	Yea	Nay
196	2	7/12/06	On the Motion (Motion to Waive the Emergency Designation Re: Schumer Amdt. No. 4587) To increase the amount appropriated for transit security by $300,000,000.	Motion Rejected (50-50, 3/5 majority required)	Yea	Nay

Vote No.	Ses-sion	Date	Vote Question Description	Result	Obama's Postion	McCain's Postion
197	2	7/13/06	On the Motion (Motion to Waive CBA Re: Dodd Amdt. No. 4641) To fund urgent priorities for our Nation's firefighters, law enforcement personnel, emergency medical personnel, and all Americans by reducing the tax breaks for individuals with annual incomes in excess of $1,000,000.	Motion Rejected (38-62, 3/5 majority required)	Yea	Nay
198	2	7/13/06	On the Amendment S.Amdt. 4634 to H.R. 5441 (Department of Homeland Security Appropriations Act, 2007) To provide that appropriations under this Act may not be used for the purpose of providing certain grants, unless all such grants meet certain conditions for allocation.	Amendment Rejected (36-64)	Yea	Yea
199	2	7/13/06	On the Motion (Motion to Waive CBA re: Schumer Amdt. No. 4600 "Emergency Designation") To increase appropriations for disaster relief, and for other purposes.	Motion Rejected (46-54, 3/5 majority required)	Yea	Nay
200	2	7/13/06	On the Amendment S.Amdt. 4659 to H.R. 5441 (Department of Homeland Security Appropriations Act, 2007) To appropriate an additional $1,829,400,000 to construct double-layered fencing and vehicle barriers along the southwest border and to offset such increase by reducing all other discretionary amounts on a prorata basis.	Amendment Rejected (29-71)	Nay	Nay
201	2	7/13/06	On the Amendment S.Amdt. 4660 to H.R. 5441 (Department of Homeland Security Appropriations Act, 2007) To appropriate an additional $85,670,000 to enable the Secretary of Homeland Security to hire 800 additional full time active duty investigators to investigate immigration laws violations and to offset such increase on a pro rata basis.	Amendment Rejected (34-66)	Nay	Nay

VOTE No.	SES- SION	DATE	VOTE QUESTION Description	RESULT	OBAMA'S POSTION	MCCAIN'S POSTION
202	2	7/13/06	On the Amendment S.Amdt. 4615 to H.R. 5441 (Department of Homeland Security Appropriations Act, 2007) To prohibit the confiscation of a firearm during an emergency or major disaster if the possession of such firearm is not prohibited under Federal or State law.	Amendment Agreed to (84-16)	Yea	Yea
203	2	7/13/06	On Passage of the Bill H.R. 5441 A bill making appropriations for the Department of Homeland Securityfor the fiscal year ending September 30, 2007, and for other purposes.	Bill Passed (100-0)	Yea	Yea
204	2	7/18/06	On Passage of the Bill S. 3504 A bill to amend the Public Health Service Act to prohibit the solicitation or acceptance of tissue from fetuses gestated for research purposes, and for other purposes.	Bill Passed (100-0)	Yea	Yea
205	2	7/18/06	On Passage of the Bill S. 2754 A bill to derive human pluripotent stem cell lines using techniques that do not knowingly harm embryos.	Bill Passed (100-0)	Yea	Yea
206	2	7/18/06	On Passage of the Bill H.R. 810 A bill to amend the Public Health Service Act to provide for human embryonic stem cell research.	Bill Passed (63-37)	Yea	Yea
207	2	7/18/06	On the Amendment S.Amdt. 680 to S. 728 (Water Resources Development Act of 2005) To modify a provision relating to Federal hopper dredges.	Amendment Agreed to (63-36)	Nay	Yea
208	2	7/19/06	On the Amendment S.Amdt. 4681 to S. 728 (Water Resources Development Act of 2005) To modify a section relating to independent peer review of water resources projects.	Amendment Agreed to (54-46)	Yea	Yea

VOTE No.	SES- SION	DATE	VOTE QUESTION *Description*	RESULT	OBAMA'S POSTION	McCAIN'S POSTION
209	2	7/19/06	On the Amendment S.Amdt. 4682 to S. 728 (Water Resources Development Act of 2005) To modify a section relating to independent reviews.	Amendment Rejected (49-51)	Nay	Nay
210	2	7/19/06	On the Amendment S.Amdt. 4684 to S. 728 (Water Resources Development Act of 2005) To provide for a water resources construction project prioritization report.	Amendment Rejected (19-80)	Nay	Yea
211	2	7/19/06	On the Amendment S.Amdt. 4683 to S. 728 (Water Resources Development Act of 2005) To modify a section relating to a fiscal transparency and prioritization report.	Amendment Rejected (43-56)	Nay	Nay
212	2	7/20/06	On Passage of the Bill H.R. 9 A bill to amend the Voting Rights Act of 1965.	Bill Passed (98-0)	Yea	Yea
213	2	7/25/06	On the Nomination PN1536 Jerome A. Holmes, of Oklahoma, to be United States Circuit Judge for the Tenth Circuit	Nomination Confirmed (67-30)	Nay	Yea
214	2	7/25/06	On the Amendment S.Amdt. 4689 to S. 403 (Child Custody Protection Act) To authorize grants to carry out programs to provide education on preventing teen pregnancies, and for other purposes.	Amendment Rejected (48-51)	Yea	Nay
215	2	7/25/06	On the Amendment S.Amdt. 4694 to S. 403 (Child Custody Protection Act) To punish parents who have committed incest.	Amendment Agreed to (98-0)	Yea	Yea
216	2	7/25/06	On Passage of the Bill S. 403 A bill to amend title 18, United States Code, to prohibit taking minors across State lines in circumvention of laws requiring the involvement of parents in abortion decisions.	Bill Passed (65-34)	Nay	Yea

VOTE No.	SES-SION	DATE	VOTE QUESTION Description	RESULT	OBAMA'S POSTION	MCCAIN'S POSTION
217	2	7/26/06	**On the Cloture Motion S. 3711** A bill to enhance the energy independence and security of the United States by providing for exploration, development, and production activities for mineral resources in the Gulf of Mexico, and for other purposes.	Cloture Motion Agreed to (86-12, 3/5 majority required)	Yea	Yea
218	2	7/31/06	**On the Cloture Motion S. 3711** A bill to enhance the energy independence and security of the United States by providing for exploration, development, and production activities for mineral resources in the Gulf of Mexico, and for other purposes.	Cloture Motion Agreed to (72-23, 3/5 majority required)	Nay	Not Voting
219	2	8/01/06	**On Passage of the Bill S. 3711** A bill to enhance the energy independence and security of the United States by providing for exploration, development, and production activities for mineral resources in the Gulf of Mexico, and for other purposes.	Bill Passed (71-25)	Nay	Yea
220	2	8/02/06	**On the Amendment S.Amdt. 4775 to H.R. 5631 (Department of Defense Appropriations Act, 2007)** To provide $1,829,100,000 for the Army National Guard for the construction of 370 miles of triple-layered fencing, and 461 miles of vehicle barriers along the southwest border.	Amendment Agreed to (94-3)	Yea	Yea
221	2	8/02/06	**On the Amendment S.Amdt. 4819 to H.R. 5631 (Department of Defense Appropriations Act, 2007)** To make available an additional $6,700,000,000 to fund equipment reset requirements resulting from continuing combat operations, including repair, depot, and procurement activities.	Amendment Agreed to (97-0)	Yea	Yea

VOTE No.	SES-SION	DATE	VOTE QUESTION *Description*	RESULT	OBAMA'S POSTION	MCCAIN'S POSTION
222	2	8/02/06	On the Motion to Table S.Amdt. 4781 to H.R. 5631 (Department of Defense Appropriations Act, 2007) To appropriate, with an offset, an additional $2,000,000 for Research, Development, Test and Evaluation, Army for the improvement of imaging for traumatic brain injuries.	Motion to Table Agreed to (54-43)	Nay	Yea
223	2	8/03/06	On the Motion to Table S.Amdt. 4787 to H.R. 5631 (Department of Defense Appropriations Act, 2007) To limit the funds available to the Department of Defense for expenses relating to conferences.	Motion to Table Failed (36-60)	Nay	Nay
224	2	8/03/06	On the Amendment S.Amdt. 4785 to H.R. 5631 (Department of Defense Appropriations Act, 2007) To ensure the fiscal integrity of travel payments made by the Department of Defense.	Amendment Agreed to (96-0)	Yea	Yea
225	2	8/03/06	On the Amendment S.Amdt. 4858 to H.R. 5631 (Department of Defense Appropriations Act, 2007) To prohibit the use of funds by the United States Government to enter into an agreement with the Government of Iraq that would subject members of the Armed Forces to the jurisdiction of Iraq criminal courts or punishment under Iraq law.	Amendment Agreed to (97-0)	Yea	Yea
226	2	8/03/06	On the Amendment S.Amdt. 4848 to H.R. 5631 (Department of Defense Appropriations Act, 2007) To require notice to Congress and the public on earmarks of funds available to the Department of Defense.	Amendment Agreed to (96-1)	Yea	Yea

Vote No.	Session	Date	Vote Question Description	Result	Obama's Postion	McCain's Postion
227	2	8/03/06	On the Amendment S.Amdt. 4844 to H.R. 5631 (Department of Defense Appropriations Act, 2007) To make available from Research, Development, Test, and Evaluation, Navy, up to $77,000,000 for the Conventional Trident Modification Program.	Amendment Rejected (31-67)	Nay	Nay
228	2	8/03/06	On the Amendment S.Amdt. 4863 to H.R. 5631 (Department of Defense Appropriations Act, 2007) To make available from Operation and Maintenance, Navy, up to an additional $3,000,000 to fund improvements to physical security at Navy recruiting stations and to improve data security.	Amendment Agreed to (96-0)	Yea	Yea
229	2	8/03/06	On the Cloture Motion H.R. 5970 A bill to amend the Internal Revenue Code of 1986 to increase the unified credit against the estate tax to an exclusion equivalent of $5,000,000, to repeal the sunset provision for the estate and generation-skipping taxes, and to extend expiring provisions, and for other purposes.	Cloture Motion Rejected (56-42, 3/5 majority required)	Nay	Yea
230	2	8/03/06	On Passage of the Bill H.R. 4 A bill to provide economic security for all Americans, and for otherpurposes.	Bill Passed (93-5)	Yea	Yea
231	2	9/05/06	On the Nomination PN1594 Kimberly Ann Moore, of Virginia, to be United States Circuit Judge for the Federal Circuit	Nomination Confirmed (92-0)	Not Voting	Yea
232	2	9/06/06	On the Amendment S.Amdt. 4882 to H.R. 5631 (Department of Defense Appropriations Act, 2007) To protect civilian lives from unexploded cluster munitions.	Amendment Rejected (30-70)	Yea	Nay

Vote No.	Ses-sion	Date	Vote Question Description	Result	Obama's Postion	McCain's Postion
233	2	9/06/06	On the Motion to Table S. Amdt. 4885 to H.R. 5631 (Department of Defense Appropriations Act, 2007) To include information on civil war in Iraq in the quarterly reports on progress toward military and political stability in Iraq.	Motion to Table Agreed to (54-44)	Nay	Yea
234	2	9/06/06	On the Motion to Table S. Amdt. 4895 to H.R. 5631 (Department of Defense Appropriations Act, 2007) To provide that none of the funds appropriated or otherwise made available by this Act may be used to enter into or carry out a contract for the performance by a contractor of any base operation support service at Walter Reed Army Medical Hospital pursuant to a private-public competition conducted under Office of Management and Budget Circular A-76 that was initiated on June 13, 2000, and has the solicitation number DADA 10-03-R-0001.	Motion to Table Agreed to (50-48)	Nay	Yea
235	2	9/07/06	On the Amendment S. Amdt. 4907 to H.R. 5631 (Department of Defense Appropriations Act, 2007) To enhance intelligence community efforts to bring Osama bin Laden and other key leaders of al Qaeda to the justice they deserve.	Amendment Agreed to (96-0)	Yea	Yea
236	2	9/07/06	On the Motion to Table S. Amdt. 4909 to H.R. 5631 (Department of Defense Appropriations Act, 2007) To prohibit the use of funds for a public relations program designed to monitor news media in the United States and the Middle East and create a database of news stories to promote positive coverage of the war in Iraq.	Motion to Table Agreed to (51-44)	Nay	Yea

VOTE No.	SES-SION	DATE	VOTE QUESTION Description	RESULT	OBAMA'S POSTION	McCAIN'S POSTION
237	2	9/07/06	On the Motion to Table S.Amdt. 4897 to H.R. 5631 (Department of Defense Appropriations Act, 2007) To make available up to an additional $700,000,000 for Drug Interdiction and Counter-Drug Activities to combat the growth of poppies in Afghanistan, to eliminate the production and trade of opium, and heroin, and to prevent terrorists from using the proceeds for terrorist activities in Afghanistan, Iraq, and elsewhere, and to designate the additional amount as emergency spending.	Motion to Table Failed (45-51)	Nay	Yea
238	2	9/07/06	On the Amendment S.Amdt. 4911 to H.R. 5631 (Department of Defense Appropriations Act, 2007) To make available an additional $65,400,000 for additional appropriations for Aircraft Procurement, Air Force, for the procurement of Predators for Special Operations forces, and to designate the amount as an emergency requirement.	Amendment Agreed to (98-0)	Yea	Yea
239	2	9/07/06	On Passage of the Bill H.R. 5631 A bill making appropriations for the Department of Defense for the fiscal year ending September 30, 2007, and for other purposes.	Bill Passed (98-0)	Yea	Yea
240	2	9/12/06	On the Amendment S.Amdt. 4921 to H.R. 4954 (Security and Accountability For Every Port Act or the SAFE Port Act) To establish a unified national hazard alert system, and for other purposes.	Amendment Agreed to (95-0)	Yea	Yea

VOTE No.	SES-SION	DATE	VOTE QUESTION Description	RESULT	OBAMA'S POSTION	MCCAIN'S POSTION
241	2	9/12/06	On the Amendment S.Amdt. 4940 to H.R. 4954 (Security and Accountability For Every Port Act or the SAFE Port Act) To provide that the limitation on the number of Transportation Security Administration employees shall not apply after the date of enactment of this Act, and for other purposes.	Amendment Agreed to (85-12)	Yea	Yea
242	2	9/12/06	On the Amendment S.Amdt. 4931 to H.R. 4954 (Security and Accountability For Every Port Act or the SAFE Port Act) To strengthen national security by adding an additional 275 Customs and Border Protection officers at United States ports.	Amendment Agreed to (97-0)	Yea	Yea
243	2	9/13/06	On the Motion (Motion to Waive CBA Re: Reid Amdt. No.4936) To provide real national security, restore United States leadership, and implement tough and smart policies to win the war on terror.	Motion Rejected (41-57, 3/5 majority required)	Yea	Nay
244	2	9/13/06	On the Motion (Motion to Table Biden Amdt. No. 4975) To establish a Homeland Security and Neighborhood Safety trust Fund and refocus Federal priorities toward securing the Homeland, and for other purposes.	Motion Agreed to (57-41)	Nay	Yea

VOTE No.	SES- SION	DATE	VOTE QUESTION Description	RESULT	OBAMA'S POSTION	MCCAIN'S POSTION
245	2	9/13/06	On the Amendment S.Amdt. 4982 to H.R. 4954 (Security and Accountability For Every Port Act or the SAFE Port Act) To require the Secretary of Homeland Security to ensure that all cargo containers are screened before arriving at a United States seaport, that all high-risk containers are scanned before leaving a United States seaport, and that integrated scanning systems are fully deployed to scan all cargo containers entering the United States before they arrive in the United States.	Amendment Agreed to (95-3)	Yea	Yea
246	2	9/13/06	On the Amendment S.Amdt. 4999 to H.R. 4954 (Security and Accountability For Every Port Act or the SAFE Port Act) To improve the security of cargo containers destined for the United States.	Amendment Rejected (43-55)	Yea	Nay
247	2	9/14/06	On the Cloture Motion H.R. 4954 A bill to improve maritime and cargo security through enhanced layered defenses, and for other purposes.	Cloture Motion Agreed to (98-0, 3/5 majority required)	Yea	Yea
248	2	9/14/06	On the Motion to Table S.Amdt. 4930 to H.R. 4954 (Security and Accountability For Every Port Act or the SAFE Port Act) To improve maritime container security by ensuring that foreign ports participating in the Container Security Initiative scan all containers shipped to the United States for nuclear and radiological weapons before loading.	Motion to Table Agreed to (61-37)	Nay	Yea
249	2	9/14/06	On Passage of the Bill H.R. 4954 A bill to improve maritime and cargo security through enhanced layered defenses, and for other purposes.	Bill Passed (98-0)	Yea	Yea

VOTE No.	SESSION	DATE	VOTE QUESTION Description	RESULT	OBAMA'S POSITION	MCCAIN'S POSITION
250	2	9/19/06	On Passage of the Bill H.R. 5684 A bill to implement the United States-Oman Free Trade Agreement.	Bill Passed (62-32)	Yea	Yea
251	2	9/19/06	On the Nomination PN358 Alice S. Fisher, of Virginia, to be an Assistant Attorney General	Nomination Confirmed (61-35)	Nay	Yea
252	2	9/20/06	On the Cloture Motion H.R. 6061 A bill to establish operational control over the international land and maritime borders of the United States.	Cloture Motion Agreed to (94-0, 3/5 majority required)	Yea	Yea
253	2	9/25/06	On the Nomination PN1586 Francisco Augusto Besosa, of Puerto Rico, to be United States District Judge for the District of Puerto Rico	Nomination Confirmed (87-0)	Yea	Not Voting
254	2	9/27/06	On the Amendment S.Amdt. 5086 to S. 3930 (Military Commissions Act of 2006) In the nature of a substitute.	Amendment Rejected (43-54)	Yea	Not Voting
255	2	9/28/06	On the Amendment S.Amdt. 5087 to S. 3930 (Military Commissions Act of 2006) To strike the provision regarding habeas review.	Amendment Rejected (48-51)	Yea	Nay
256	2	9/28/06	On the Amendment S.Amdt. 5095 to S. 3930 (Military Commissions Act of 2006) To provide for congressional oversight of certain Central Intelligence Agency programs.	Amendment Rejected (46-53)	Yea	Nay
257	2	9/28/06	On the Amendment S.Amdt. 5104 to S. 3930 (Military Commissions Act of 2006) To prohibit the establishment of new military commissions after December 31, 2011.	Amendment Rejected (47-52)	Yea	Nay

VOTE No.	SES-SION	DATE	VOTE QUESTION *Description*	RESULT	OBAMA'S POSTION	MCCAIN'S POSTION
258	2	9/28/06	On the Amendment S.Amdt. 5088 to S. 3930 (Military Commissions Act of 2006) To provide for the protection of United States persons in the implementation of treaty obligations.	Amendment Rejected (46-53)	Yea	Nay
259	2	9/28/06	On Passage of the Bill S. 3930 A bill to authorize trial by military commission for violations of the law of war, and for other purposes.	Bill Passed (65-34)	Nay	Yea
260	2	9/28/06	On the Cloture Motion H.R. 6061 A bill to establish operational control over the international land and maritime borders of the United States.	Cloture Motion Agreed to (71-28, 3/5 majority required)	Nay	Yea
261	2	9/29/06	On the Conference Report H.R. 5631 A bill making appropriations for the Department of Defense for the fiscal year ending September 30, 2007, and for other purposes.	Conference Report Agreed to (100-0)	Yea	Yea
262	2	9/29/06	On Passage of the Bill H.R. 6061 A bill to establish operational control over the international land and maritime borders of the United States.	Bill Passed (80-19)	Yea	Yea
263	2	9/29/06	On the Cloture Motion S. 403 A bill to amend title 18, United States Code, to prohibit taking minors across State lines in circumvention of laws requiring the involvement of parents in abortion decisions.	Cloture Motion Rejected (57-42, 3/5 majority required)	Nay	Yea
264	2	11/14/06	On the Motion (Motion to Instruct Sgt. At Arms) An act making appropriations for Military Construction and Veterans Affairs, and Related Agencies for the fiscal year ending September 30, 2007, and for other purposes.	Motion Agreed to (95-1)	Yea	Yea

Vote No.	Ses-sion	Date	Vote Question Description	Result	Obama's Position	McCain's Position
265	2	11/16/06	On the Amendment S.Amdt. 5174 to S. 3709 (United States-India Peaceful Atomic Energy Cooperation Act) To limit the waiver authority of the President.	Amendment Rejected (26-73)	Yea	Nay
266	2	11/16/06	On the Amendment S.Amdt. 5178 to S. 3709 (United States-India Peaceful Atomic Energy Cooperation Act) To declare that it is the policy of the United States to continue to support implementation of United Nations Security Council Resolution 1172 (1998).	Amendment Rejected (27-71)	Yea	Not Voting
267	2	11/16/06	On the Amendment S.Amdt. 5181 to S. 3709 (United States-India Peaceful Atomic Energy Cooperation Act) To ensure that IAEA inspection equipment is not used for espionage purposes.	Amendment Rejected (27-71)	Nay	Nay
268	2	11/16/06	On the Amendment S.Amdt. 5183 to S. 3709 (United States-India Peaceful Atomic Energy Cooperation Act) To require as a precondition to United States-India peaceful atomic energy cooperation determinations by the President that United States nuclear cooperation with India does nothing to assist, encourage, or induce India to manufacture or acquire nuclear weapons or other nuclear explosive devices.	Amendment Rejected (25-71)	Yea	Not Voting
269	2	11/16/06	On the Amendment S.Amdt. 5187 to S. 3709 (United States-India Peaceful Atomic Energy Cooperation Act) To make the waiver authority of the President contingent upon a certification that India has agreed to suspend military-to-military cooperation with Iran, including training exercises, until such time as Iran is no longer designated as a state sponsor of terrorism.	Amendment Rejected (38-59)	Yea	Nay

VOTE No.	SES-SION	DATE	VOTE QUESTION *Description*	RESULT	OBAMA'S POSTION	McCAIN'S POSTION
270	2	11/16/06	**On Passage of the Bill H.R. 5682** A bill to exempt from certain requirements of the Atomic Energy Act of 1954 a proposed nuclear agreement for cooperation with India.	Bill Passed (85-12)	Yea	Yea
271	2	12/05/06	**On the Motion (Motion to Waive CBA "Emergency Designation" Re: Conrad Amdt. No. 5205)** To provide emergency agricultural disaster assistance.	Motion Rejected (56-38, 3/5 majority required)	Yea	Nay
272	2	12/06/06	**On the Nomination PN2191** Robert M. Gates, of Texas, to be Secretary of Defense	Nomination Confirmed (95-2)	Yea	Yea
273	2	12/07/06	**On the Cloture Motion PN1396** Andrew von Eschenbach, of Texas, to be Commissioner of Food and Drugs, Department of Health and Human Services	Cloture Motion Agreed to (89-6, 3/5 majority required)	Yea	Yea
274	2	12/07/06	**On the Nomination PN1396** Andrew von Eschenbach, of Texas, to be Commissioner of Food and Drugs, Department of Health and Human Services	Nomination Confirmed (80-11)	Yea	Not Voting
275	2	12/08/06	**On the Cloture Motion PN1746** Kent A. Jordan, of Delaware, to be United States Circuit Judge for the Third Circuit	Cloture Motion Agreed to (93-0, 3/5 majority required)	Yea	Not Voting
276	2	12/08/06	**On the Nomination PN1746** Kent A. Jordan, of Delaware, to be United States Circuit Judge for the Third Circuit	Nomination Confirmed (91-0)	Yea	Not Voting

Vote No.	Ses-sion	Date	Vote Question Description	Result	Obama's Postion	McCain's Postion
277	2	12/09/06	On the Motion (Motion to Waive CBA Re: Motion to Concur in House Amendment to the Senate Amendment to H.R.6111.) An act to amend the Internal Revenue Code of 1986 to extend expiring provisions, and for other purposes.	Motion Agreed to (67-21, 3/5 majority required)	Yea	Not Voting
278	2	12/09/06	On the Cloture Motion H.R. 6111 An act to amend the Internal Revenue Code of 1986 to extend expiring provisions, and for other purposes.	Cloture Motion Agreed to (78-10, 3/5 majority required)	Yea	Not Voting
279	2	12/09/06	On the Motion (Motion to Concur in the House Amendment to the Senate Amendment to H.R. 6111) An act to amend the Internal Revenue Code of 1986 to extend expiring provisions, and for other purposes.	Motion Agreed to (79-9)	Yea	Not Voting

THE 110TH CONGRESS

1ST SESSION

VOTE No.	SES-SION	DATE	VOTE QUESTION Description	RESULT	OBAMA'S POSTION	MCCAIN'S POSTION
1	1	1/08/07	On the Resolution S.Res. 19 A resolution honoring President Gerald Rudolph Ford.	Resolution Agreed to (88-0)	Yea	Not Voting
2	1	1/10/07	On the Amendment S.Amdt. 7 to S.Amdt. 3 to S. 1 (No short title on file) To amend the Ethics in Government Act of 1978 to establish criminal penalties for knowingly and willfully falsifying or failing to file or report certain information required to be reported under that Act, and for other purposes.	Amendment Agreed to (93-2)	Yea	Yea
3	1	1/10/07	On the Motion to Table S.Amdt. 5 to S.Amdt. 3 to S. 1 (No short title on file) To modify the application of the Federal Election Campaign Act of 1971 to Indian tribes.	Motion to Table Agreed to (56-40)	Yea	Nay
4	1	1/10/07	On the Motion to Table S.Amdt. 6 to S.Amdt. 3 to S. 1 (No short title on file) to prohibit authorized committees and leadership PACs from employing the spouse or immediate family members of any candidate or Federal office holder connected to the committee.	Motion to Table Agreed to (54-41)	Nay	Nay

VOTE No.	SES-SION	DATE	VOTE QUESTION Description	RESULT	OBAMA'S POSITION	MCCAIN'S POSITION
5	1	1/11/07	On the Motion to Table S.Amdt. 11 to S.Amdt. 3 to S. 1 (No short title on file) To strengthen earmark reform.	Motion to Table Failed (46-51)	Nay	Nay
6	1	1/11/07	On the Motion (Motion to Waive CBA DeMint Amdt. No. 13) To prevent government shutdowns.	Motion Rejected (25-72, 3/5 majority required)	Nay	Yea
7	1	1/11/07	On the Motion (Motion to Instruct Sgt. at Arms) A bill to provide greater transparency in the legislative process.	Motion Agreed to (90-6)	Yea	Nay
8	1	1/12/07	On the Amendment S.Amdt. 1 to S.Amdt. 3 to S. 1 (No short title on file) To amend title 5, United States Code, to deny Federal retirement benefits to individuals convicted of certain offenses, and for other purposes.	Amendment Agreed to (87-0)	Yea	Yea
9	1	1/12/07	On the Amendment S.Amdt. 10 to S.Amdt. 3 to S. 1 (No short title on file) To increase the penalty for failure to comply with lobbying disclosure requirements.	Amendment Agreed to (81-6)	Yea	Yea
10	1	1/16/07	On the Amendment S.Amdt. 44 to S.Amdt. 11 to S.Amdt. 3 to S. 1 To strengthen earmark reform.	Amendment Agreed to (98-0)	Yea	Yea
11	1	1/16/07	On the Amendment S.Amdt. 11 to S.Amdt. 3 to S. 1 (No short title on file) To strengthen earmark reform.	Amendment Agreed to (98-0)	Yea	Yea
12	1	1/16/07	On the Cloture Motion S.Amdt. 4 to S.Amdt. 3 to S. 1 (No short title on file) To strengthen the gift and travel bans.	Cloture Motion Agreed to (95-2, 2/3 majority required)	Yea	Yea

Vote No.	Ses-sion	Date	Vote Question Description	Result	Obama's Postion	McCain's Postion
13	1	1/17/07	On the Amendment S.Amdt. 65 to S.Amdt. 4 to S.Amdt. 3 to S. 1 To prohibit lobbyists and entities that retain or employ lobbyists from throwing lavish parties honoring Members at party conventions.	Amend-ment Agreed to (89-5)	Yea	Yea
14	1	1/17/07	On the Amendment S.Amdt. 81 to S.Amdt. 4 to S.Amdt. 3 to S. 1 To permit travel hosted by preap-proved 501(c)(3) organizations.	Amend-ment Agreed to (51-46)	Nay	Yea
15	1	1/17/07	On the Amendment S.Amdt. 4 to S.Amdt. 3 to S. 1 (No short title on file) To strengthen the gift and travel bans.	Amend-ment Agreed to (88-9)	Yea	Yea
16	1	1/17/07	On the Cloture Motion S.Amdt. 3 to S. 1 (No short title on file) In the nature of a substitute.	Cloture Motion Rejected (51-46, 2/3 majority required)	Yea	Nay
17	1	1/18/07	On the Amendment S.Amdt. 20 to S.Amdt. 3 to S. 1 (No short title on file) To strike a provision relating to paid efforts to stimulate grassroots lobbying.	Amend-ment Agreed to (55-43)	Nay	Yea
18	1	1/18/07	On the Amendment S.Amdt. 30 to S.Amdt. 3 to S. 1 (No short title on file) To establish a Senate Office of Public Integrity.	Amend-ment Rejected (27-71)	Yea	Yea
19	1	1/18/07	On Passage of the Bill S. 1 A bill to provide greater transparency in the legislative process.	Bill Passed (96-2)	Yea	Yea
20	1	1/23/07	On the Amendment S.Amdt. 103 to S.Amdt. 100 to H.R. 2 (Fair Mini-mum Wage Act of 2007) In the nature of a substitute.	Amend-ment Agreed to (99-0)	Yea	Yea

Vote No.	Ses-sion	Date	Vote Question Description	Result	Obama's Postion	McCain's Postion
21	1	1/23/07	On the Amendment S.Amdt. 106 to S.Amdt. 100 to H.R. 2 (Fair Minimum Wage Act of 2007) To express the sense of the Senate that increasing personal savings is a necessary step toward ensuring the economic security of all the people of the United States upon retirement.	Amendment Agreed to (98-0)	Yea	Yea
22	1	1/24/07	On the Cloture Motion S.Amdt. 101 to S.Amdt. 100 to H.R. 2 (Fair Minimum Wage Act of 2007) To provide Congress a second look at wasteful spending by establishing enhance rescission authority under fast-track procedures.	Cloture Motion Rejected (49-48, 3/5 majority required)	Nay	Yea
23	1	1/24/07	On the Cloture Motion H.R. 2 A bill to amend the Fair Labor Standards Act of 1938 to provide for an increase in the Federal minimum wage.	Cloture Motion Rejected (54-43, 3/5 majority required)	Yea	Nay
24	1	1/24/07	On the Amendment S.Amdt. 116 to S.Amdt. 100 to H.R. 2 (Fair Minimum Wage Act of 2007) To afford States the rights and flexibility to determine minimum wage.	Amendment Rejected (28-69)	Nay	Yea
25	1	1/25/07	On the Motion (Motion to Waive Re: DeMint Amdt. No. 158) To increase the Federal minimum wage by an amount that is based on applicable State minimum wages.	Motion Rejected (18-76, 3/5 majority required)	Nay	Nay
26	1	1/25/07	On the Motion (Motion to Waive CBA, Ensign Amdt. No. 154) To improve access to affordable health care.	Motion Rejected (47-48, 3/5 majority required)	Nay	Yea

VOTE No.	SES-SION	DATE	VOTE QUESTION Description	RESULT	OBAMA'S POSTION	McCAIN'S POSTION
27	1	1/25/07	On the Amendment S.Amdt. 207 to S.Amdt. 100 to H.R. 2 (Fair Minimum Wage Act of 2007) To express the sense of the Senate that Congress should repeal the 1993 tax increase on Social Security benefits and eliminate wasteful spending, such as spending on unnecessary tax loopholes, in order to fully offset the cost of such repeal and avoid forcing taxpayers to pay substantially more interest to foreign creditors.	Amendment Agreed to (93-0)	Yea	Yea
28	1	1/25/07	On the Motion (Motion to Waive CBA, Bunning Amdt. No. 119) To amend the Internal Revenue Code of 1986 to repeal the 1993 income tax increase on Social Security benefits.	Motion Rejected (42-51, 3/5 majority required)	Nay	Yea
29	1	1/25/07	On the Amendment S.Amdt. 206 to S.Amdt. 100 to H.R. 2 (Fair Minimum Wage Act of 2007) To express the sense of the Senate that Congress should make permanent the tax incentives to make education more affordable and more accessible for American families and eliminate wasteful spending, such as spending on unnecessary tax loopholes, in order to fully offset the cost of such incentives and avoid forcing taxpayers to pay substantially more interest to foreign creditors.	Amendment Agreed to (90-0)	Yea	Yea
30	1	1/25/07	On the Motion (Motion to Waive CBA, Smith Amdt. No. 113, As Amended) To make permanent certain education-related tax incentives.	Motion Rejected (43-50, 3/5 majority required)	Nay	Yea

Vote No.	Ses- sion	Date	Vote Question Description	Result	Obama's Postion	McCain's Postion
31	1	1/25/07	On the Amendment S.Amdt. 148 to S.Amdt. 100 to H.R. 2 (Fair Minimum Wage Act of 2007) To prohibit employers who unlawfully employ aliens from receiving government contracts.	Amendment Agreed to (94-0)	Yea	Yea
32	1	1/25/07	On the Motion to Table S.Amdt. 205 to S.Amdt. 100 to H.R. 2 (Fair Minimum Wage Act of 2007) To extend through December 31, 2008, the depreciation treatment of leasehold, restaurant, and retail space improvements, and for other purposes.	Motion to Table Agreed to (50-42)	Yea	Nay
33	1	1/26/07	On the Nomination PN178 Lt. Gen. David H. Petraeus, in the Army, to be General	Nomination Confirmed (81-0)	Yea	Not Voting
34	1	1/30/07	On the Motion (Motion to Invoke Cloture on the Baucus Amdt. No. 100) In the nature of a substitute.	Motion Agreed to (87-10, 3/5 majority required)	Yea	Yea
35	1	1/30/07	On the Nomination PN31 Lisa Godbey Wood, of Georgia, to be United States District Judge for the Southern District of Georgia	Nomination Confirmed (97-0)	Yea	Yea
36	1	1/30/07	On the Nomination PN17 Philip S. Gutierrez, of California, to be United States District Judge for the Central District of California	Nomination Confirmed (97-0)	Yea	Yea
37	1	1/31/07	On the Motion to Table S.Amdt. 209 to S.Amdt. 100 to H.R. 2 (Fair Minimum Wage Act of 2007) To extend through December 31, 2012, the increased expensing for small businesses.	Motion to Table Agreed to (49-48)	Yea	Nay
38	1	1/31/07	On the Motion (Motion to Waive C.B.A. Re: Kyl Amdt. No. 115) To extend through December 31, 2008, the depreciation treatment of leasehold, restaurant, and retail space improvements.	Motion Rejected (46-50, 3/5 majority required)	Nay	Yea

Vote No.	Ses- sion	Date	Vote Question Description	Result	Obama's Postion	McCain's Postion
39	1	1/31/07	On the Motion (Motion to Invoke Cloture on H.R.2, As Amended) A bill to amend the Fair Labor Standards Act of 1938 to provide for an increase in the Federal minimum wage.	Motion Agreed to (88-8, 3/5 majority required)	Yea	Yea
40	1	2/01/07	On the Nomination PN24 Lawrence Joseph O'Neill, of California, to be United States District Judge for the Eastern District of California	Nomination Confirmed (88-0)	Yea	Yea
41	1	2/01/07	On the Nomination PN16 Gregory Kent Frizzell, of Oklahoma, to be United States District Judge for the Northern District of Oklahoma	Nomination Confirmed (99-0)	Yea	Yea
42	1	2/01/07	On Passage of the Bill H.R. 2 A bill to amend the Fair Labor Standards Act of 1938 to provide for an increase in the Federal minimum wage.	Bill Passed (94-3)	Yea	Yea
43	1	2/01/07	On the Motion (Motion to Invoke Cloture on the Motion to Proceed to S.Con.Res.2) A concurrent resolution expressing the bipartisan resolution on Iraq.	Motion Rejected (0-97, 3/5 majority required)	Nay	Nay
44	1	2/05/07	On the Cloture Motion S. 470 A bill to express the sense of Congress on Iraq.	Cloture Motion Rejected (49-47, 3/5 majority required)	Yea	Not Voting
45	1	2/08/07	On the Nomination PN177 Gen. George W. Casey, Jr., in the Army, to be General	Nomination Confirmed (83-14)	Yea	Nay
46	1	2/13/07	On the Motion (Motion to Invoke Cloture on H.J.Res. 20) A joint resolution making further continuing appropriations for the fiscal year 2007, and for other purposes.	Motion Agreed to (71-26, 3/5 majority required)	Yea	Nay

Vote No.	Session	Date	Vote Question Description	Result	Obama's Position	McCain's Position
47	1	2/14/07	**On the Nomination PN15** Nora Barry Fischer, of Pennsylvania, to be United States District Judge for the Western District of Pennsylvania	Nomination Confirmed (96-0)	Yea	Yea
48	1	2/14/07	**On the Joint Resolution H.J.Res. 20** A joint resolution making further continuing appropriations for the fiscal year 2007, and for other purposes.	Joint Resolution Passed (81-15)	Yea	Yea
49	1	2/15/07	**On the Nomination PN183** Norman Randy Smith, of Idaho, to be United States Circuit Judge for the Ninth Circuit	Nomination Confirmed (94-0)	Yea	Yea
50	1	2/15/07	**On the Nomination PN18** Marcia Morales Howard, of Florida, to be United States District Judge for the Middle District of Florida	Nomination Confirmed (93-0)	Yea	Yea
51	1	2/17/07	**On the Cloture Motion S. 574** A bill to express the sense of Congress on Iraq.	Cloture Motion Rejected (56-34, 3/5 majority required)	Yea	Not Voting
52	1	2/17/07	**On Passage of the Bill H.Con.Res. 67** A concurrent resolution providing for a conditional adjournment of the House of Representatives and a conditional recess or adjournment of the Senate.	Bill Passed (47-33)	Yea	Not Voting
53	1	2/27/07	**On the Cloture Motion S. 4** A bill to make the United States more secure by implementing unfinished recommendations of the 9/11 Commission to fight the war on terror more effectively, to improve homeland security, and for other purposes.	Cloture Motion Agreed to (97-0, 3/5 majority required)	Yea	Yea

VOTE NO.	SES-SION	DATE	VOTE QUESTION *Description*	RESULT	OBAMA'S POSTION	MCCAIN'S POSTION
54	1	2/28/07	On the Amendment S.Amdt. 285 to S.Amdt. 275 to S. 4 (Improving America's Security Act of 2007) To specify the criminal offenses that disqualify an applicant from the receipt of a transportation security card.	Amendment Agreed to (58-37)	Yea	Not Voting
55	1	2/28/07	On the Amendment S.Amdt. 279 to S.Amdt. 275 to S. 4 (Improving America's Security Act of 2007) To specify the criminal offenses that disqualify an applicant from the receipt of a transportation security card.	Amendment Agreed to (94-2)	Yea	Not Voting
56	1	3/01/07	On the Motion to Table S.Amdt. 298 to S.Amdt. 275 to S. 4 (Improving America's Security Act of 2007) To strengthen the security of cargo containers.	Motion to Table Agreed to (58-38)	Nay	Not Voting
57	1	3/02/07	On the Amendment S.Amdt. 292 to S.Amdt. 275 to S. 4 (Improving America's Security Act of 2007) To expand the reporting requirement on cross border interoperability, and to prevent lengthy delays in the accessing frequencies and channels for public safety communication users and others.	Amendment Agreed to (82-0)	Not Voting	Not Voting
58	1	3/02/07	On the Amendment S.Amdt. 280 to S.Amdt. 275 to S. 4 (Improving America's Security Act of 2007) To create a Rural Policing Institute as part of the Federal Law Enforcement Training Center.	Amendment Agreed to (82-1)	Not Voting	Not Voting
59	1	3/05/07	On the Nomination PN104 Carl Joseph Artman, of Colorado, to be an Assistant Secretary of the Interior	Nomination Confirmed (87-1)	Not Voting	Not Voting

Vote No.	Ses-sion	Date	Vote Question Description	Result	Obama's Postion	McCain's Postion
60	1	3/06/07	On the Motion to Table S.Amdt. 314 to S.Amdt. 275 to S. 4 (Improving America's Security Act of 2007) To strike the provision that revises the personnel management practices of the Transportation Security Administration.	Motion to Table Agreed to (51-46)	Yea	Nay
61	1	3/06/07	On the Motion to Table S.Amdt. 335 to S.Amdt. 275 to S. 4 (Improving America's Security Act of 2007) To improve the allocation of grants through the Department of Homeland Security, and for other purposes.	Motion to Table Agreed to (56-43)	Nay	Nay
62	1	3/06/07	On the Motion to Table S.Amdt. 338 to S.Amdt. 275 to S. 4 (Improving America's Security Act of 2007) To require consideration of high-risk qualifying criteria in allocating funds under the State Homeland Security Grant Program.	Motion to Table Agreed to (58-41)	Nay	Nay
63	1	3/06/07	On the Amendment S.Amdt. 333 to S.Amdt. 275 to S. 4 (Improving America's Security Act of 2007) To increase the minimum allocation for States under the State Homeland Security Grant Program.	Amend-ment Rejected (49-50)	Nay	Nay
64	1	3/07/07	On the Amendment S.Amdt. 316 to S.Amdt. 275 to S. 4 (Improving America's Security Act of 2007) To provide appeal rights and employee engagement mechanisms for passenger and property screeners.	Amend-ment Agreed to (51-48)	Yea	Nay
65	1	3/07/07	On the Amendment S.Amdt. 342 to S.Amdt. 275 to S. 4 (Improving America's Security Act of 2007) To provide certain employment rights and an employee engagement mechanism for passenger and property screeners, and for other purposes.	Amend-ment Rejected (47-52)	Nay	Yea

Vote No.	Session	Date	Vote Question Description	Result	Obama's Postion	McCain's Postion
66	1	3/07/07	On the Motion to Table S.Amdt. 345 to S.Amdt. 275 to S. 4 (Improving America's Security Act of 2007) To authorize funding for the Emergency Communications and Interoperability Grants program, to require the Secretary to examine the possibility of allowing commercial entities to develop public safety communications networks, and for other purposes.	Motion to Table Agreed to (71-25)	Yea	Nay
67	1	3/08/07	On the Nomination PN19 John Alfred Jarvey, of Iowa, to be United States District Judge for the Southern District of Iowa	Nomination Confirmed (95-0)	Yea	Not Voting
68	1	3/09/07	On the Cloture Motion S.Amdt. 312 to S.Amdt. 275 to S. 4 (Improving America's Security Act of 2007) To prohibit the recruitment of persons to participate in terrorism, to clarify that the revocation of an alien's visa or other documentation is not subject to judicial review, to strengthen the Federal Government's ability to detain dangerous criminal aliens, including murderers, rapists, and child molesters, until they can be removed from the United States, to prohibit the rewarding of suicide bombings and allow adequate punishments for terrorists murders, kidnappings, and sexual assaults, and for other purposes.	Cloture Motion Rejected (46-49, 3/5 majority required)	Nay	Not Voting
69	1	3/09/07	On the Cloture Motion S.Amdt. 275 to S. 4 (Improving America's Security Act of 2007) In the nature of a substitute.	Cloture Motion Agreed to (69-26, 3/5 majority required)	Yea	Not Voting

Vote No.	Session	Date	Vote Question Description	Result	Obama's Postion	McCain's Postion
70	1	3/13/07	On the Motion to Table S.Amdt. 294 to S.Amdt. 275 to S. 4 (Improving America's Security Act of 2007) To provide that the provisions of the Act shall cease to have any force or effect on and after December, 31, 2012, to ensure congressional review and oversight of the Act.	Motion to Table Agreed to (60-38)	Nay	Not Voting
71	1	3/13/07	On the Motion to Table S.Amdt. 325 to S.Amdt. 275 to S. 4 (Improving America's Security Act of 2007) To ensure the fiscal integrity of grants awarded by the Department of Homeland Security.	Motion to Table Agreed to (66-31)	Yea	Not Voting
72	1	3/13/07	On the Motion to Table S.Amdt. 383 to S.Amdt. 275 to S. 4 (Improving America's Security Act of 2007) To require the Secretary of Homeland Security to develop regulations regarding the transportation of high hazard materials, and for other purposes.	Motion to Table Agreed to (73-25)	Nay	Not Voting
73	1	3/13/07	On Passage of the Bill S. 4 A bill to make the United States more secure by implementing unfinished recommendations of the 9/11 Commission to fight the war on terror more effectively, to improve homeland security, and for other purposes.	Bill Passed (60-38)	Yea	Not Voting
74	1	3/14/07	On the Cloture Motion S.J.Res. 9 A joint resolution to revise United States policy on Iraq.	Cloture Motion Agreed to (89-9, 3/5 majority required)	Yea	Yea
75	1	3/15/07	On the Joint Resolution S.J.Res. 9 A joint resolution to revise United States policy on Iraq.	Joint Resolution Defeated (48-50, 3/5 majority required)	Yea	Not Voting

Vote No.	Session	Date	Vote Question / Description	Result	Obama's Position	McCain's Position
76	1	3/15/07	On the Resolution S.Res. 107 A resolution expressing the sense of the Senate that no action should be taken to undermine the safety of the Armed Forces of the United States or impact their ability to complete their assigned or future missions.	Resolution Agreed to (96-2, 3/5 majority required)	Yea	Not Voting
77	1	3/15/07	On the Concurrent Resolution S.Con. Res. 20 A concurrent resolution expressing the sense of Congress that no funds should be cut off or reduced for American Troops in the field which would result in undermining their safety or their ability to complete their assigned mission.	Concurrent Resolution Agreed to (82-16, 3/5 majority required)	Yea	Not Voting
78	1	3/15/07	On the Nomination PN8 Thomas M. Hardiman, of Pennsylvania, to be United States Circuit Judge for the Third Circuit	Nomination Confirmed (95-0)	Yea	Not Voting
79	1	3/20/07	On the Amendment S.Amdt. 459 to S. 214 (Preserving United States Attorney Independence Act of 2007) To ensure that United States attorneys are promptly nominated by the President, and are appointed by and with the advice and consent of the Senate.	Amendment Rejected (40-56)	Nay	Not Voting
80	1	3/20/07	On the Amendment S.Amdt. 460 to S. 214 (Preserving United States Attorney Independence Act of 2007) To require appropriate qualifications for interim United States attorneys.	Amendment Rejected (47-50)	Nay	Not Voting
81	1	3/20/07	On Passage of the Bill S. 214 A bill to amend chapter 35 of title 28, United States Code, to preserve the independence of United States attorneys.	Bill Passed (94-2)	Yea	Not Voting

VOTE NO.	SESSION	DATE	VOTE QUESTION Description	RESULT	OBAMA'S POSTION	McCAIN'S POSTION
82	1	3/21/07	On the Amendment S.Amdt. 492 to S.Con.Res. 21 (No short title on file) To provide tax relief to middle class families and small businesses and to expand health insurance coverage for children.	Amendment Agreed to (97-1)	Yea	Yea
83	1	3/21/07	On the Amendment S.Amdt. 507 to S.Con.Res. 21 (No short title on file) To protect families, family farms and small businesses by raising the death tax exemption to $5 million and reducing the maximum death tax rate to no more than 35%, to extend college tuition deduction, to extend the student loan interest deduction, to extend the teacher classroom deduction, to protect senior citizens from higher taxes on their retirement income, to maintain U.S. financial market competitiveness, and to promote economic growth by extending the lower tax rates on dividends and capital gains.	Amendment Rejected (47-51)	Nay	Yea
84	1	3/21/07	On the Amendment S.Amdt. 477 to S.Con.Res. 21 (No short title on file) To provide for a budget point of order against legislation that increases income taxes on taxpayers, including hard-working middle-income families, entrepreneurs, and college students.	Amendment Agreed to (63-35)	Nay	Yea
85	1	3/21/07	On the Amendment S.Amdt. 466 to S.Con.Res. 21 (No short title on file) To exclude the extension of tax relief provided in 2001 and 2003 from points of order provided in the resolution and other budget points of order.	Amendment Rejected (46-52)	Nay	Yea

Vote No.	Ses- sion	Date	Vote Question Description	Result	Obama's Postion	McCain's Postion
86	1	3/21/07	On the Amendment S.Amdt. 476 to S.Con.Res. 21 (No short title on file) To ensure that our troops serving in harms way remain Americas top budget priority by ensuring full funding for the Department of Defense within the regular appropriations process, reducing reliance on supplemental appropriations bills, and by improving the integrity of the Congressional budget process.	Amend- ment Rejected (47-51)	Nay	Yea
87	1	3/21/07	On the Amendment S.Amdt. 483 to S.Con.Res. 21 (No short title on file) To provide a point of order against any budget resolution that fails to achieve an on-budget balance within 5 years.	Amend- ment Agreed to (98-0)	Yea	Yea
88	1	3/21/07	On the Amendment S.Amdt. 486 to S.Con.Res. 21 (No short title on file) To provide additional funding resources in FY2008 for investments in innovation and education in order to improve the competitiveness of the United States.	Amend- ment Agreed to (97-1)	Yea	Yea
89	1	3/22/07	On the Amendment S.Amdt. 489 to S.Con.Res. 21 (No short title on file) To establish a reserve fund for Social Security.	Amend- ment Rejected (45-52)	Nay	Not Voting
90	1	3/22/07	On the Amendment S.Amdt. 491 to S.Con.Res. 21 (No short title on file) To pay down the Federal debt and eliminate government waste by reducing spending on programs rated ineffective by the Program Assessment Rating Tool.	Amend- ment Rejected (33-64)	Nay	Not Voting
91	1	3/22/07	On the Amendment S.Amdt. 511 to S.Con.Res. 21 (No short title on file) To provide a deficit-neutral reserve fund for the reauthorization of the State Children's Health Insurance Program (SCHIP) that will cover kids first.	Amend- ment Rejected (38-59)	Nay	Not Voting

Vote No.	Session	Date	Vote Question / Description	Result	Obama's Postion	McCain's Postion
92	1	3/22/07	On the Amendment S.Amdt. 525 to S.Con.Res. 21 (No short title on file) To provide reconciliation instructions of $33.8 billion to make provider payments more accurate, to improve Medicare Part B income relation provisions, expand those provisions to Medicare Part D and reduce the deficit.	Amendment Rejected (23-74)	Nay	Not Voting
93	1	3/22/07	On the Amendment S.Amdt. 472 to S.Con.Res. 21 (No short title on file) To require wealthy Medicare beneficiaries to pay a greater share of their Medicare Part D premiums.	Amendment Rejected (44-52)	Nay	Not Voting
94	1	3/22/07	On the Amendment S.Amdt. 545 to S.Con.Res. 21 (No short title on file) To restore the top marginal tax rate to pre-2001 levels on taxable income in excess of $1 million and use the increased revenue to increase funding for the Individuals with Disabilities Act.	Amendment Rejected (38-58)	Yea	Not Voting
95	1	3/22/07	On the Amendment S.Amdt. 497 to S.Con.Res. 21 (No short title on file) To establish a 60-vote point of order for legislation that creates unfunded mandates on small business concerns.	Amendment Rejected (47-49)	Nay	Not Voting
96	1	3/22/07	On the Amendment S.Amdt. 498 to S.Con.Res. 21 (No short title on file) To strike the reserve funds.	Amendment Rejected (29-67)	Nay	Not Voting
97	1	3/22/07	On the Amendment S.Amdt. 598 to S.Con.Res. 21 (No short title on file) To create a deficit-neutral reserve fund for extending certain energy tax incentives.	Amendment Agreed to (54-42)	Yea	Not Voting

Vote No.	Session	Date	Vote Question Description	Result	Obama's Position	McCain's Position
98	1	3/22/07	On the Amendment S.Amdt. 577 to S.Con.Res. 21 (No short title on file) To provide budget levels to extend through 2012 the production tax credit for electricity produced from renewable resources, the Clean Renewable Energy Bonds, and energy tax provisions for energy efficient buildings and power plants.	Amendment Rejected (42-53)	Nay	Not Voting
99	1	3/23/07	On the Amendment S.Amdt. 513 to S.Con.Res. 21 (No short title on file) To provide for true deficit reduction in appropriation bills.	Amendment Rejected (38-61)	Nay	Yea
100	1	3/23/07	On the Amendment S.Amdt. 473 to S.Con.Res. 21 (No short title on file) To save families from the Alternative Minimum Tax (AMT) first by permitting a deduction for personal exemptions for purposes of computing the AMT.	Amendment Rejected (46-53)	Nay	Yea
101	1	3/23/07	On the Amendment S.Amdt. 626 to S.Con.Res. 21 (No short title on file) To reform the estate tax to avoid subjecting thousands of families, family businesses, and family farms and ranches to the estate tax, and to promote continued economic growth and job creation.	Amendment Rejected (25-74)	Nay	Nay
102	1	3/23/07	On the Amendment S.Amdt. 583 to S.Con.Res. 21 (No short title on file) To reform the death tax by setting the exemption at $5 million per estate, indexed for inflation, and the top death tax rate at no more than 35% beginning in 2010; to avoid subjecting an estimated 119,200 families, family businesses, and family farms to the death tax each and every year; to promote continued economic growth and job creation; and to make the enhanced teacher deduction permanent.	Amendment Rejected (48-51)	Nay	Yea

VOTE No.	SES-SION	DATE	VOTE QUESTION *Description*	RESULT	OBAMA'S POSTION	MCCAIN'S POSTION
103	1	3/23/07	On the Amendment S.Amdt. 508 to S.Con.Res. 21 (No short title on file) To establish a reserve fund for protecting coverage choices, additional benefits, and lower cost-sharing for Medicare beneficiaries.	Amendment Rejected (49-50)	Nay	Yea
104	1	3/23/07	On the Motion (Motion to Waive CBA Re: Allard Amendment No. 521) To improve the economy, efficiency, and effectiveness of Federal programs and reduce the Federal debt by eliminating waste, fraud, and abuse.	Motion Rejected (39-60, 3/5 majority required)	Nay	Yea
105	1	3/23/07	On the Amendment S.Amdt. 510 to S.Con.Res. 21 (No short title on file) To provide for the consideration of an increase in the tobacco products user fee rate, but only to the extent that such rate increase does not result in an increase of more than 61 cents per pack of cigarettes, with all revenue generated by such increase dedicated to the reauthorization and expansion of the State Children's Health Insurance Program.	Amendment Agreed to (59-40)	Yea	Nay
106	1	3/23/07	On the Amendment S.Amdt. 515 to S.Con.Res. 21 (No short title on file) To prevent the adding of extraneous earmarks to an emergency war supplemental.	Amendment Rejected (39-59)	Nay	Yea
107	1	3/23/07	On the Amendment S.Amdt. 478 to S.Con.Res. 21 (No short title on file) To extend the 35, 33, 28, and 25 percent income tax rate structure and protect nearly 28,000,000 families and individuals, including small business owners, from having their tax rates increase to 39.6, 36, 31, or 28 percent.	Amendment Rejected (46-52)	Nay	Yea

Vote No.	Session	Date	Vote Question *Description*	Result	Obama's Postion	McCain's Postion
108	1	3/23/07	**On the Amendment S.Amdt. 471 to S.Con.Res. 21 (No short title on file)** To amend the budget resolution for fiscal year 2008 in order to accommodate the full repeal of the Alternative Minimum Tax preventing 23 million families and individuals from being subject to the AMT in 2007, and millions of families and individuals in subsequent years.	Amendment Rejected (44-53)	Nay	Yea
109	1	3/23/07	**On the Amendment S.Amdt. 578 to S.Con.Res. 21 (No short title on file)** To repeal the death tax.	Amendment Rejected (44-55)	Nay	Yea
110	1	3/23/07	**On the Amendment S.Amdt. 529 to S.Con.Res. 21 (No short title on file)** To increase funding for the COPS Program to $1.15 billion for FY 2008 to provide state and local law enforcement with critical resources necessary to prevent and respond to violent crime and acts of terrorism and is offset by an unallocated reduction to non-defense discretionary spending and/or reduction to administrative expenses.	Amendment Agreed to (65-33)	Yea	Not Voting
111	1	3/23/07	**On the Amendment S.Amdt. 594 to S.Con.Res. 21 (No short title on file)** To provide a deficit-neutral reserve fund for protecting State flexibility in Medicaid.	Amendment Rejected (44-55)	Nay	Yea
112	1	3/23/07	**On the Amendment S.Amdt. 536 to S.Con.Res. 21 (No short title on file)** To provide a deficit-neutral reserve fund for the reauthorization of the State Children's Health Insurance Program (SCHIP) that eliminates enhanced Federal matching payments for coverage of nonpregnant adults and permits States to offer supplemental dental and mental health benefits for children enrolled in SCHIP.	Amendment Rejected (44-55)	Nay	Yea

Vote No.	Session	Date	Vote Question *Description*	Result	Obama's Position	McCain's Position
113	1	3/23/07	**On the Amendment S.Amdt. 606 to S.Con.Res. 21 (No short title on file)** To repeal section 13203 of the Omnibus Budget Reconciliation Act of 1993 by restoring the Alternative Minimum Tax rates that had been in effect prior thereto.	Amendment Rejected (49-50)	Nay	Yea
114	1	3/23/07	**On the Resolution S.Con.Res. 21** An original concurrent resolution setting forth the congressional budget for the United States Government for fiscal year 2008 and including the appropriate budgetary levels for fiscal years 2007 and 2009 through 2012.	Resolution Agreed to (52-47)	Yea	Nay
115	1	3/27/07	**On the Nomination PN33** George H. Wu, of California, to be United States District Judge for the Central District of California	Nomination Confirmed (95-0)	Yea	Not Voting
116	1	3/27/07	**On the Amendment S.Amdt. 643 to H.R. 1591 (U.S. Troop Readiness, Veterans' Health, and Iraq Accountability Act, 2007)** To strike language that would tie the hands of the Commander-in-Chief by imposing an arbitrary timetable for the withdrawal of U.S. forces from Iraq, thereby undermining the position of American Armed Forces and jeopardizing the successful conclusion of Operation Iraqi Freedom.	Amendment Rejected (48-50)	Nay	Yea
117	1	3/28/07	**On the Cloture Motion H.R. 1591** A bill making emergency supplemental appropriations for the fiscal year ending September 30, 2007, and for other purposes.	Cloture Motion Agreed to (97-0, 3/5 majority required)	Yea	Not Voting

Vote No.	Ses-sion	Date	Vote Question / Description	Result	Obama's Postion	McCain's Postion
118	1	3/28/07	On the Amendment S.Amdt. 709 to H.R. 1591 (U.S. Troop Readiness, Veterans' Health, and Iraq Accountability Act, 2007) To reauthorize the secure rural schools and community self-determination program and to provide funding for the payments in lieu of taxes program.	Amendment Agreed to (74-23)	Yea	Not Voting
119	1	3/28/07	On the Amendment S.Amdt. 716 to H.R. 1591 (U.S. Troop Readiness, Veterans' Health, and Iraq Accountability Act, 2007) To reauthorize the secure rural schools and community self-determination program and to provide funding for the payments in lieu of taxes program.	Amendment Rejected (8-89)	Nay	Not Voting
120	1	3/28/07	On the Amendment S.Amdt. 657 to H.R. 1591 (U.S. Troop Readiness, Veterans' Health, and Iraq Accountability Act, 2007) To provide farm assistance in a fiscally responsible manner.	Amendment Rejected (23-74)	Nay	Not Voting
121	1	3/28/07	On the Amendment S.Amdt. 648 to H.R. 1591 (U.S. Troop Readiness, Veterans' Health, and Iraq Accountability Act, 2007) To remove $100 million in funding for the Republican and Democrat party conventions in 2008.	Amendment Rejected (45-51)	Yea	Not Voting

VOTE No.	SES-SION	DATE	VOTE QUESTION _Description_	RESULT	OBAMA'S POSTION	MCCAIN'S POSTION
122	1	3/29/07	On the Amendment S.Amdt. 752 to H.R. 1591 (U.S. Troop Readiness, Veterans' Health, and Iraq Accountability Act, 2007) To provide additional funding for certain programs under the Adam Walsh Child Safety and Protection Act of 2006, by increasing funding for the United States Marshals Service to track down convicted sex offenders who have failed to register as a sex offender as required by law and by increasing funding for United States attorneys to prosecute child exploitation and child pornography cases as part of Project Safe Childhood.	Amendment Agreed to (93-0)	Yea	Yea
123	1	3/29/07	On the Amendment S.Amdt. 704 to H.R. 1591 (U.S. Troop Readiness, Veterans' Health, and Iraq Accountability Act, 2007) To prohibit the use of funds to make payments to certain spinach growers and first handlers.	Amendment Agreed to (97-0)	Yea	Yea
124	1	3/29/07	On the Amendment S.Amdt. 739 to H.R. 1591 (U.S. Troop Readiness, Veterans' Health, and Iraq Accountability Act, 2007) To appropriate an additional $1,500,000,000 for Procurement, Marine Corps, to accelerate the procurement of an additional 2,500 Mine Resistant Ambush Protected vehicles for the Armed Forces.	Amendment Agreed to (98-0)	Yea	Yea
125	1	3/29/07	Whether the Amendment is Germane S.Amdt. 641 to H.R. 1591 (U.S. Troop Readiness, Veterans' Health, and Iraq Accountability Act, 2007) In the nature of a substitute.	Amendment Germane (57-41)	Yea	Nay

VOTE No.	SES-SION	DATE	VOTE QUESTION Description	RESULT	OBAMA'S POSTION	McCAIN'S POSTION
126	1	3/29/07	On Passage of the Bill H.R. 1591 A bill making emergency supplemental appropriations for the fiscal year ending September 30, 2007, and for other purposes.	Bill Passed (51-47)	Yea	Nay
127	1	4/11/07	On Passage of the Bill S. 5 A bill to amend the Public Health Service Act to provide for human embryonic stem cell research.	Bill Passed (63-34, 3/5 majority required)	Yea	Yea
128	1	4/11/07	On Passage of the Bill S. 30 A bill to intensify research to derive human pluripotent stem cell lines.	Bill Passed (70-28, 3/5 majority required)	Nay	Yea
129	1	4/12/07	On the Cloture Motion S. 372 An original bill to authorize appropriations for fiscal year 2007 for the intelligence and intelligence-related activities of the United States Government, the Intelligence Community Management Account, and the Central Intelligence Agency Retirement and Disability System, and for other purposes.	Cloture Motion Agreed to (94-3, 3/5 majority required)	Yea	Yea
130	1	4/16/07	On the Cloture Motion S. 372 An original bill to authorize appropriations for fiscal year 2007 for the intelligence and intelligence-related activities of the United States Government, the Intelligence Community Management Account, and the Central Intelligence Agency Retirement and Disability System, and for other purposes.	Cloture Motion Rejected (41-40, 3/5 majority required)	Not Voting	Not Voting

VOTE No.	SES- SION	DATE	VOTE QUESTION Description	RESULT	OBAMA'S POSTION	McCAIN'S POSTION
131	1	4/17/07	On the Cloture Motion S. 372 An original bill to authorize appropriations for fiscal year 2007 for the intelligence and intelligence-related activities of the United States Government, the Intelligence Community Management Account, and the Central Intelligence Agency Retirement and Disability System, and for other purposes.	Cloture Motion Rejected (50-45, 3/5 majority required)	Not Voting	Not Voting
132	1	4/18/07	On the Cloture Motion S. 3 A bill to amend part D of title XVIII of the Social Security Act to provide for fair prescription drug prices for Medicare beneficiaries.	Cloture Motion Rejected (55-42, 3/5 majority required)	Yea	Not Voting
133	1	4/18/07	On the Cloture Motion S. 378 A bill to amend title 18, United States Code, to protect judges, prosecutors, witnesses, victims, and their family members, and for other purposes.	Cloture Motion Agreed to (93-3, 3/5 majority required)	Yea	Not Voting
134	1	4/18/07	On the Motion to Table S.Amdt. 891 to S. 378 (Court Security Improvement Act of 2007) To express the sense of the Senate that Congress should offset the cost of new spending.	Motion to Table Agreed to (59-38)	Yea	Not Voting
135	1	4/19/07	On Passage of the Bill S. 378 A bill to amend title 18, United States Code, to protect judges, prosecutors, witnesses, victims, and their family members, and for other purposes.	Bill Passed (97-0)	Yea	Not Voting
136	1	4/24/07	On the Nomination PN26 Halil Suleyman Ozerden, of Mississippi, to be United States District Judge for the Southern District of Mississippi	Nomination Confirmed (95-0)	Not Voting	Not Voting

Vote No.	Session	Date	Vote Question Description	Result	Obama's Position	McCain's Position
137	1	4/24/07	**On the Amendment S.Amdt. 929 to S. 761 (No short title on file)** To require the study on barriers to innovation to include an examination of the impact of the Internal Revenue Code of 1986 on innovation.	Amendment Agreed to (96-0)	Not Voting	Not Voting
138	1	4/24/07	**On the Amendment S.Amdt. 947 to S. 761 (No short title on file)** To express the sense of the Senate with respect to small business growth and capital markets.	Amendment Agreed to (97-0)	Yea	Not Voting
139	1	4/24/07	**On the Motion to Table S.Amdt. 928 to S. 761 (No short title on file)** To amend the Sarbanes-Oxley Act of 2002, with respect to smaller public company options regarding internal controls.	Motion to Table Agreed to (62-35)	Yea	Not Voting
140	1	4/24/07	**On the Motion to Table S.Amdt. 917 to S. 761 (No short title on file)** To express the sense of the Senate that Congress has a moral obligation to offset the cost of new Government programs and initiatives.	Motion to Table Agreed to (54-43)	Yea	Not Voting
141	1	4/25/07	**On the Amendment S.Amdt. 938 to S. 761 (No short title on file)** To strike the provisions regarding strengthening the education and human resources directorate of the National Science Foundation.	Amendment Rejected (24-74)	Nay	Not Voting
142	1	4/25/07	**On the Amendment S.Amdt. 930 to S. 761 (No short title on file)** To prohibit congressional earmarks of funds appropriated pursuant to authorizations in the bill.	Amendment Rejected (22-71)	Nay	Not Voting
143	1	4/25/07	**On the Amendment S.Amdt. 918 to S. 761 (No short title on file)** To provide a sunset date.	Amendment Rejected (27-67)	Nay	Not Voting

Vote No.	Ses-sion	Date	Vote Question Description	Result	Obama's Postion	McCain's Postion
144	1	4/25/07	On the Amendment S.Amdt. 921 to S. 761 (No short title on file) To discontinue the Advanced Technology Program of the National Institute of Standards and Technology.	Amendment Rejected (39-57)	Nay	Not Voting
145	1	4/25/07	On the Amendment S.Amdt. 922 to S. 761 (No short title on file) To promote transparency at the National Oceanic and Atmospheric Administration.	Amendment Agreed to (82-14)	Yea	Not Voting
146	1	4/25/07	On Passage of the Bill S. 761 A bill to invest in innovation and education to improve the competitiveness of the United States in the global economy.	Bill Passed (88-8)	Yea	Not Voting
147	1	4/26/07	On the Conference Report H.R. 1591 A bill making emergency supplemental appropriations for the fiscal year ending September 30, 2007, and for other purposes.	Conference Report Agreed to (51-46)	Yea	Not Voting
148	1	5/02/07	On the Amendment S.Amdt. 982 to S. 1082 (Prescription Drug User Fee Amendments of 2007) To strike provisions related to market exclusivity.	Amendment Rejected (41-53)	Nay	Not Voting
149	1	5/02/07	On the Amendment S.Amdt. 1022 to S. 1082 (Prescription Drug User Fee Amendments of 2007) To ensure the safety of human and pet food.	Amendment Agreed to (94-0)	Yea	Not Voting
150	1	5/03/07	On the Cloture Motion S.Amdt. 990 to S. 1082 (Prescription Drug User Fee Amendments of 2007) To provide for the importation of prescription drugs.	Cloture Motion Agreed to (63-28, 3/5 majority required)	Yea	Not Voting

VOTE No.	SES-SION	DATE	VOTE QUESTION Description	RESULT	OBAMA'S POSITION	MCCAIN'S POSITION
151	1	5/07/07	On the Amendment S.Amdt. 1010 to S.Amdt. 990 to S. 1082 (Prescription Drug User Fee Amendments of 2007) To protect the health and safety of the public.	Amendment Agreed to (49-40)	Not Voting	Not Voting
152	1	5/07/07	On the Cloture Motion S. 1082 A bill to amend the Federal Food, Drug, and Cosmetic Act to reauthorize and amend the prescription drug user fee provisions, and for other purposes.	Cloture Motion Agreed to (82-8, 3/5 majority required)	Not Voting	Not Voting
153	1	5/08/07	On the Nomination PN20 Frederick J. Kapala, of Illinois, to be United States District Judge for the Northern District of Illinois	Nomination Confirmed (91-0)	Yea	Not Voting
154	1	5/09/07	On the Amendment S.Amdt. 1039 to S. 1082 (Prescription Drug User Fee Amendments of 2007) To clarify the authority of the Office of Surveillance and Epidemiology with respect to postmarket drug safety pursuant to recommendations by the Institute of Medicine.	Amendment Rejected (46-47)	Yea	Not Voting
155	1	5/09/07	On the Amendment S.Amdt. 998 to S. 1082 (Prescription Drug User Fee Amendments of 2007) To provide for the application of stronger civil penalties for violations of approved risk evaluation and mitigation strategies.	Amendment Agreed to (64-30)	Yea	Not Voting
156	1	5/09/07	On the Amendment S.Amdt. 1034 to S. 1082 (Prescription Drug User Fee Amendments of 2007) To reduce financial conflict of interest in FDA Advisory Panels.	Amendment Rejected (47-47)	Yea	Not Voting

Vote No.	Session	Date	Vote Question Description	Result	Obama's Postion	McCain's Postion
157	1	5/09/07	On Passage of the Bill S. 1082 An act to amend the Federal Food, Drug, and cosmetic Act and the Public Health Service Act to reauthorize drug and device user fees and ensure the safety of medical products, and for other purposes.	Bill Passed (93-1)	Yea	Not Voting
158	1	5/09/07	On the Nomination PN11 Debra Ann Livingston, of New York, to be United States Circuit Judge for the Second Circuit	Nomination Confirmed (91-0)	Yea	Not Voting
159	1	5/09/07	On the Motion (Kyl Motion to Instruct Conferees Re: S. Con. Res. 21) An original concurrent resolution setting forth the congressional budget for the United States Government for fiscal year 2008 and including the appropriate budgetary levels for fiscal years 2007 and 2009 through 2012.	Motion Agreed to (54-41)	Nay	Not Voting
160	1	5/09/07	On the Motion (Conrad Motion to Instruct Conferees Re: S. Con. Res.21) An original concurrent resolution setting forth the congressional budget for the United States Government for fiscal year 2008 and including the appropriate budgetary levels for fiscal years 2007 and 2009 through 2012.	Motion Agreed to (51-44)	Yea	Not Voting
161	1	5/09/07	On the Motion (Gregg Motion to Instruct Conferees Re: S. Con. Res. 21) An original concurrent resolution setting forth the congressional budget for the United States Government for fiscal year 2008 and including the appropriate budgetary levels for fiscal years 2007 and 2009 through 2012.	Motion Rejected (44-51)	Nay	Not Voting

Vote No.	Ses-sion	Date	Vote Question Description	Result	Obama's Postion	McCain's Postion
162	1	5/10/07	On the Cloture Motion H.R. 1495 A bill to provide for the conservation and development of water and related resources, to authorize the Secretary of the Army to construct various projects for improvements to rivers and harbors of the United States, and for other purposes.	Cloture Motion Agreed to (89-7, 3/5 majority required)	Yea	Not Voting
163	1	5/15/07	On the Amendment S.Amdt. 1090 to S.Amdt. 1065 to H.R. 1495 (Water Resources Development Act of 2007) To prioritize Federal spending to ensure the residents of the city of Sacramento are protected from the threat of floods before spending money to add sand to beaches in San Diego.	Amend-ment Rejected (12-77)	Not Voting	Not Voting
164	1	5/15/07	On the Amendment S.Amdt. 1089 to S.Amdt. 1065 to H.R. 1495 (Water Resources Development Act of 2007) To prioritize Federal spending to ensure the needs of Louisiana residents who lost their homes as a result of Hurricane Katrina and Rita are met before spending money to design or construct a nonessential visitors center.	Amend-ment Rejected (11-79)	Nay	Not Voting
165	1	5/15/07	On the Amendment S.Amdt. 1086 to S.Amdt. 1065 to H.R. 1495 (Water Resources Development Act of 2007) To establish a Water Resources Commission to prioritize water resources projects in the United States.	Amend-ment Rejected (22-69)	Nay	Not Voting
166	1	5/15/07	On the Amendment S.Amdt. 1094 to S.Amdt. 1065 to H.R. 1495 (Water Resources Development Act of 2007) To require the consideration of certain factors relating to global climate change.	Amend-ment Rejected (51-42, 3/5 majority required)	Yea	Not Voting

VOTE No.	SES-SION	DATE	VOTE QUESTION Description	RESULT	OBAMA'S POSTION	MCCAIN'S POSTION
167	1	5/16/07	On the Cloture Motion S.Amdt. 1098 to S.Amdt. 1097 to H.R. 1495 (Water Resources Development Act of 2007) To provide for a transition of the Iraq mission.	Cloture Motion Rejected (29-67, 3/5 majority required)	Yea	Not Voting
168	1	5/16/07	On the Cloture Motion S.Amdt. 1134 to H.R. 1495 (Water Resources Development Act of 2007) Relative to the President's strategy in Iraq.	Cloture Motion Rejected (52-44, 3/5 majority required)	Nay	Not Voting
169	1	5/16/07	On the Cloture Motion S.Amdt. 1135 to H.R. 1495 (Water Resources Development Act of 2007) To express the sense of the Senate that Congress must send to the President acceptable legislation to continue funds for Operation Iraqi Freedom and Operation Enduring Freedom by not later than May 28, 2007.	Cloture Motion Agreed to (87-9, 3/5 majority required)	Yea	Not Voting
170	1	5/16/07	On Passage of the Bill H.R. 1495 A bill to provide for the conservation and development of water and related resources, to authorize the Secretary of the Army to construct various proj-ects for improvements to rivers and harbors of the United States, and for other purposes.	Bill Passed (91-4)	Not Voting	Not Voting
171	1	5/17/07	On the Cloture Motion S.Amdt. 1123 to H.R. 2206 (U.S. Troop Readiness, Veterans' Care, Katrina Recovery, and Iraq Accountability Appropriations Act, 2007) Expressing the sense of the Congress that no action should be taken to undermine the safety of the Armed Forces of the United States or impact their ability to complete their assigned or future missions.	Cloture Motion Agreed to (94-1, 3/5 majority required)	Yea	Not Voting

VOTE No.	SES-SION	DATE	VOTE QUESTION Description	RESULT	OBAMA'S POSTION	MCCAIN'S POSTION
172	1	5/17/07	On the Conference Report S.Con. Res. 21 An original concurrent resolution setting forth the congressional budget for the United States Government for fiscal year 2008 and including the appropriate budgetary levels for fiscal years 2007 and 2009 through 2012.	Conference Report Agreed to (52-40)	Yea	Not Voting
173	1	5/21/07	On the Cloture Motion S. 1348 A bill to provide for comprehensive immigration reform and for other purposes.	Cloture Motion Agreed to (69-23, 3/5 majority required)	Not Voting	Not Voting
174	1	5/22/07	On the Amendment S.Amdt. 1153 to S.Amdt. 1150 to S. 1348 (Comprehensive Immigration Reform Act of 2007) To strike the Y nonimmigrant guestworker program.	Amendment Rejected (31-64)	Not Voting	Not Voting
175	1	5/23/07	On the Amendment S.Amdt. 1169 to S.Amdt. 1150 to S. 1348 (Comprehensive Immigration Reform Act of 2007) To reduce to 200,000 the number of certain non-immigrants permitted to be admitted during a fiscal year.	Amendment Agreed to (74-24)	Yea	Not Voting
176	1	5/24/07	On the Amendment S.Amdt. 1186 to S.Amdt. 1150 to S. 1348 (Comprehensive Immigration Reform Act of 2007) To exempt children of certain Filipino World War II veterans from the numerical limitations on immigrant visas.	Amendment Agreed to (87-9)	Yea	Yea
177	1	5/24/07	On the Amendment S.Amdt. 1158 to S.Amdt. 1150 to S. 1348 (Comprehensive Immigration Reform Act of 2007) To amend the Illegal Immigration Reform and Immigrant Responsibility Act of 1996 to facilitate information sharing between federal and local law enforcement officials related to an individual's immigration status.	Amendment Rejected (48-49)	Nay	Yea

VOTE No.	SES-SION	DATE	VOTE QUESTION *Description*	RESULT	OBAMA'S POSTION	MCCAIN'S POSTION
178	1	5/24/07	On the Amendment S.Amdt. 1181 to S.Amdt. 1150 to S. 1348 (Comprehensive Immigration Reform Act of 2007) To sunset the Y-1 nonimmigrant visa program after a 5-year period.	Amendment Rejected (48-49)	Yea	Nay
179	1	5/24/07	On the Amendment S.Amdt. 1223 to S.Amdt. 1150 to S. 1348 (Comprehensive Immigration Reform Act of 2007) To establish the American Competitiveness Scholarship Program.	Amendment Agreed to (59-35)	Yea	Not Voting
180	1	5/24/07	On the Amendment S.Amdt. 1157 to S.Amdt. 1150 to S. 1348 (Comprehensive Immigration Reform Act of 2007) To strike title VI (related to Nonimmigrants in the United States Previously in Unlawful Status).	Amendment Rejected (29-66)	Nay	Nay
181	1	5/24/07	On the Motion (Motion to Concur in House Amdt. to Senate Amdt to H.R.2206) Making emergency supplemental appropriations and additional supplemental appropriations for agricultural and other emergency assistance for the fiscal year ending September 30, 2007, and for other purposes.	Motion Agreed to (80-14)	Nay	Yea
182	1	6/05/07	On the Amendment S.Amdt. 1189 to S.Amdt. 1150 to S. 1348 (Comprehensive Immigration Reform Act of 2007) To eliminate the preference given to people who entered the United States illegally over people seeking to enter the country legally in the merit-based evaluation system for visas.	Amendment Rejected (31-62)	Not Voting	Not Voting
183	1	6/05/07	On the Amendment S.Amdt. 1231 to S.Amdt. 1150 to S. 1348 (Comprehensive Immigration Reform Act of 2007) To ensure that employers make efforts to recruit American workers.	Amendment Agreed to (71-22)	Not Voting	Not Voting

VOTE No.	SES-SION	DATE	VOTE QUESTION Description	RESULT	OBAMA'S POSTION	McCAIN'S POSTION
184	1	6/05/07	On the Amendment S.Amdt. 1170 to S.Amdt. 1150 to S. 1348 (Comprehensive Immigration Reform Act of 2007) To amend the Help America Vote Act of 2002 to require individuals voting in person to present photo identification.	Amendment Rejected (41-52, 3/5 majority required)	Not Voting	Not Voting
185	1	6/05/07	On the Amendment S.Amdt. 1176 to S.Amdt. 1150 to S. 1348 (Comprehensive Immigration Reform Act of 2007) To establish commissions to review the facts and circumstances surrounding injustices suffered by European Americans, European Latin Americans, and Jewish refugees during World War II.	Amendment Agreed to (67-26, 3/5 majority required)	Not Voting	Not Voting
186	1	6/06/07	On the Amendment S.Amdt. 1333 to S.Amdt. 1150 to S. 1348 (Comprehensive Immigration Reform Act of 2007) To increase the immigration-related penalties associated with various criminal activities.	Amendment Agreed to (66-32)	Yea	Yea
187	1	6/06/07	On the Amendment S.Amdt. 1184 to S.Amdt. 1150 to S. 1348 (Comprehensive Immigration Reform Act of 2007) To establish a permanent bar for gang members, terrorists, and other criminals.	Amendment Rejected (46-51)	Nay	Nay
188	1	6/06/07	On the Amendment S.Amdt. 1197 to S.Amdt. 1150 to S. 1348 (Comprehensive Immigration Reform Act of 2007) To require health care coverage for holders of Z nonimmigrant visas.	Amendment Rejected (43-55)	Nay	Nay
189	1	6/06/07	On the Amendment S.Amdt. 1267 to S.Amdt. 1150 to S. 1348 (Comprehensive Immigration Reform Act of 2007) To remove the requirement that Y-1 nonimmigrant visa holders leave the United States before they are able to renew their visa.	Amendment Rejected (41-57)	Yea	Nay

VOTE No.	SES-SION	DATE	VOTE QUESTION Description	RESULT	OBAMA'S POSTION	MCCAIN'S POSTION
190	1	6/06/07	On the Amendment S.Amdt. 1250 to S.Amdt. 1150 to S. 1348 (Comprehensive Immigration Reform Act of 2007) To address documentation of employment and to make an amendment with respect to mandatory disclosure of information.	Amendment Agreed to (57-39)	Nay	Yea
191	1	6/06/07	On the Amendment S.Amdt. 1331 to S.Amdt. 1150 to S. 1348 (Comprehensive Immigration Reform Act of 2007) To clarify the application of the earned income tax credit.	Amendment Agreed to (57-40)	Yea	Nay
192	1	6/06/07	On the Amendment S.Amdt. 1234 to S.Amdt. 1150 to S. 1348 (Comprehensive Immigration Reform Act of 2007) To save American taxpayers up to $24 billion in the 10 years after passage of this Act, by preventing the earned income tax credit, which is, according to the Congressional Research Service, the largest anti-poverty entitlement program of the Federal Government, from being claimed by Y temporary workers or illegal aliens given status by this Act until they adjust to legal permanent resident status.	Amendment Agreed to (56-41)	Nay	Yea
193	1	6/06/07	On the Motion (Motion to Waive CBA Re: Menendez Amdt. No 1194) To modify the deadline for the family backlog reduction.	Motion Rejected (53-44, 3/5 majority required)	Yea	Nay
194	1	6/06/07	On the Amendment S.Amdt. 1460 to S.Amdt. 1150 to S. 1348 (Comprehensive Immigration Reform Act of 2007) To modify the allocation of visas with respect to the backlog of family-based visa petitions.	Amendment Agreed to (51-46)	Nay	Yea

Vote No.	Session	Date	Vote Question / Description	Result	Obama's Postion	McCain's Postion
195	1	6/06/07	On the Motion (Motion to Waive CBA Re: Clinton Amdt. No. 1183, As Further Modified) To reclassify the spouses and minor children of lawful permanent residents as immediate relatives.	Motion Rejected (44-53, 3/5 majority required)	Yea	Nay
196	1	6/06/07	On the Amendment S.Amdt. 1374 to S.Amdt. 1150 to S. 1348 (Comprehensive Immigration Reform Act of 2007) To improve the criteria and weights of the merit-based evaluation system.	Amendment Rejected (42-55)	Nay	Nay
197	1	6/06/07	On the Amendment S.Amdt. 1384 to S.Amdt. 1150 to S. 1348 (Comprehensive Immigration Reform Act of 2007) To preserve and enhance the role of the English language.	Amendment Agreed to (58-39)	Yea	Nay
198	1	6/06/07	On the Amendment S.Amdt. 1151 to S.Amdt. 1150 to S. 1348 (Comprehensive Immigration Reform Act of 2007) To amend title 4, United States Code, to declare English as the national language of the Government of the United States, and for other purposes.	Amendment Agreed to (64-33)	Nay	Yea
199	1	6/06/07	On the Amendment S.Amdt. 1339 to S.Amdt. 1150 to S. 1348 (Comprehensive Immigration Reform Act of 2007) To require that the U.S. VISIT system- the biometric border check-in/check-out system first required by Congress in 1996 that is already well past its already postponed 2005 implementation due date- be finished as part of the enforcement trigger.	Amendment Rejected (48-49)	Nay	Nay

VOTE No.	SES-SION	DATE	VOTE QUESTION Description	RESULT	OBAMA's POSTION	McCAIN's POSTION
200	1	6/06/07	On the Amendment S.Amdt. 1202 to S.Amdt. 1150 to S. 1348 (Comprehensive Immigration Reform Act of 2007) To provide a date on which the authority of the section relating to the increasing of American competitiveness through a merit-based evaluation system for immigrants shall be terminated.	Amendment Rejected (42-55)	Yea	Nay
201	1	6/06/07	On the Amendment S.Amdt. 1316 to S.Amdt. 1150 to S. 1348 (Comprehensive Immigration Reform Act of 2007) To sunset the Y-1 nonimmigrant visa program after a 5-yer period.	Amendment Agreed to (49-48)	Yea	Nay
202	1	6/07/07	On the Amendment S.Amdt. 1311 to S.Amdt. 1150 to S. 1348 (Comprehensive Immigration Reform Act of 2007) To require the enforcement of existing border security and immigration laws and Congressional approval before amnesty can be granted.	Amendment Rejected (42-54)	Nay	Not Voting
203	1	6/07/07	On the Cloture Motion S.Amdt. 1150 to S. 1348 (Comprehensive Immigration Reform Act of 2007) In the nature of a substitute.	Cloture Motion Rejected (33-63, 3/5 majority required)	Yea	Not Voting
204	1	6/07/07	On the Cloture Motion S. 1348 A bill to provide for comprehensive immigration reform and for other purposes.	Cloture Motion Rejected (34-61, 3/5 majority required)	Yea	Not Voting
205	1	6/07/07	On the Motion (Motion to Instruct Sgt. at Arms) A bill to provide for comprehensive immigration reform and for other purposes.	Motion Agreed to (72-13)	Yea	Not Voting

VOTE No.	SES-SION	DATE	VOTE QUESTION Description	RESULT	OBAMA'S POSTION	McCAIN'S POSTION
206	1	6/07/07	On the Cloture Motion S.Amdt. 1150 to S. 1348 (Comprehensive Immigration Reform Act of 2007) In the nature of a substitute.	Cloture Motion Rejected (45-50, 3/5 majority required)	Yea	Yea
207	1	6/11/07	On the Cloture Motion S.J.Res. 14 A joint resolution expressing the sense of the Senate that Attorney General Alberto Gonzales no longer holds the confidence of the Senate and of the American people.	Cloture Motion Rejected (53-38, 3/5 majority required)	Not Voting	Not Voting
208	1	6/11/07	On the Cloture Motion H.R. 6 A bill to reduce our Nation's dependency on foreign oil by investing in clean, renewable, and alternative energy resources, promoting new-emerging energy technologies, developing greater efficiency, and creating a Strategic Energy Efficiency and Renewables Reserve to invest in alternative energy, and for other purposes.	Cloture Motion Agreed to (91-0, 3/5 majority required)	Not Voting	Not Voting
209	1	6/12/07	On the Amendment S.Amdt. 1508 to S.Amdt. 1502 to H.R. 6 (CLEAN Energy Act of 2007) To provide for the publication and implementation of an action plan to reduce the quantity of oil used annually in the United States.	Amendment Agreed to (63-30)	Not Voting	Not Voting
210	1	6/13/07	On the Amendment S.Amdt. 1505 to S.Amdt. 1502 to H.R. 6 (CLEAN Energy Act of 2007) To improve domestic fuels security.	Amendment Rejected (43-52)	Nay	Not Voting
211	1	6/14/07	On the Motion to Table S.Amdt. 1538 to S.Amdt. 1537 to S.Amdt. 1502 to H.R. 6 To provide for the establishment of a Federal clean portfolio standard.	Motion to Table Agreed to (56-39)	Yea	Not Voting

VOTE No.	SES-SION	DATE	VOTE QUESTION *Description*	RESULT	OBAMA'S POSTION	MCCAIN'S POSTION
212	1	6/14/07	**On the Amendment S.Amdt. 1566 to S.Amdt. 1502 to H.R. 6 (CLEAN Energy Act of 2007)** To authorize the State of Virginia to petition for authorization to conduct natural gas exploration and drilling activities in the coastal zone of the State.	Amendment Rejected (43-44, 3/5 majority required)	Not Voting	Not Voting
213	1	6/19/07	**On the Amendment S.Amdt. 1628 to S.Amdt. 1502 to H.R. 6 (CLEAN Energy Act of 2007)** To provide standards for clean coal-derived fuels.	Amendment Rejected (39-55)	Nay	Not Voting
214	1	6/19/07	**On the Amendment S.Amdt. 1614 to S.Amdt. 1502 to H.R. 6 (CLEAN Energy Act of 2007)** To establish a program to provide loans for projects to produce syngas from coal and other feedstocks while simultaneously reducing greenhouse gas emissions and reliance of the United States on petroleum and natural gas.	Amendment Rejected (33-61)	Yea	Not Voting
215	1	6/19/07	**On the Amendment S.Amdt. 1519 to S.Amdt. 1502 to H.R. 6 (CLEAN Energy Act of 2007)** To amend the Sherman Act to make oil-producing and exporting cartels illegal.	Amendment Agreed to (70-23)	Yea	Not Voting
216	1	6/19/07	**On the Amendment S.Amdt. 1610 to S.Amdt. 1502 to H.R. 6 (CLEAN Energy Act of 2007)** To provide for the siting, construction, expansion, and operation of liquefied natural gas terminals.	Amendment Rejected (37-56)	Yea	Not Voting
217	1	6/20/07	**On the Motion (Motion to Waive C.B.A. re: DeMint Amdt. No. 1546)** To provide that legislation that would increase the national average fuel prices for automobiles is subject to a point of order in the Senate.	Motion Rejected (37-55, 3/5 majority required)	Not Voting	Not Voting

Vote No.	Ses-sion	Date	Vote Question Description	Result	Obama's Postion	McCain's Postion
218	1	6/20/07	On the Motion (Motion to Waive C.B.A. re: Gregg Amdt. No. 1718) To strike the provision extending the additional duty on ethanol and for other purposes.	Motion Rejected (36-56, 3/5 majority required)	Not Voting	Not Voting
219	1	6/20/07	On the Amendment S.Amdt. 1693 to S.Amdt. 1502 to H.R. 6 (CLEAN Energy Act of 2007) To ensure that the renewable fuel standard does not harm the environment.	Amendment Agreed to (58-34)	Yea	Not Voting
220	1	6/20/07	On the Motion (Motion to Waive C.B.A. re: Inhofe Amdt. No. 1666) To ensure agricultural equity with respect to the renewable fuels standard.	Motion Rejected (31-63, 3/5 majority required)	Nay	Not Voting
221	1	6/20/07	On the Amendment S.Amdt. 1800 to S.Amdt. 1704 to S.Amdt. 1502 to H.R. 6 To disallow the credit for renewable diesel for fuel that is coprocessed with petroleum.	Amendment Rejected (45-49)	Yea	Not Voting
222	1	6/21/07	On the Motion (Motion to Waive CBA Re: Kyl Amdt. No. 1733 as Modified) To provide a condition precedent for the effective date of the revenue raisers.	Motion Rejected (38-55, 3/5 majority required)	Nay	Not Voting
223	1	6/21/07	On the Cloture Motion S.Amdt. 1704 to S.Amdt. 1502 to H.R. 6 (CLEAN Energy Act of 2007) To amend the Internal Revenue Code of 1986 to provide for energy advancement and investment, and for other purposes.	Cloture Motion Rejected (57-36, 3/5 majority required)	Yea	Not Voting
224	1	6/21/07	On the Cloture Motion S.Amdt. 1502 to H.R. 6 (CLEAN Energy Act of 2007) In the nature of a substitute.	Cloture Motion Agreed to (61-32, 3/5 majority required)	Yea	Not Voting

VOTE No.	SES-SION	DATE	VOTE QUESTION Description	RESULT	OBAMA'S POSTION	McCAIN'S POSTION
225	1	6/21/07	On the Cloture Motion H.R. 6 An Act to move the United States toward greater energy independence and security, to increase the production of clean renewable fuels, to protect consumers from price gouging, to increase the energy efficiency of products, buildings, and vehicles, to promote research on and deploy greenhouse gas capture and storage options, and to improve the energy performance of the Federal Government, and for other purposes.	Cloture Motion Agreed to (62-32, 3/5 majority required)	Yea	Not Voting
226	1	6/21/07	On Passage of the Bill H.R. 6 An Act to move the United States toward greater energy independence and security, to increase the production of clean renewable fuels, to protect consumers from price gouging, to increase the energy efficiency of products, buildings, and vehicles, to promote research on and deploy greenhouse gas capture and storage options, and to improve the energy performance of the Federal Government, and for other purposes.	Bill Passed (65-27)	Yea	Not Voting
227	1	6/26/07	On the Cloture Motion H.R. 800 A bill to amend the National Labor Relations Act to establish an efficient system to enable employees to form, join, or assist labor organizations, to provide for mandatory injunctions for unfair labor practices during organizing efforts, and for other purposes.	Cloture Motion Rejected (51-48, 3/5 majority required)	Yea	Nay
228	1	6/26/07	On the Cloture Motion S. 1639 A bill to provide for comprehensive immigration reform and for other purposes.	Cloture Motion Agreed to (64-35, 3/5 majority required)	Yea	Yea
229	1	6/27/07	On the Motion to Table S.Amdt. 1934 to S. 1639 (No short title on file) Of a perfecting nature.	Motion to Table Agreed to (53-45)	Yea	Not Voting

Vote No.	Session	Date	Vote Question Description	Result	Obama's Postion	McCain's Postion
230	1	6/27/07	On the Motion to Table S.Amdt. 1934 to S. 1639 (No short title on file) Of a perfecting nature.	Motion to Table Agreed to (79-18)	Yea	Not Voting
231	1	6/27/07	On the Motion to Table S.Amdt. 1934 to S. 1639 (No short title on file) Of a perfecting nature.	Motion to Table Agreed to (57-40)	Yea	Not Voting
232	1	6/27/07	On the Motion to Table S.Amdt. 1934 to S. 1639 (No short title on file) Of a perfecting nature.	Motion to Table Agreed to (56-41)	Nay	Not Voting
233	1	6/27/07	On the Motion to Table S.Amdt. 1934 to S. 1639 (No short title on file) Of a perfecting nature.	Motion to Table Agreed to (55-40)	Nay	Not Voting
234	1	6/27/07	On the Motion to Table S.Amdt. 1934 to S. 1639 (No short title on file) Of a perfecting nature.	Motion to Table Failed (45-52)	Nay	Not Voting
235	1	6/28/07	On the Cloture Motion S. 1639 A bill to provide for comprehensive immigration reform and for other purposes.	Cloture Motion Rejected (46-53, 3/5 majority required)	Yea	Yea
236	1	6/28/07	On the Nomination PN599 Lt. Gen. Douglas E. Lute, in the Army, to be Lieutenant General	Nomination Confirmed (94-4)	Yea	Yea
237	1	6/28/07	On the Nomination PN30 Benjamin Hale Settle, of Washington, to be United States District Judge for the Western District of Washington	Nomination Confirmed (99-0)	Yea	Yea
238	1	6/28/07	On the Nomination PN252 Richard Sullivan, of New York, to be United States District Judge for the Southern District of New York	Nomination Confirmed (99-0)	Yea	Yea
239	1	7/09/07	On the Nomination PN23 Liam O'Grady, of Virginia, to be United States District Judge for the Eastern District of Virginia	Nomination Confirmed (88-0)	Not Voting	Not Voting

VOTE No.	SES- SION	DATE	VOTE QUESTION *Description*	RESULT	OBAMA'S POSTION	MCCAIN'S POSTION
240	1	7/09/07	On the Nomination PN347 Janet T. Neff, of Michigan, to be United States District Judge for the Western District of Michigan	Nomination Confirmed (83-4)	Not Voting	Not Voting
241	1	7/11/07	On the Cloture Motion S.Amdt. 2012 to S.Amdt. 2011 to H.R. 1585 (National Defense Authorization Act for Fiscal Year 2008) To specify minimum periods between deployment of units and members of the Armed Forces for Operation Iraqi Freedom and Operation Enduring Freedom.	Cloture Motion Rejected (56-41, 3/5 majority required)	Yea	Nay
242	1	7/11/07	On the Amendment S.Amdt. 2073 to S.Amdt. 2011 to H.R. 1585 (National Defense Authorization Act for Fiscal Year 2008) To require a report on support provided by the Government of Iran for attacks against coalition forces in Iraq.	Amendment Agreed to (97-0)	Yea	Yea
243	1	7/11/07	On the Amendment S.Amdt. 2032 to S.Amdt. 2011 to H.R. 1585 (National Defense Authorization Act for Fiscal Year 2008) To limit the length of deployment of members of the Armed Forced for Operation Iraqi Freedom.	Amendment Rejected (52-45, 3/5 majority required)	Yea	Nay
244	1	7/11/07	On the Amendment S.Amdt. 2078 to H.R. 1585 (National Defense Authorization Act for Fiscal Year 2008) To express the sense of Congress on length of time between deployments for members of the Armed Forces.	Amendment Rejected (41-55, 3/5 majority required)	Nay	Yea
245	1	7/12/07	On the Amendment S.Amdt. 2024 to S.Amdt. 2011 to H.R. 1585 (National Defense Authorization Act for Fiscal Year 2008) To state the policy of the United States on the protection of the United States and its allies against Iranian ballistic missiles.	Amendment Agreed to (90-5)	Not Voting	Yea

Vote No.	Session	Date	Vote Question Description	Result	Obama's Postion	McCain's Postion
246	1	7/12/07	On the Amendment S.Amdt. 2019 to S.Amdt. 2011 to H.R. 1585 (National Defense Authorization Act for Fiscal Year 2008) To provide for the care and management of wounded warriors.	Amendment Agreed to (94-0)	Not Voting	Yea
247	1	7/13/07	On the Amendment S.Amdt. 2135 to S.Amdt. 2011 to H.R. 1585 (National Defense Authorization Act for Fiscal Year 2008) Relative to bringing Osama bin Laden and other leaders of al Qaeda to justice.	Amendment Agreed to (87-1)	Not Voting	Not Voting
248	1	7/17/07	On the Amendment S.Amdt. 2100 to S.Amdt. 2011 to H.R. 1585 (National Defense Authorization Act for Fiscal Year 2008) To express the sense of the Senate that it is in the national security interest of the United States that Iraq not become a failed state and a safe haven for terrorists.	Amendment Agreed to (94-3)	Yea	Yea
249	1	7/17/07	On the Motion (Motion to Instruct the Sgt. At Arms) To authorize appropriations for fiscal year 2008 for military activities of the Department of Defense, for military construction, and for defense activities of the Department of Energy, to prescribe military personnel strengths for such fiscal year, and for other purposes.	Motion Rejected (44-47)	Not Voting	Nay
250	1	7/17/07	On the Motion (Motion to Instruct the Sgt. at Arms) To authorize appropriations for fiscal year 2008 for military activities of the Department of Defense, for military construction, and for defense activities of the Department of Energy, to prescribe military personnel strengths for such fiscal year, and for other purposes.	Motion Agreed to (41-37)	Yea	Not Voting

Vote No.	Session	Date	Vote Question Description	Result	Obama's Postion	McCain's Postion
251	1	7/18/07	On the Motion (Motion to Instruct Sgt. At Arms) To authorize appropriations for fiscal year 2008 for military activities of the Department of Defense, for military construction, and for defense activities of the Department of Energy, to prescribe military personnel strengths for such fiscal year, and for other purposes.	Motion Agreed to (37-23)	Yea	Not Voting
252	1	7/18/07	On the Motion (Motion to Invoke Cloture on the Levin Amdt. No. 2087) To provide for a reduction and transition of United States forces in Iraq.	Motion Rejected (52-47, 3/5 majority required)	Yea	Nay
253	1	7/18/07	On the Motion to Proceed H.R. 2669 A bill to provide for reconciliation pursuant to section 601 of the concurrent resolution on the budget for fiscal year 2008.	Motion to Proceed Agreed to (49-48)	Not Voting	Nay
254	1	7/19/07	On the Amendment S.Amdt. 2329 to S.Amdt. 2327 to H.R. 2669 (College Cost Reduction Act of 2007) To increase the amount appropriated for the college access partnership grant program.	Amendment Agreed to (73-24)	Yea	Nay
255	1	7/19/07	On the Amendment S.Amdt. 2330 to S.Amdt. 2327 to H.R. 2669 (College Cost Reduction Act of 2007) To amend the amounts appropriated for Promise Grants for fiscal years 2014 through 2017.	Amendment Agreed to (52-45)	Yea	Nay
256	1	7/19/07	On the Amendment S.Amdt. 2337 to S.Amdt. 2327 to H.R. 2669 (College Cost Reduction Act of 2007) To amend the special allowance payments.	Amendment Rejected (35-62)	Nay	Yea

Vote No.	Ses-sion	Date	Vote Question Description	Result	Obama's Postion	McCain's Postion
257	1	7/19/07	On the Amendment S.Amdt. 2333 to S.Amdt. 2327 to H.R. 2669 (College Cost Reduction Act of 2007) To strike the provisions relating to loan forgiveness for public service employees.	Amend-ment Rejected (42-55)	Not Voting	Yea
258	1	7/19/07	On the Motion (Motion to Waive CBA Re: Coleman Amdt. No. 2334) To prevent the Federal Communications Commission from repromulgating the fairness doctrine.	Motion Rejected (49-48, 3/5 majority required)	Not Voting	Yea
259	1	7/19/07	On the Amendment S.Amdt. 2351 to S.Amdt. 2327 to H.R. 2669 (College Cost Reduction Act of 2007) To express the sense of the Senate on the detainees of Guantanamo Bay, Cuba.	Amend-ment Agreed to (94-3)	Not Voting	Yea
260	1	7/19/07	On the Motion (Motion to Waive CBA DeMint Amdt. No. 2352) To amend the National Labor Relations Act to ensure the right of employees to a secret-ballot election conducted by the National Labor Relations Board.	Motion Rejected (42-54, 3/5 majority required)	Not Voting	Yea
261	1	7/19/07	On the Motion (Motion to Waive CBA Collins Amdt. No. 2340) To provide limited immunity for reports of suspicious behavior and response.	Motion Rejected (57-39, 3/5 majority required)	Not Voting	Yea
262	1	7/19/07	On the Motion (Motion to Waive CBA Stabenow Amdt. No 2358) Relative to illegal aliens qualifying for Social Security benefits; and Relative to I. Lewis "Scooter" Libby.	Motion Rejected (53-44, 3/5 majority required)	Not Voting	Yea
263	1	7/19/07	On the Motion (Motion to Waive CBA Ensign Amdt. No. 2355) To reduce document fraud, prevent identity theft, and preserve the integrity of the Social Security system, by ensuring that individuals are not able to receive Social Security benefits as a result of unlawful activity.	Motion Rejected (57-40, 3/5 majority required)	Not Voting	Yea

VOTE No.	SESSION	DATE	VOTE QUESTION *Description*	RESULT	OBAMA'S POSITION	McCAIN'S POSITION
264	1	7/19/07	On the Motion (Motion to Waive CBA Schumer Amdt. No. 2361) A sense of the Senate relative to tax policy.	Motion Rejected (48-48, 3/5 majority required)	Not Voting	Nay
265	1	7/19/07	On the Motion (Motion to Waive CBA Sununu Amdt. No. 2341) To permanently extend certain education-related tax incentives.	Motion Rejected (47-48, 3/5 majority required)	Not Voting	Yea
266	1	7/19/07	On the Motion (Motion to Waive CBA Cornyn Amdt No. 2339) To provide interim relief for shortages in employment-based visas for aliens with extraordinary ability and advanced degrees and for nurses.	Motion Rejected (55-40, 3/5 majority required)	Not Voting	Yea
267	1	7/19/07	On the Motion (Motion to Waive CBA Landrieu Amdt. No. 2363) A sense of the Senate relative to the adoption tax credit	Motion Rejected (48-48, 3/5 majority required)	Not Voting	Nay
268	1	7/19/07	On the Motion (Motion to Waive CBA DeMint Amdt. 2362) To repeal the sunset of the Economic Growth and Tax Relief Reconciliation Act of 2001 with respect to the expansion of the adoption credit and adoption assistance programs.	Motion Rejected (48-48, 3/5 majority required)	Not Voting	Yea
269	1	7/19/07	On the Motion (Motion to Waive CBA Dole Amdt. No. 2350) To amend the Help America Vote Act of 2002 to require individuals voting in person to present photo identification.	Motion Rejected (42-54, 3/5 majority required)	Not Voting	Yea
270	1	7/20/07	On the Motion (Motion to Waive CBA Kerry Amdt. No. 2364.) A sense of the Senate relative to the Alternative Minimum Tax.	Motion Rejected (48-48, 3/5 majority required)	Not Voting	Nay

Vote No.	Ses-sion	Date	Vote Question Description	Result	Obama's Postion	McCain's Postion
271	1	7/20/07	On the Motion (Motion to Waive C.B.A. re: Kyl Amdt. No. 2353) To amend the Internal Revenue Code of 1986 to repeal the individual alternative minimum tax.	Motion Rejected (47-49, 3/5 majority required)	Not Voting	Yea
272	1	7/20/07	On Passage of the Bill H.R. 2669 A bill to provide for reconciliation pursuant to section 601 of the concurrent resolution on the budget for fiscal year 2008.	Bill Passed (78-18)	Not Voting	Nay
273	1	7/23/07	On the Amendment S.Amdt. 2376 to S. 1642 (Higher Education Amendments of 2007) To provide for a Federal supplemental loan program.	Amendment Rejected (37-54)	Not Voting	Not Voting
274	1	7/24/07	On the Amendment S.Amdt. 2381 to S.Amdt. 2369 to S. 1642 (Higher Education Amendments of 2007) To provide for a demonstration and certification regarding the use of certain Federal funds.	Amendment Agreed to (93-0)	Not Voting	Not Voting
275	1	7/24/07	On Passage of the Bill S. 1642 A bill to extend the authorization of programs under the Higher Education Act of 1965, and for other purposes.	Bill Passed (95-0)	Not Voting	Not Voting
276	1	7/24/07	On the Joint Resolution H.J.Res. 44 Joint resolution approving the renewal of import restrictions contained in the Burmese Freedom and Democracy Act of 2003, and for other purposes.	Joint Resolution Passed (93-1)	Not Voting	Not Voting
277	1	7/25/07	On the Decision of the Chair S.Amdt. 2412 to S.Amdt. 2383 to H.R. 2638 (Department of Homeland Security Appropriations Act, 2008) To ensure control over the United States borders and strengthen enforcement of the immigration laws.	Decision of Chair Sustained (52-44)	Yea	Not Voting

VOTE No.	SES-SION	DATE	VOTE QUESTION *Description*	RESULT	OBAMA'S POSTION	MCCAIN'S POSTION
278	1	7/26/07	On the Amendment S.Amdt. 2480 to S.Amdt. 2383 to H.R. 2638 (Department of Homeland Security Appropriations Act, 2008) To ensure control over the United States borders and strengthen enforcement of the immigration laws.	Amend-ment Agreed to (89-1)	Not Voting	Not Voting
279	1	7/26/07	On the Motion to Table S.Amdt. 2405 to S.Amdt. 2383 to H.R. 2638 (Department of Homeland Security Appropriations Act, 2008) To make $300,000,000 available for grants to States to carry out the REAL ID Act of 2005.	Motion to Table Agreed to (50-44)	Not Voting	Not Voting
280	1	7/26/07	On the Amendment S.Amdt. 2498 to S.Amdt. 2383 to H.R. 2638 (Department of Homeland Security Appropriations Act, 2008) To prohibit funds made available in this Act from being used to implement a rule or regulation related to certain petitions for aliens to perform temporary labor in the United States.	Amend-ment Agreed to (51-43)	Not Voting	Not Voting
281	1	7/26/07	On the Amendment S.Amdt. 2481 to S.Amdt. 2383 to H.R. 2638 (Department of Homeland Security Appropriations Act, 2008) To prohibit the use of funds to remove offenses from the list of criminal offenses disqualifying individuals from receiving TWIC cards.	Amend-ment Agreed to (93-1)	Not Voting	Not Voting
282	1	7/26/07	On Passage of the Bill H.R. 2638 A bill making appropriations for the Department of Homeland Securityfor the fiscal year ending September 30, 2008, and for other purposes.	Bill Passed (89-4)	Not Voting	Not Voting

Vote No.	Ses-sion	Date	Vote Question Description	Result	Obama's Postion	McCain's Postion
283	1	7/26/07	On the Motion to Recommit H.R. 1 A bill to provide for the implementation of the recommendations of the National Commission on Terrorist Attacks Upon the United States.	Motion to Recommit Rejected (26-67)	Not Voting	Not Voting
284	1	7/26/07	On the Conference Report H.R. 1 A bill to provide for the implementation of the recommendations of the National Commission on Terrorist Attacks Upon the United States.	Conference Report Agreed to (85-8)	Not Voting	Not Voting
285	1	7/30/07	On the Cloture Motion H.R. 976 A bill to amend the Internal Revenue Code of 1986 to provide tax relief for small businesses, and for other purposes.	Cloture Motion Agreed to (80-0, 3/5 majority required)	Not Voting	Not Voting
286	1	7/31/07	On the Amendment S.Amdt. 2536 to S.Amdt. 2530 to H.R. 976 (Small Business Tax Relief Act of 2007) To standardize the determination of income for purposes of eligibility for SCHIP.	Amendment Rejected (37-59)	Nay	Not Voting
287	1	8/01/07	On the Amendment S.Amdt. 2538 to S.Amdt. 2530 to H.R. 976 (Small Business Tax Relief Act of 2007) To amend the Internal Revenue Code of 1986 to create a Disease Prevention and Treatment Research Trust Fund.	Amendment Rejected (26-58)	Nay	Not Voting
288	1	8/01/07	On the Amendment S.Amdt. 2587 to S.Amdt. 2530 to H.R. 976 (Small Business Tax Relief Act of 2007) To limit the matching rate for coverage other than for low-income children or pregnant women covered through a waiver and to prohibit any new waivers for coverage of adults other than pregnant women.	Amendment Rejected (42-53)	Not Voting	Not Voting

VOTE No.	SES-SION	DATE	VOTE QUESTION Description	RESULT	OBAMA'S POSTION	MCCAIN'S POSTION
289	1	8/01/07	**On the Amendment S.Amdt. 2554 to S.Amdt. 2530 to H.R. 976 (Small Business Tax Relief Act of 2007)** To amend the Congressional Budget Act of 1974 to provide for a 60-vote point of order against legislation that includes a Federal excise tax rate increase which disproportionately affects taxpayers with earned income of less than 200 percent of the Federal poverty level.	Amend-ment Rejected (32-64)	Nay	Not Voting
290	1	8/01/07	**On the Motion to Table S.Amdt. 2547 to S.Amdt. 2530 to H.R. 976 (Small Business Tax Relief Act of 2007)** To eliminate the exception for certain States to cover children under SCHIP whose income exceeds 300 percent of the Federal poverty level.	Motion to Table Agreed to (53-43)	Yea	Not Voting
291	1	8/01/07	**On the Amendment S.Amdt. 2593 to S.Amdt. 2530 to H.R. 976 (Small Business Tax Relief Act of 2007)** To provide a perfecting amendment.	Amend-ment Rejected (35-61)	Nay	Not Voting
292	1	8/01/07	**On the Amendment S.Amdt. 2602 to S.Amdt. 2530 to H.R. 976 (Small Business Tax Relief Act of 2007)** To provide sufficient funding and incentives to increase the enrollment of uninsured children.	Amend-ment Rejected (36-60)	Yea	Not Voting
293	1	8/02/07	**On the Cloture Motion S. 1** A bill to provide greater transparency in the legislative process.	Cloture Motion Agreed to (80-17, 2/3 majority required)	Yea	Nay
294	1	8/02/07	**On the Motion (Motion to Concur in the Amendment of the House to S.1)** A bill to provide greater transparency in the legislative process.	Motion Agreed to (83-14)	Yea	Nay

Vote No.	Session	Date	Vote Question Description	Result	Obama's Postion	McCain's Postion
295	1	8/02/07	On the Motion (Motion to Waive CBA Specter Amdt. 2557) To amend the Internal Revenue Code of 1986 to reset the rate of tax under the alternative minimum tax at 24 percent.	Motion Rejected (47-52, 3/5 majority required)	Nay	Yea
296	1	8/02/07	On the Motion (Motion to Waive CBA Graham Amdt. No 2558 As Modified) To sunset the increase in the tax on tobacco products on September 30, 2012.	Motion Rejected (39-60, 3/5 majority required)	Nay	Yea
297	1	8/02/07	On the Amendment S.Amdt. 2540 to S.Amdt. 2530 to H.R. 976 (Small Business Tax Relief Act of 2007) To prohibit a State from using SCHIP funds to provide coverage for non-pregnant adults until the State first demonstrates that it has adequately covered targeted low-income children who reside in the State.	Amendment Rejected (43-55)	Nay	Yea
298	1	8/02/07	On the Amendment S.Amdt. 2579 to S.Amdt. 2530 to H.R. 976 (Small Business Tax Relief Act of 2007) To exclude individuals with alternative minimum tax liability from eligibility for SCHIP coverage.	Amendment Rejected (42-57)	Nay	Yea
299	1	8/02/07	On the Amendment S.Amdt. 2537 to S.Amdt. 2530 to H.R. 976 (Small Business Tax Relief Act of 2007) To minimize the erosion of private health coverage.	Amendment Rejected (37-62)	Nay	Yea
300	1	8/02/07	On the Amendment S.Amdt. 2627 to S.Amdt. 2530 to H.R. 976 (Small Business Tax Relief Act of 2007) To ensure that children and pregnant women whose family income exceeds 200 percent of the poverty line and who have access to employer-sponsored coverage receive premium assistance.	Amendment Rejected (37-62)	Nay	Yea

Vote No.	Ses-sion	Date	Vote Question Description	Result	Obama's Postion	McCain's Postion
301	1	8/02/07	On the Amendment S.Amdt. 2596 to S.Amdt. 2530 to H.R. 976 (Small Business Tax Relief Act of 2007) To require individuals who are eligible for SCHIP and employer-sponsored coverage to use the employer-sponsored coverage instead of SCHIP.	Amendment Rejected (35-64)	Nay	Nay
302	1	8/02/07	On the Amendment S.Amdt. 2535 to S.Amdt. 2530 to H.R. 976 (Small Business Tax Relief Act of 2007) To codify the unborn child rule.	Amendment Rejected (49-50)	Nay	Yea
303	1	8/02/07	On the Amendment S.Amdt. 2620 to S.Amdt. 2530 to H.R. 976 (Small Business Tax Relief Act of 2007) To increase access to health insurance for low-income children based on actual need, as adjusted for cost-of-living.	Amendment Rejected (21-78)	Nay	Yea
304	1	8/02/07	On the Amendment S.Amdt. 2562 to S.Amdt. 2530 to H.R. 976 (Small Business Tax Relief Act of 2007) To amend the Internal Revenue Code of 1986 to extend and modify the 15-year straight-line cost recovery for qualified leasehold improvements and qualified restaurant improvements and to provide a 15-year straight-line cost recovery for certain improvements to retail space.	Amendment Rejected (49-50, 3/5 majority required)	Nay	Yea
305	1	8/02/07	On the Amendment S.Amdt. 2577 to S.Amdt. 2530 to H.R. 976 (Small Business Tax Relief Act of 2007) To amend the Public Health Service Act to provide for cooperative governing of individual health insurance coverage offered in interstate commerce.	Amendment Rejected (37-62)	Nay	Yea
306	1	8/02/07	On the Motion (Motion to Waive CBA on Baucus Amdt. No. 2530) In the nature of a substitute.	Motion Agreed to (67-32, 3/5 majority required)	Yea	Nay

VOTE No.	SES-SION	DATE	VOTE QUESTION Description	RESULT	OBAMA'S POSTION	MCCAIN'S POSTION
307	1	8/02/07	On Passage of the Bill H.R. 976 A bill to amend title XXI of the Social Security Act to reauthorize the State Children's Health Insurance Program, and for other purposes.	Bill Passed (68-31)	Yea	Nay
308	1	8/03/07	On the Nomination PN253 Timothy D. DeGiusti, of Oklahoma, to be United States District Judge for the Western District of Oklahoma	Nomination Confirmed (96-0)	Yea	Yea
309	1	8/03/07	On Passage of the Bill S. 1927 A bill to amend the Foreign Intelligence Surveillance Act of 1978 to provide additional procedures for authorizing certain acquisitions of foreign intelligence information and for other purposes.	Bill Passed (60-28, 3/5 majority required)	Nay	Not Voting
310	1	8/03/07	On Passage of the Bill S. 2011 A bill entitled "The Protect America Act of 2007".	Bill Defeated (43-45, 3/5 majority required)	Yea	Not Voting
311	1	9/04/07	On the Nomination PN688 Jim Nussle, of Iowa, to be Director of the Office of Management and Budget	Nomination Confirmed (69-24)	Not Voting	Not Voting
312	1	9/05/07	On the Motion to Table S.Amdt. 2686 to H.R. 2642 (Military Construction and Veterans Affairs Appropriations Act, 2008) To strike section 225, relating to a prohibition on the disposal of Department of Veterans Affairs lands and improvements at West Los Angeles Medical Center, California.	Motion to Table Agreed to (66-25)	Not Voting	Not Voting
313	1	9/06/07	On the Amendment S.Amdt. 2687 to H.R. 2642 (Military Construction and Veterans Affairs Appropriations Act, 2008) To provide funding for security associated with the national party conventions.	Amendment Agreed to (76-15)	Not Voting	Yea

VOTE No.	SES- SION	DATE	VOTE QUESTION Description	RESULT	OBAMA'S POSTION	McCAIN'S POSTION
314	1	9/06/07	On the Amendment S.Amdt. 2662 to H.R. 2642 (Military Construction and Veterans Affairs Appropriations Act, 2008) To prohibit the use of funds to expand the boundaries or size of the Pinon Canyon Maneuver Site, Colorado.	Amend- ment Agreed to (47-45)	Not Voting	Nay
315	1	9/06/07	On the Amendment S.Amdt. 2673 to H.R. 2642 (Military Construc- tion and Veterans Affairs Appro- priations Act, 2008) To limit the cases in which funds appropriated or otherwise made available by this Act may be used to convert to contractor performance an activity or function of the De- partment of Veterans Affairs that is performed by more than 10 Federal employees.	Amend- ment Agreed to (52-39)	Not Voting	Nay
316	1	9/06/07	On Passage of the Bill H.R. 2642 A bill making appropriations for military construction, the Depart- ment of Veterans Affairs, and related agencies for the fiscal year ending September 30, 2008, and for other purposes.	Bill Passed (92-1)	Not Voting	Yea
317	1	9/06/07	On the Amendment S.Amdt. 2700 to H.R. 2764 (Department of State, Foreign Operations, and Related Pro- grams Appropriations Act, 2008) To strike the provision in section 113 that increases the limit on the United States' share for United Na- tions peacekeeping operations dur- ing fiscal year 2008 from 25 percent to 27.1 percent so that the United States does not pay more than its fair share for United Nations peace- keeping.	Amend- ment Rejected (30-63)	Not Voting	Not Voting

Vote No.	Session	Date	Vote Question Description	Result	Obama's Postion	McCain's Postion
318	1	9/06/07	On the Amendment S.Amdt. 2707 to H.R. 2764 (Department of State, Foreign Operations, and Related Programs Appropriations Act, 2008) To prohibit funding of organizations that support coercive abortion.	Amendment Agreed to (48-45)	Not Voting	Not Voting
319	1	9/06/07	On the Amendment S.Amdt. 2719 to H.R. 2764 (Department of State, Foreign Operations, and Related Programs Appropriations Act, 2008) To prohibit the application of certain restrictive eligibility requirements to foreign nongovernmental organizations with respect to the provision of assistance under part I of the Foreign Assistance Act of 1961.	Amendment Agreed to (53-41)	Not Voting	Not Voting
320	1	9/06/07	On the Amendment S.Amdt. 2708 to H.R. 2764 (Department of State, Foreign Operations, and Related Programs Appropriations Act, 2008) To prevent contributions to organizations that perform or promote abortion as a method of family planning.	Amendment Rejected (40-54)	Not Voting	Not Voting
321	1	9/06/07	On the Amendment S.Amdt. 2774 to H.R. 2764 (Department of State, Foreign Operations, and Related Programs Appropriations Act, 2008) To prohibit the use of funds by international organizations, agencies, and entities that require the registration of, or taxes guns owned by citizens of the United States.	Amendment Agreed to (81-10)	Not Voting	Not Voting

VOTE No.	SES-SION	DATE	VOTE QUESTION *Description*	RESULT	OBAMA'S POSTION	MCCAIN'S POSTION
322	1	9/06/07	**On the Amendment S.Amdt. 2773 to H.R. 2764 (Department of State, Foreign Operations, and Related Programs Appropriations Act, 2008)** To ensure that the United States contribution to the United Nations is not being lost to waste, fraud, abuse or corruption by maximizing the public transparency of all United Nations spending.	Amend-ment Agreed to (92-1)	Not Voting	Not Voting
323	1	9/06/07	**On the Amendment S.Amdt. 2716 to H.R. 2764 (Department of State, Foreign Operations, and Related Programs Appropriations Act, 2008)** To provide for the spending of $106,763,000 on programs that save children's lives, such as the President's Malaria Initiative, rather than lower priority programs, such as the Global Environment Facility, which produce few results and are managed by the United Nations Development Program, which utilizes corrupt procurement practices, operates contrary to United Nations rules, and retaliates against whistleblowers.	Amend-ment Rejected (46-47)	Not Voting	Not Voting
324	1	9/06/07	**On the Amendment S.Amdt. 2704 to H.R. 2764 (Department of State, Foreign Operations, and Related Programs Appropriations Act, 2008)** To provide that none of the funds appropriated or otherwise made available by this Act for "Contribution to the International Development Association" may be made available for the World Bank malaria control or prevention programs.	Amend-ment Rejected (33-60)	Not Voting	Not Voting

Vote No.	Session	Date	Vote Question Description	Result	Obama's Position	McCain's Position
325	1	9/06/07	On Passage of the Bill H.R. 2764 A bill making appropriations for the Department of State, foreign operations, and related programs for the fiscal year ending September 30, 2008, and for other purposes.	Bill Passed (81-12)	Not Voting	Not Voting
326	1	9/07/07	On the Conference Report H.R. 2669 A bill to provide for reconciliation pursuant to section 601 of the concurrent resolution on the budget for fiscal year 2008.	Conference Report Agreed to (79-12)	Not Voting	Not Voting
327	1	9/10/07	On the Nomination PN25 William Lindsay Osteen, Jr., of North Carolina, to be United States District Judge for the Middle District of North Carolina	Nomination Confirmed (86-0)	Not Voting	Not Voting
328	1	9/10/07	On the Nomination PN353 Janis Lynn Sammartino, of California, to be United States District Judge for the Southern District of California	Nomination Confirmed (90-0)	Not Voting	Not Voting
329	1	9/10/07	On the Amendment S.Amdt. 2792 to S.Amdt. 2791 to H.R. 3074 (Transportation, Housing and Urban Development, and Related Agencies Appropriations Act, 2008) To expand the extension of authority of the Secretary of Transportation and provide additional obligation authority for the highway bridge program.	Amendment Agreed to (60-33)	Not Voting	Not Voting
330	1	9/11/07	On the Motion to Table S.Amdt. 2810 to H.R. 3074 (Transportation, Housing and Urban Development, and Related Agencies Appropriations Act, 2008) To prohibit funds appropriated under title I from being used for earmarks until all structurally deficient and functionally obsolete bridges have been repaired, with limited exceptions.	Motion to Table Agreed to (82-14)	Not Voting	Not Voting

VOTE No.	SES-SION	DATE	VOTE QUESTION Description	RESULT	OBAMA'S POSTION	McCAIN'S POSTION
331	1	9/11/07	On the Amendment S.Amdt. 2797 to H.R. 3074 (Transportation, Housing and Urban Development, and Related Agencies Appropriations Act, 2008) To prohibit the establishment of a program that allows Mexican truck drivers to operate beyond the commercial zones near the Mexican border.	Amend-ment Agreed to (75-23)	Yea	Not Voting
332	1	9/11/07	On the Amendment S.Amdt. 2842 to H.R. 3074 (Transportation, Housing and Urban Development, and Related Agencies Appropriations Act, 2008) To ensure that every motor carrier entering the United States through the cross-border motor carrier demonstration program is inspected and meets all applicable safety standards established for United States commercial motor vehicles.	Amend-ment Rejected (29-69)	Nay	Not Voting
333	1	9/11/07	On the Motion to Table S.Amdt. 2811 to H.R. 3074 (Transportation, Housing and Urban Development, and Related Agencies Appropriations Act, 2008) To prohibit the use of funds made available under this Act for bicycle paths so that the funds can be used to improve bridge and road safety.	Motion to Table Agreed to (80-18)	Yea	Not Voting
334	1	9/12/07	On the Motion to Table S.Amdt. 2844 to H.R. 3074 (Transportation, Housing and Urban Development, and Related Agencies Appropriations Act, 2008) To provide a system for better construction and maintenance of America's aging bridge infrastructure by spending American tax dollars more effectively and efficiently.	Motion to Table Agreed to (56-37)	Yea	Not Voting

VOTE No.	SES-SION	DATE	VOTE QUESTION Description	RESULT	OBAMA'S POSTION	MCCAIN'S POSTION
335	1	9/12/07	On the Motion to Table S.Amdt. 2814 to H.R. 3074 (Transportation, Housing and Urban Development, and Related Agencies Appropriations Act, 2008) and S.Amdt. 2813 to H.R. 3074 (Transportation, Housing and Urban Development, and Related Agencies Appropriations Act, 2008) and S.Amdt. 2812 to H.R. 3074 (Transportation, Housing and Urban Development, and Related Agencies Appropriations Act, 2008) To prohibit the use of funds for the construction of a baseball facility in Billings, Montana, and to reduce the amounts made available for the Economic Development Initiative and the Community Development Fund; and To ensure that no funds made available under this Act shall be used to carry out any activity relating to the design or construction of the America's Wetland Center in Lake Charles, Louisiana, until the date on which the Secretary, in consultation with the Administrator of the Federal Emergency Management Agency and the State of Louisiana, certifies to Congress that all residents of the State of Louisiana who were displaced as a result of Hurricane Katrina or Rita in 2005 are no longer living in temporary housing; and To remove an unnecessary earmark for the International Peace Garden in Dunseith, North Dakota.	Motion to Table Agreed to (63-32)	Yea	Not Voting
336	1	9/12/07	On Passage of the Bill H.R. 3074 A bill making appropriations for the Departments of Transportation, and Housing and Urban Development, and related agencies for the fiscal year ending September 30, 2008, and for other purposes.	Bill Passed (88-7)	Yea	Not Voting

VOTE No.	SES-SION	DATE	VOTE QUESTION Description	RESULT	OBAMA'S POSTION	MCCAIN'S POSTION
337	1	9/18/07	On the Amendment S.Amdt. 2888 to H.R. 1124 (No short title on file) To prohibit the Federal Government from favoring public colleges and universities over private colleges and universities under the District of Columbia College Access Act of 1999.	Amendment Rejected (38-59)	Not Voting	Yea
338	1	9/18/07	On Passage of the Bill H.R. 1124 A bill to extend the District of Columbia College Access Act of 1999.	Bill Passed (96-0)	Not Voting	Yea
339	1	9/18/07	On Cloture on the Motion to Proceed S. 1257 A bill to provide the District of Columbia a voting seat and the State of Utah an additional seat in the House of Representatives.	Cloture on the Motion to Proceed Rejected (57-42, 3/5 majority required)	Yea	Nay
340	1	9/19/07	On the Cloture Motion S.Amdt. 2022 to S.Amdt. 2011 to H.R. 1585 (National Defense Authorization Act for Fiscal Year 2008) To restore habeas corpus for those detained by the United States.	Cloture Motion Rejected (56-43, 3/5 majority required)	Yea	Nay
341	1	9/19/07	On the Amendment S.Amdt. 2909 to S.Amdt. 2011 to H.R. 1585 (National Defense Authorization Act for Fiscal Year 2008) To specify minimum periods between deployment of units and members of the Armed Forces deployed for Operation Iraqi Freedom and Operation Enduring Freedom.	Amendment Rejected (56-44, 3/5 majority required)	Yea	Nay
342	1	9/19/07	On the Amendment S.Amdt. 2918 to S.Amdt. 2011 to H.R. 1585 (National Defense Authorization Act for Fiscal Year 2008) To express the sense of Congress on Department of Defense policy regarding dwell time.	Amendment Rejected (55-45, 3/5 majority required)	Nay	Yea

VOTE No.	SES-SION	DATE	VOTE QUESTION *Description*	RESULT	OBAMA'S POSTION	MCCAIN'S POSTION
343	1	9/20/07	On the Amendment S.Amdt. 2947 to S.Amdt. 2011 to H.R. 1585 (National Defense Authorization Act for Fiscal Year 2008) To reaffirm strong support for all the men and women of the United States Armed Forces and to strongly condemn attacks on the honor, integrity, and patriotism of any individual who is serving or has served honorably in the United States Armed Forces, by any person or organization.	Amendment Rejected (50-47, 3/5 majority required)	Yea	Nay
344	1	9/20/07	On the Amendment S.Amdt. 2934 to S.Amdt. 2011 to H.R. 1585 (National Defense Authorization Act for Fiscal Year 2008) To express the sense of the Senate that General David H. Petraeus, Commanding General, Multi-National Force-Iraq, deserves the full support of the Senate and strongly condemn personal attacks on the honor and integrity of General Petraeus and all members of the United States Armed Forces.	Amendment Agreed to (72-25, 3/5 majority required)	Not Voting	Yea
345	1	9/20/07	On the Amendment S.Amdt. 2924 to S.Amdt. 2011 to H.R. 1585 (National Defense Authorization Act for Fiscal Year 2008) To safely redeploy United States troops from Iraq.	Amendment Rejected (28-70, 3/5 majority required)	Yea	Nay
346	1	9/21/07	On the Amendment S.Amdt. 2898 to S.Amdt. 2011 to H.R. 1585 (National Defense Authorization Act for Fiscal Year 2008) To provide for a reduction and transition of United States forces in Iraq.	Amendment Rejected (47-47, 3/5 majority required)	Yea	Nay

VOTE No.	SES-SION	DATE	VOTE QUESTION Description	RESULT	OBAMA'S POSTION	MCCAIN'S POSTION
347	1	9/24/07	On the Conference Report H.R. 1495 A bill to provide for the conservation and development of water and related resources, to authorize the Secretary of the Army to construct various projects for improvements to rivers and harbors of the United States, and for other purposes.	Conference Report Agreed to (81-12)	Not Voting	Not Voting
348	1	9/26/07	On the Amendment S.Amdt. 2997 to S.Amdt. 2011 to H.R. 1585 (National Defense Authorization Act for Fiscal Year 2008) To express the sense of Congress on federalism in Iraq.	Amendment Agreed to (75-23, 3/5 majority required)	Not Voting	Not Voting
349	1	9/26/07	On the Amendment S.Amdt. 3017 to S.Amdt. 2011 to H.R. 1585 (National Defense Authorization Act for Fiscal Year 2008) To express the sense of the Senate regarding Iran.	Amendment Agreed to (76-22, 3/5 majority required)	Not Voting	Not Voting
350	1	9/27/07	On the Cloture Motion S.Amdt. 3035 to H.R. 1585 (National Defense Authorization Act for Fiscal Year 2008) To provide Federal assistance to States, local jurisdictions, and Indian tribes to prosecute hate crimes, and for other purposes.	Cloture Motion Agreed to (60-39, 3/5 majority required)	Yea	Not Voting
351	1	9/27/07	On the Amendment S.Amdt. 3047 to S.Amdt. 2011 to H.R. 1585 (National Defense Authorization Act for Fiscal Year 2008) To require comprehensive study and support for criminal investigations and prosecutions by State and local law enforcement officials.	Amendment Agreed to (96-3)	Yea	Not Voting

Vote No.	Ses-sion	Date	Vote Question Description	Result	Obama's Postion	McCain's Postion
352	1	9/27/07	On the Cloture Motion H.R. 976 An act to amend title XXI of the Social Security Act to extend and improve the Children's Health Insurance Program, and for other purposes.	Cloture Motion Agreed to (69-30, 3/5 majority required)	Yea	Not Voting
353	1	9/27/07	On the Motion (Motion to Concur in the Amendments of the House to the Amendments of the Senate to H.R.976) An act to amend title XXI of the Social Security Act to extend and improve the Children's Health Insurance Program, and for other purposes.	Motion Agreed to (67-29)	Not Voting	Not Voting
354	1	9/27/07	On the Joint Resolution H.J.Res. 43 A joint resolution increasing the statutory limit on the public debt.	Joint Resolution Passed (53-42)	Not Voting	Not Voting
355	1	9/27/07	On the Joint Resolution H.J.Res. 52 A joint resolution making continuing appropriations for the fiscal year 2008, and for other purposes.	Joint Resolution Passed (94-1)	Not Voting	Not Voting
356	1	9/27/07	On the Amendment S.Amdt. 2196 to S.Amdt. 2011 to H.R. 1585 (National Defense Authorization Act for Fiscal Year 2008) To eliminate wasteful spending and improve the management of counter-drug intelligence.	Amendment Rejected (26-69)	Not Voting	Not Voting
357	1	9/27/07	On the Cloture Motion S.Amdt. 2011 to H.R. 1585 (National Defense Authorization Act for Fiscal Year 2008) In the nature of a substitute.	Cloture Motion Agreed to (89-6, 3/5 majority required)	Not Voting	Not Voting
358	1	10/01/07	On the Amendment S.Amdt. 3058 to S.Amdt. 2011 to H.R. 1585 (National Defense Authorization Act for Fiscal Year 2008) To provide for certain public-private competition requirements.	Amendment Agreed to (51-44)	Not Voting	Not Voting

VOTE No.	SES-SION	DATE	VOTE QUESTION *Description*	RESULT	OBAMA'S POSTION	MCCAIN'S POSTION
359	1	10/01/07	On Passage of the Bill H.R. 1585 To authorize appropriations for fiscal year 2008 for military activities of the Department of Defense, for military construction, and for defense activities of the Department of Energy, to prescribe military personnel strengths for such fiscal year, and for other purposes.	Bill Passed (92-3)	Not Voting	Not Voting
360	1	10/02/07	On the Motion to Table S.Amdt. 3126 to H.R. 3222 (Department of Defense Appropriations Act, 2008) To prohibit waivers for enlistment in the Armed Forces of individuals with certain felony offenses.	Motion to Table Agreed to (53-41)	Not Voting	Not Voting
361	1	10/03/07	On the Amendment S.Amdt. 3117 to H.R. 3222 (Department of Defense Appropriations Act, 2008) To improve the security of United States borders.	Amend-ment Agreed to (95-1)	Not Voting	Not Voting
362	1	10/03/07	On the Amendment S.Amdt. 3164 to H.R. 3222 (Department of Defense Appropriations Act, 2008) To safely redeploy United States troops from Iraq.	Amend-ment Rejected (28-68, 3/5 majority required)	Not Voting	Not Voting
363	1	10/04/07	On the Motion to Table S.Amdt. 3243 to H.R. 3093 (Commerce, Justice, Science, and Related Agencies Appropriations Act, 2008) To provide $1,680,000 to investigate and prosecute unsolved civil rights crimes in a fiscally responsible manner by prioritizing spending.	Motion to Table Agreed to (61-31)	Not Voting	Nay

Vote No.	Ses-sion	Date	Vote Question *Description*	Result	Obama's Postion	McCain's Postion
364	1	10/15/07	On the Amendment S.Amdt. 3260 to H.R. 3093 (Commerce, Justice, Science, and Related Agencies Appropriations Act, 2008) To prohibit the use of any funds made available in this Act in a manner that is inconsistent with the trade remedy laws of the United States, and for other purposes.	Amendment Agreed to (85-3)	Not Voting	Yea
365	1	10/16/07	On the Amendment S.Amdt. 3289 to H.R. 3093 (Commerce, Justice, Science, and Related Agencies Appropriations Act, 2008) To prevent Federal employees from purchasing unnecessary first-class or premium-class airline tickets at taxpayers' expense.	Amendment Agreed to (90-0)	Not Voting	Yea
366	1	10/16/07	On the Amendment S.Amdt. 3294 to H.R. 3093 (Commerce, Justice, Science, and Related Agencies Appropriations Act, 2008) To increase funding for the United States Marshals Service to ensure full funding for the Adam Walsh Child Protection and Safety Act of 2006 and offset the increase by reducing funding for the Advanced Technology Program.	Amendment Agreed to (91-0)	Not Voting	Yea
367	1	10/16/07	On the Motion to Table S.Amdt. 3295 to H.R. 3093 (Commerce, Justice, Science, and Related Agencies Appropriations Act, 2008) To increase funding for the State Criminal Alien Assistance Program and offset the increase by reducing NASA funding.	Motion to Table Agreed to (68-25)	Not Voting	Nay

Vote No.	Session	Date	Vote Question Description	Result	Obama's Postion	McCain's Postion
368	1	10/16/07	On the Motion to Table S.Amdt. 3317 to H.R. 3093 (Commerce, Justice, Science, and Related Agencies Appropriations Act, 2008) To provide, in a fiscally responsible manner, additional funding for United States attorneys to prosecute violent crimes in Indian country.	Motion to Table Agreed to (62-31)	Not Voting	Nay
369	1	10/16/07	On the Motion to Table S.Amdt. 3313 to H.R. 3093 (Commerce, Justice, Science, and Related Agencies Appropriations Act, 2008) To set aside $75,000,000 of the funds appropriated under the heading State and Local Law Enforcement Assistance for activities that support State and local law enforcement agencies in their efforts to assist the Federal Government's enforcement of immigration laws.	Motion to Table Agreed to (50-42)	Not Voting	Nay
370	1	10/16/07	On the Motion to Table S.Amdt. 3277 to H.R. 3093 (Commerce, Justice, Science, and Related Agencies Appropriations Act, 2008) To prohibit funds from being used in contravention of section 642(a) of the Illegal Immigration Reform and Immigrant Responsibility Act of 1996.	Motion to Table Agreed to (52-42)	Not Voting	Nay
371	1	10/16/07	On the Motion (Motion to Commit H.R.3093 to the Committee on Appropriations, with Instructions) A bill making appropriations for the Departments of Commerce and Justice, and Science, and Related Agencies for the fiscal year ending September 30, 2008, and for other purposes.	Motion Rejected (44-50)	Not Voting	Yea

Vote No.	Ses-sion	Date	Vote Question *Description*	Result	Obama's Postion	McCain's Postion
372	1	10/16/07	On Passage of the Bill H.R. 3093 A bill making appropriations for the Departments of Commerce and Justice, and Science, and Related Agencies for the fiscal year ending September 30, 2008, and for other purposes.	Bill Passed (75-19)	Not Voting	Nay
373	1	10/18/07	On the Amendment S.Amdt. 3338 to S.Amdt. 3325 to H.R. 3043 (Departments of Labor, Health and Human Services, and Education, and Related Agencies Appropriations Act, 2008) To provide a limitation on funds with respect to the Charles B. Rangel Center for Public Service.	Amend-ment Rejected (34-61)	Not Voting	Not Voting
374	1	10/18/07	On the Amendment S.Amdt. 3368 to S.Amdt. 3325 to H.R. 3043 (Departments of Labor, Health and Human Services, and Education, and Related Agencies Appropriations Act, 2008) To provide funding for activities to reduce infections from methicillin-resistant staphylococcus aureus (MRSA) and related infections.	Amend-ment Agreed to (90-3)	Not Voting	Not Voting
375	1	10/18/07	On the Amendment S.Amdt. 3362 to S.Amdt. 3325 to H.R. 3043 (Departments of Labor, Health and Human Services, and Education, and Related Agencies Appropriations Act, 2008) To increase funding for the Mine Safety and Health Administration.	Amend-ment Agreed to (89-4)	Not Voting	Not Voting
376	1	10/18/07	On the Amendment S.Amdt. 3348 to S.Amdt. 3325 to H.R. 3043 (Departments of Labor, Health and Human Services, and Education, and Related Agencies Appropriations Act, 2008) To provide funding for the Underground Railroad Educational and Cultural Program.	Amend-ment Agreed to (81-12)	Not Voting	Not Voting

Vote No.	Ses-sion	Date	Vote Question Description	Result	Obama's Postion	McCain's Postion
377	1	10/18/07	On the Motion to Table S.Amdt. 3321 to S.Amdt. 3325 to H.R. 3043 (Departments of Labor, Health and Human Services, and Education, and Related Agencies Appropriations Act, 2008) To provide additional care for pregnant women, mothers, and infants by eliminating a $1,000,000 earmark for a museum dedicated to Woodstock.	Motion to Table Failed (42-52)	Not Voting	Not Voting
378	1	10/18/07	On the Amendment S.Amdt. 3395 to S.Amdt. 3325 to H.R. 3043 (Departments of Labor, Health and Human Services, and Education, and Related Agencies Appropriations Act, 2008) To clarify the application of current law.	Amendment Agreed to (68-25)	Not Voting	Yea
379	1	10/18/07	On the Amendment S.Amdt. 3330 to S.Amdt. 3325 to H.R. 3043 (Departments of Labor, Health and Human Services, and Education, and Related Agencies Appropriations Act, 2008) To prohibit the provision of funds to grantees who perform abortions.	Amendment Rejected (41-52)	Not Voting	Yea
380	1	10/18/07	On the Amendment S.Amdt. 3373 to S.Amdt. 3325 to H.R. 3043 (Departments of Labor, Health and Human Services, and Education, and Related Agencies Appropriations Act, 2008) To increase the amount of funds available for the Office of Labor Management Standards.	Amendment Rejected (46-47)	Not Voting	Yea

Vote No.	Ses-sion	Date	Vote Question *Description*	Result	Obama's Postion	McCain's Postion
381	1	10/22/07	On the Motion to Table S.Amdt. 3369 to S.Amdt. 3325 to H.R. 3043 (Departments of Labor, Health and Human Services, and Education, and Related Agencies Appropriations Act, 2008) To reduce the total amount appropriated to any program that is rated ineffective by the Office of Management and Budget through the Program Assessment Rating Tool (PART).	Motion to Table Agreed to (68-21)	Not Voting	Not Voting
382	1	10/22/07	On the Amendment S.Amdt. 3347 to S.Amdt. 3325 to H.R. 3043 (Departments of Labor, Health and Human Services, and Education, and Related Agencies Appropriations Act, 2008) To provide funding for the activities under the Patient Navigator Outreach and Chronic Disease Prevention Act of 2005.	Amendment Agreed to (88-3)	Not Voting	Not Voting
383	1	10/23/07	On the Amendment S.Amdt. 3437 to S.Amdt. 3325 to H.R. 3043 (Departments of Labor, Health and Human Services, and Education, and Related Agencies Appropriations Act, 2008) To prohibit the use of funds to modify certain HIV/AIDS funding formulas.	Amendment Agreed to (65-28)	Not Voting	Not Voting
384	1	10/23/07	On the Motion to Table S.Amdt. 3358 to S.Amdt. 3325 to H.R. 3043 (Departments of Labor, Health and Human Services, and Education, and Related Agencies Appropriations Act, 2008) To require Congress to provide health care for all children in the U.S. before funding special interest pork projects.	Motion to Table Agreed to (68-26)	Not Voting	Not Voting

Vote No.	Ses-sion	Date	Vote Question Description	Result	Obama's Postion	McCain's Postion
385	1	10/23/07	On the Motion to Table S.Amdt. 3387 to S.Amdt. 3325 to H.R. 3043 (Departments of Labor, Health and Human Services, and Education, and Related Agencies Appropriations Act, 2008) To replace non-competitive earmarks for the AFL-CIO with competitive grants.	Motion to Table Agreed to (60-34)	Not Voting	Not Voting
386	1	10/23/07	On the Amendment S.Amdt. 3400 to S.Amdt. 3325 to H.R. 3043 (Departments of Labor, Health and Human Services, and Education, and Related Agencies Appropriations Act, 2008) To provide support to Iraqis and Afghans who arrives in the United States under the Special Immigrant Visa program.	Amendment Agreed to (92-0)	Not Voting	Not Voting
387	1	10/23/07	On the Amendment S.Amdt. 3342 to S.Amdt. 3325 to H.R. 3043 (Departments of Labor, Health and Human Services, and Education, and Related Agencies Appropriations Act, 2008) To prohibit the use of funds to administer Social Security benefit payments under a totalization agreement with Mexico.	Amendment Agreed to (91-3)	Not Voting	Not Voting
388	1	10/23/07	On the Amendment S.Amdt. 3352 to S.Amdt. 3325 to H.R. 3043 (Departments of Labor, Health and Human Services, and Education, and Related Agencies Appropriations Act, 2008) To prohibit the use of funds to process claims based on illegal work for purposes of receiving Social Security benefits.	Amendment Agreed to (92-2)	Not Voting	Not Voting

VOTE No.	SES-SION	DATE	VOTE QUESTION *Description*	RESULT	OBAMA'S POSTION	MCCAIN'S POSTION
389	1	10/23/07	On the Amendment S.Amdt. 3440 to S.Amdt. 3325 to H.R. 3043 (Departments of Labor, Health and Human Services, and Education, and Related Agencies Appropriations Act, 2008) Of a perfecting nature.	Amendment Agreed to (88-6)	Not Voting	Not Voting
390	1	10/23/07	On the Motion (McConnell Motion to Commit H.R. 3043 to the Committee on Appropriations, with Instructions) A bill making appropriations for the Departments of Labor, Health and Human Services, and Education, and related agencies for the fiscal year ending September 30, 2008, and for other purposes.	Motion Rejected (40-54)	Not Voting	Not Voting
391	1	10/23/07	On Passage of the Bill H.R. 3043 A bill making appropriations for the Departments of Labor, Health and Human Services, and Education, and related agencies for the fiscal year ending September 30, 2008, and for other purposes.	Bill Passed (75-19)	Not Voting	Not Voting
392	1	10/24/07	On the Cloture Motion PN2 Leslie Southwick, of Mississippi, to be United States Circuit Judge for the Fifth Circuit	Cloture Motion Agreed to (62-35, 3/5 majority required)	Nay	Yea
393	1	10/24/07	On the Nomination PN2 Leslie Southwick, of Mississippi, to be United States Circuit Judge for the Fifth Circuit	Nomination Confirmed (59-38)	Nay	Yea
394	1	10/24/07	On the Cloture Motion S. 2205 A bill to authorize the cancellation of removal and adjustment of status of certain alien students who are long-term United States residents and who entered the United States as children, and for other purposes.	Cloture Motion Rejected (52-44, 3/5 majority required)	Yea	Not Voting

VOTE No.	SES-SION	DATE	VOTE QUESTION Description	RESULT	OBAMA'S POSTION	MCCAIN'S POSTION
395	1	10/25/07	On the Amendment S.Amdt. 3453 to S. 294 (Passenger Rail Investment and Improvement Act of 2007) To prohibit Federal subsidies in excess of specified amounts on any Amtrak train route.	Amendment Rejected (28-66)	Not Voting	Not Voting
396	1	10/25/07	On the Amendment S.Amdt. 3456 to S. 294 (Passenger Rail Investment and Improvement Act of 2007) To remove the limitation on the number of Amtrak routes available for competitive bid.	Amendment Rejected (27-64)	Not Voting	Not Voting
397	1	10/30/07	On the Amendment S.Amdt. 3474 to S. 294 (Passenger Rail Investment and Improvement Act of 2007) To require Amtrak to regularly report to Congress on the profits or losses relating to the provision of food and beverage service and to limit such service on Amtrak rail lines that incur losses.	Amendment Rejected (24-67)	Not Voting	Not Voting
398	1	10/30/07	On the Cloture Motion S. 294 A bill to reauthorize Amtrak, and for other purposes.	Cloture Motion Agreed to (79-13, 3/5 majority required)	Not Voting	Not Voting
399	1	10/30/07	On the Amendment S.Amdt. 3467 to S. 294 (Passenger Rail Investment and Improvement Act of 2007) To require Amtrak to disclose the Federal subsidy of every ticket sold for transportation on Amtrak.	Amendment Rejected (27-65)	Not Voting	Not Voting
400	1	10/30/07	On Passage of the Bill S. 294 A bill to reauthorize Amtrak, and for other purposes.	Bill Passed (70-22)	Not Voting	Not Voting

Vote No.	Session	Date	Vote Question Description	Result	Obama's Postion	McCain's Postion
401	1	10/31/07	On the Cloture Motion H.R. 3963 A bill to amend title XXI of the Social Security Act to extend and improve the Children's Health Insurance Program, and for other purposes.	Cloture Motion Agreed to (62-33, 3/5 majority required)	Not Voting	Nay
402	1	11/01/07	On the Cloture Motion H.R. 3963 A bill to amend title XXI of the Social Security Act to extend and improve the Children's Health Insurance Program, and for other purposes.	Cloture Motion Agreed to (65-30, 3/5 majority required)	Not Voting	Not Voting
403	1	11/01/07	On Passage of the Bill H.R. 3963 A bill to amend title XXI of the Social Security Act to extend and improve the Children's Health Insurance Program, and for other purposes.	Bill Passed (64-30)	Not Voting	Not Voting
404	1	11/07/07	On the Motion (Motion to Waive Rule XXVIII, Paragraph 3, Re: H.R. 3043 Conference Report) A bill making appropriations for the Departments of Labor, Health and Human Services, and Education, and related agencies for the fiscal year ending September 30, 2008, and for other purposes.	Motion Rejected (47-46, 3/5 majority required)	Not Voting	Not Voting
405	1	11/07/07	On the Motion (Motion to Recede and Amend the Bill) A bill making appropriations for the Departments of Labor, Health and Human Services, and Education, and related agencies for the fiscal year ending September 30, 2008, and for other purposes.	Motion Agreed to (56-37)	Not Voting	Not Voting
406	1	11/08/07	On Overriding the Veto H.R. 1495 A bill to provide for the conservation and development of water and related resources, to authorize the Secretary of the Army to construct various projects for improvements to rivers and harbors of the United States, and for other purposes.	Veto Overridden (79-14, 2/3 majority required)	Not Voting	Not Voting

Vote No.	Session	Date	Vote Question Description	Result	Obama's Position	McCain's Postion
407	1	11/08/07	On the Nomination PN958 Michael B. Mukasey, of New York, to be Attorney General	Nomination Confirmed (53-40)	Not Voting	Not Voting
408	1	11/13/07	On the Nomination PN776 Robert M. Dow, Jr., of Illinois, to be United States District Judge for the Northern District of Illinois	Nomination Confirmed (86-0)	Not Voting	Not Voting
409	1	11/14/07	On the Conference Report H.R. 1429 A bill to reauthorize the Head Start Act, to improve program quality, to expand access, and for other purposes.	Conference Report Agreed to (95-0)	Not Voting	Not Voting
410	1	11/16/07	On the Cloture Motion S. 2340 A bill making emergency supplemental appropriations for the Department of Defense for the fiscal year ending September 30, 2008, and for other purposes.	Cloture Motion Rejected (45-53, 3/5 majority required)	Nay	Not Voting
411	1	11/16/07	On the Cloture Motion H.R. 4156 A bill making emergency supplemental appropriations for the Department of Defense for the fiscal year ending September 30, 2008, and for other purposes.	Cloture Motion Rejected (53-45, 3/5 majority required)	Yea	Not Voting
412	1	11/16/07	On the Cloture Motion S.Amdt. 3500 to H.R. 2419 (Farm, Nutrition, and Bioenergy Act of 2007) In the nature of a substitute.	Cloture Motion Rejected (55-42, 3/5 majority required)	Yea	Not Voting
413	1	12/04/07	On Passage of the Bill H.R. 3688 A bill to implement the United States-Peru Trade Promotion Agreement.	Bill Passed (77-18)	Not Voting	Not Voting
414	1	12/06/07	On the Cloture Motion H.R. 3996 A bill to amend the Internal Revenue Code of 1986 to extend certain expiring provisions, and for other purposes.	Cloture Motion Rejected (46-48, 3/5 majority required)	Not Voting	Not Voting

Vote No.	Session	Date	Vote Question Description	Result	Obama's Position	McCain's Position
415	1	12/06/07	**On Passage of the Bill H.R. 3996** A bill to amend the Internal Revenue Code of 1986 to extend certain expiring provisions, and for other purposes.	Bill Passed (88-5)	Not Voting	Not Voting
416	1	12/07/07	**On the Cloture Motion H.R. 6** An Act to move the United States toward greater energy independence and security, to increase the production of clean renewable fuels, to protect consumers, to increase the efficiency of products, buildings, and vehicles, to promote research on and deploy greenhouse gas capture and storage options, and to improve the energy performance of the Federal Government, and for other purposes.	Cloture Motion Rejected (53-42, 3/5 majority required)	Yea	Not Voting
417	1	12/11/07	**On the Amendment S.Amdt. 3711 to S.Amdt. 3500 to H.R. 2419 (Farm, Nutrition, and Bioenergy Act of 2007)** Relative to traditional payments and loans.	Amendment Rejected (37-58)	Not Voting	Not Voting
418	1	12/12/07	**On the Amendment S.Amdt. 3671 to S.Amdt. 3500 to H.R. 2419 (Farm, Nutrition, and Bioenergy Act of 2007)** To strike the section requiring the establishment of a Farm and Ranch Stress Assistance Network.	Amendment Rejected (37-58)	Not Voting	Not Voting
419	1	12/12/07	**On the Amendment S.Amdt. 3672 to S.Amdt. 3500 to H.R. 2419 (Farm, Nutrition, and Bioenergy Act of 2007)** To strike a provision relating to market loss assistance for asparagus producers.	Amendment Rejected (39-56)	Not Voting	Not Voting
420	1	12/12/07	**On the Amendment S.Amdt. 3551 to S.Amdt. 3500 to H.R. 2419 (Farm, Nutrition, and Bioenergy Act of 2007)** To increase funding for the Initiative for Future Agriculture and Food Systems, with an offset.	Amendment Rejected (19-75)	Not Voting	Not Voting

VOTE No.	SES-SION	DATE	VOTE QUESTION Description	RESULT	OBAMA'S POSTION	MCCAIN'S POSTION
421	1	12/12/07	On the Amendment S.Amdt. 3553 to S.Amdt. 3500 to H.R. 2419 (Farm, Nutrition, and Bioenergy Act of 2007) To limit the tax credit for small wind energy property expenditures to property placed in service in connection with a farm or rural small business.	Amendment Rejected (14-79)	Not Voting	Not Voting
422	1	12/12/07	On the Amendment S.Amdt. 3673 to S.Amdt. 3500 to H.R. 2419 (Farm, Nutrition, and Bioenergy Act of 2007) To improve women's access to heath care services in rural areas and provide improved medical care by reducing the excessive burden the liability system places on the delivery of obstetrical and gynecological services.	Amendment Rejected (41-53, 3/5 majority required)	Not Voting	Not Voting
423	1	12/12/07	On the Amendment S.Amdt. 3596 to S.Amdt. 3500 to H.R. 2419 (Farm, Nutrition, and Bioenergy Act of 2007) To amend the Internal Revenue Code of 1986 to establish a pilot program under which agricultural producers may establish and contribute to tax-exempt farm savings accounts in lieu of obtaining federally subsidized crop insurance or noninsured crop assistance, to provide for contributions to such accounts by the Secretary of Agriculture, to specify the situations in which amounts may be paid to producers from such accounts, and to limit the total amount of such distributions to a producer during a taxable year, and for other purposes.	Amendment Rejected (35-58)	Not Voting	Not Voting
424	1	12/13/07	On the Amendment S.Amdt. 3695 to S.Amdt. 3500 to H.R. 2419 (Farm, Nutrition, and Bioenergy Act of 2007) To strengthen payment limitations and direct the savings to increase funding for certain programs.	Amendment Rejected (56-43, 3/5 majority required)	Yea	Not Voting

Vote No.	Session	Date	Vote Question Description	Result	Obama's Postion	McCain's Postion
425	1	12/13/07	On the Cloture Motion H.R. 6 An Act to move the United States toward greater energy independence and security, to increase the production of clean renewable fuels, to protect consumers, to increase the efficiency of products, buildings, and vehicles, to promote research on and deploy greenhouse gas capture and storage options, and to improve the energy performance of the Federal Government, and for other purposes.	Cloture Motion Rejected (59-40, 3/5 majority required)	Yea	Not Voting
426	1	12/13/07	On the Amendment S.Amdt. 3810 to S.Amdt. 3500 to H.R. 2419 (Farm, Nutrition, and Bioenergy Act of 2007) To improve the adjusted gross income limitation and use the savings to provide additional funding for certain programs and reduce the Federal deficit.	Amendment Rejected (48-47, 3/5 majority required)	Not Voting	Not Voting
427	1	12/13/07	On the Amendment S.Amdt. 3666 to S.Amdt. 3500 to H.R. 2419 (Farm, Nutrition, and Bioenergy Act of 2007) To modify the provisions relating to unlawful practices under the Packers and Stockyards Act.	Amendment Rejected (40-55, 3/5 majority required)	Not Voting	Not Voting
428	1	12/13/07	On the Amendment S.Amdt. 3819 to S.Amdt. 3500 to H.R. 2419 (Farm, Nutrition, and Bioenergy Act of 2007) To increase funding for critical Farm Bill programs and improve crop insurance.	Amendment Rejected (32-63, 3/5 majority required)	Not Voting	Not Voting
429	1	12/13/07	On the Amendment S.Amdt. 3640 to S.Amdt. 3500 to H.R. 2419 (Farm, Nutrition, and Bioenergy Act of 2007) To prohibit the involuntary acquisition of farmland and grazing land by Federal, State, and local governments for parks, open space, or similar purposes.	Amendment Rejected (37-58, 3/5 majority required)	Not Voting	Not Voting

VOTE No.	SES-SION	DATE	VOTE QUESTION Description	RESULT	OBAMA'S POSTION	MCCAIN'S POSTION
430	1	12/13/07	On the Motion (Motion to Concur in the Amendment of the House to the Amendment of the Senate to the Text of H.R. 6, with an Amendment) An Act to move the United States toward greater energy independence and security, to increase the production of clean renewable fuels, to protect consumers, to increase the efficiency of products, buildings, and vehicles, to promote research on and deploy greenhouse gas capture and storage options, and to improve the energy performance of the Federal Government, and for other purposes.	Motion Agreed to (86-8)	Not Voting	Not Voting
431	1	12/13/07	On the Cloture Motion S.Amdt. 3500 to H.R. 2419 (Farm, Nutrition, and Bioenergy Act of 2007) In the nature of a substitute.	Cloture Motion Agreed to (78-12, 3/5 majority required)	Not Voting	Not Voting
432	1	12/14/07	On Passage of the Bill S. 2338 An original bill to modernize and update the National Housing Act and enable the Federal Housing Administration to more effectively reach underserved borrowers, and for other purposes.	Bill Passed (93-1)	Not Voting	Not Voting
433	1	12/14/07	On the Conference Report H.R. 1585 To authorize appropriations for fiscal year 2008 for military activities of the Department of Defense, for military construction, and for defense activities of the Department of Energy, to prescribe military personnel strengths for such fiscal year, and for other purposes.	Conference Report Agreed to (90-3)	Not Voting	Not Voting
434	1	12/14/07	On Passage of the Bill H.R. 2419 A bill to provide for the continuation of agricultural programs through fiscal year 2012, and for other purposes.	Bill Passed (79-14)	Not Voting	Not Voting

Vote No.	Ses-sion	Date	Vote Question Description	Result	Obama's Postion	McCain's Postion
435	1	12/17/07	On the Cloture Motion S. 2248 An original bill to amend the Foreign Intelligence Surveillance Act of 1978, to modernize and streamline the provisions of that Act, and for other purposes.	Cloture Motion Agreed to (76-10, 3/5 majority required)	Not Voting	Not Voting
436	1	12/18/07	On the Cloture Motion H.R. 2764 A bill making appropriations for the Department of State, foreign operations, and related programs for the fiscal year ending September 30, 2008, and for other purposes.	Cloture Motion Rejected (44-51, 3/5 majority required)	Not Voting	Nay
437	1	12/18/07	On the Amendment S.Amdt. 3875 to S.Amdt. 3874 to H.R. 2764 (Department of State, Foreign Operations, and Related Programs Appropriations Act, 2008) To provide for the safe redeployment of United States troops from Iraq.	Amendment Rejected (24-71, 3/5 majority required)	Not Voting	Nay
438	1	12/18/07	On the Amendment S.Amdt. 3876 to S.Amdt. 3874 to H.R. 2764 (Department of State, Foreign Operations, and Related Programs Appropriations Act, 2008) To express the sense of Congress on the transition of the missions of United States Forces in Iraq to a more limited set of missions as specified by the President on September 13, 2007.	Amendment Rejected (50-45, 3/5 majority required)	Not Voting	Nay
439	1	12/18/07	On the Motion (McConnell Motion to Concur in House Amdt. No. 2 to the Senate Amdt. to H.R. 2764, with an Amdt. No. 3874) A bill making appropriations for the Department of State, foreign operations, and related programs for the fiscal year ending September 30, 2008, and for other purposes.	Motion Agreed to (70-25, 3/5 majority required)	Not Voting	Yea

Vote No.	Session	Date	Vote Question Description	Result	Obama's Postion	McCain's Postion
440	1	12/18/07	On the Motion (Reid Motion to Concur in House Amdt. No. 1 to Senate Amdt. To H.R. 2764, with an Amdt. No. 3877) A bill making appropriations for the Department of State, foreign operations, and related programs for the fiscal year ending September 30, 2008, and for other purposes.	Motion Rejected (48-46, 3/5 majority required)	Not Voting	Not Voting
441	1	12/18/07	On the Motion (Reid Motion to Concur in House Amdt. No. 1 to Senate Amdt. to H.R. 2764) A bill making appropriations for the Department of State, foreign operations, and related programs for the fiscal year ending September 30, 2008, and for other purposes.	Motion Agreed to (76-17)	Not Voting	Not Voting
442	1	12/18/07	On the Nomination PN768 John Daniel Tinder, of Indiana, to be United States Circuit Judge for the Seventh Circuit	Nomination Confirmed (93-0)	Not Voting	Not Voting

2ND SESSION

Vote No.	Session	Date	Vote Question Description	Result	Obama's Postion	McCain's Postion
1	2	1/22/08	On Passage of the Bill H.R. 4986 A bill to provide for the enactment of the National Defense Authorization Act for Fiscal Year 2008, as previously enrolled, with certain modifications to address the foreign sovereign immunities provisions of title 28, United States Code, with respect to the attachment of property in certain judgements against Iraq, the lapse of statutory authorities for the payment of bonuses, special pays, and similar benefits for members of the uniformed services, and for other purposes.	Bill Passed (91-3)	Not Voting	Not Voting
2	2	1/24/08	On the Motion to Table S. 2248 An original bill to amend the Foreign Intelligence Surveillance Act of 1978, to modernize and streamline the provisions of that Act, and for other purposes.	Motion to Table Agreed to (60-36)	Not Voting	Not Voting

Vote No.	Session	Date	Vote Question Description	Result	Obama's Postion	McCain's Postion
3	2	1/28/08	On the Cloture Motion S.Amdt. 3911 to S. 2248 (FISA Amendments Act of 2007) In the nature of a substitute.	Cloture Motion Rejected (48-45, 3/5 majority required)	Nay	Not Voting
4	2	1/28/08	On the Cloture Motion S.Amdt. 3918 to S. 2248 (FISA Amendments Act of 2007) Relative to the extension of the Protect America Act of 2007.	Cloture Motion Rejected (48-45, 3/5 majority required)	Yea	Not Voting
5	2	2/04/08	On the Cloture Motion H.R. 5140 A bill to provide economic stimulus through recovery rebates to individuals, incentives for business investment, and an increase in conforming and FHA loan limits.	Cloture Motion Agreed to (80-4, 3/5 majority required)	Not Voting	Not Voting
6	2	2/05/08	On the Motion (Motion to Instruct Sgt. At Arms) A bill to provide economic stimulus through recovery rebates to individuals, incentives for business investment, and an increase in conforming and FHA loan limits.	Motion Agreed to (73-12)	Not Voting	Not Voting
7	2	2/06/08	On the Amendment S.Amdt. 3930 to S.Amdt. 3911 to S. 2248 (FISA Amendments Act of 2007) To modify the sunset provision.	Amendment Rejected (49-46, 3/5 majority required)	Yea	Not Voting
8	2	2/06/08	On the Cloture Motion S.Amdt. 3983 to H.R. 5140 (Recovery Rebates and Economic Stimulus for the American People Act of 2008) Of a perfecting nature.	Cloture Motion Rejected (58-41, 3/5 majority required)	Yea	Not Voting
9	2	2/07/08	On the Amendment S.Amdt. 4010 to H.R. 5140 (Economic Stimulus Act of 2008) To revise the eligibility criteria for the 2008 recovery rebates for individuals.	Amendment Agreed to (91-6)	Not Voting	Yea

Vote No.	Session	Date	Vote Question Description	Result	Obama's Postion	McCain's Postion
10	2	2/07/08	On Passage of the Bill H.R. 5140 A bill to provide economic stimulus through recovery rebates to individuals, incentives for business investment, and an increase in conforming and FHA loan limits.	Bill Passed (81-16)	Not Voting	Yea
11	2	2/07/08	On the Amendment S.Amdt. 3915 to S.Amdt. 3911 to S. 2248 (FISA Amendments Act of 2007) To place flexible limits on the use of information obtained using unlawful procedures.	Amendment Rejected (40-56)	Not Voting	Not Voting
12	2	2/07/08	On the Amendment S.Amdt. 3913 to S.Amdt. 3911 to S. 2248 (FISA Amendments Act of 2007) To prohibit reverse targeting and protect the rights of Americans who are communicating with people abroad.	Amendment Rejected (38-57)	Not Voting	Not Voting
13	2	2/12/08	On the Amendment S.Amdt. 3910 to S.Amdt. 3911 to S. 2248 (FISA Amendments Act of 2007) To provide a statement of the exclusive means by which electronic surveillance and interception of certain communications may be conducted.	Amendment Rejected (57-41, 3/5 majority required)	Yea	Nay
14	2	2/12/08	On the Amendment S.Amdt. 3979 to S.Amdt. 3911 to S. 2248 (FISA Amendments Act of 2007) To provide safeguards for communications involving persons inside the United States.	Amendment Rejected (35-63)	Yea	Nay
15	2	2/12/08	On the Amendment S.Amdt. 3907 to S.Amdt. 3911 to S. 2248 (FISA Amendments Act of 2007) To strike the provisions providing immunity from civil liability to electronic communication service providers for certain assistance provided to the Government.	Amendment Rejected (31-67)	Yea	Nay

Vote No.	Session	Date	Vote Question / Description	Result	Obama's Postion	McCain's Postion
16	2	2/12/08	On the Amendment S.Amdt. 3912 to S.Amdt. 3911 to S. 2248 (FISA Amendments Act of 2007) To modify the requirements for certifications made prior to the initiation of certain acquisitions.	Amendment Rejected (37-60)	Yea	Nay
17	2	2/12/08	On the Amendment S.Amdt. 3927 to S.Amdt. 3911 to S. 2248 (FISA Amendments Act of 2007) To provide for the substitution of the United States in certain civil actions.	Amendment Rejected (30-68)	Yea	Nay
18	2	2/12/08	On the Amendment S.Amdt. 3919 to S.Amdt. 3911 to S. 2248 (FISA Amendments Act of 2007) To provide for the review of certifications by the Foreign Intelligence Surveillance Court.	Amendment Rejected (41-57, 3/5 majority required)	Yea	Nay
19	2	2/12/08	On the Cloture Motion S. 2248 An original bill to amend the Foreign Intelligence Surveillance Act of 1978, to modernize and streamline the provisions of that Act, and for other purposes.	Cloture Motion Agreed to (69-29, 3/5 majority required)	Nay	Yea
20	2	2/12/08	On Passage of the Bill S. 2248 An original bill to amend the Foreign Intelligence Surveillance Act of 1978, to modernize and streamline the provisions of that Act, and for other purposes.	Bill Passed (68-29)	Not Voting	Yea
21	2	2/13/08	On the Cloture Motion H.R. 2082 A bill to authorize appropriations for fiscal year 2008 for intelligence and intelligence-related activities of the United States Government, the Community Management Account, and the Central Intelligence Agency Retirement and Disability System, and for other purposes.	Cloture Motion Agreed to (92-4, 3/5 majority required)	Not Voting	Yea

VOTE No.	SES-SION	DATE	VOTE QUESTION Description	RESULT	OBAMA'S POSITION	MCCAIN'S POSITION
22	2	2/13/08	On the Conference Report H.R. 2082 A bill to authorize appropriations for fiscal year 2008 for intelligence and intelligence-related activities of the United States Government, the Community Management Account, and the Central Intelligence Agency Retirement and Disability System, and for other purposes.	Conference Report Agreed to (51-45)	Not Voting	Nay
23	2	2/13/08	On the Amendment S.Amdt. 4020 to S.Amdt. 3899 to S. 1200 (Indian Health Care Improvement Act Amendments of 2007) To express the sense of Congress regarding law enforcement and methamphetamine issues in Indian country.	Amendment Agreed to (95-0)	Not Voting	Yea
24	2	2/14/08	On the Amendment S.Amdt. 4082 to S.Amdt. 3899 to S. 1200 (Indian Health Care Improvement Act Amendments of 2007) Of a perfecting nature.	Amendment Agreed to (95-0)	Not Voting	Not Voting
25	2	2/14/08	On the Amendment S.Amdt. 4034 to S.Amdt. 3899 to S. 1200 (Indian Health Care Improvement Act Amendments of 2007) To allow tribal members to make their own health care choices.	Amendment Rejected (28-67)	Not Voting	Not Voting
26	2	2/14/08	On the Amendment S.Amdt. 4036 to S.Amdt. 3899 to S. 1200 (Indian Health Care Improvement Act Amendments of 2007) To prioritize scarce resources to basic medical services for Indians.	Amendment Rejected (21-73)	Not Voting	Not Voting
27	2	2/14/08	On the Amendment S.Amdt. 4032 to S.Amdt. 3899 to S. 1200 (Indian Health Care Improvement Act Amendments of 2007) To protect rape and sexual assault victims from HIV/AIDS and other sexually transmitted diseases.	Amendment Agreed to (94-0)	Not Voting	Not Voting

Vote No.	Session	Date	Vote Question / Description	Result	Obama's Position	McCain's Position
28	2	2/25/08	On the Cloture Motion S.Amdt. 3899 to S. 1200 (Indian Health Care Improvement Act Amendments of 2007) In the nature of a substitute.	Cloture Motion Agreed to (85-2, 3/5 majority required)	Not Voting	Not Voting
29	2	2/25/08	On the Amendment S.Amdt. 4070 to S.Amdt. 3899 to S. 1200 (Indian Health Care Improvement Act Amendments of 2007) Of a perfecting nature.	Amendment Agreed to (78-11)	Not Voting	Not Voting
30	2	2/26/08	On the Amendment S.Amdt. 3896 to S.Amdt. 3899 to S. 1200 (Indian Health Care Improvement Act Amendments of 2007) To modify a section relating to limitation on use of funds appropriated to the Service.	Amendment Agreed to (52-42)	Not Voting	Not Voting
31	2	2/26/08	On the Amendment S.Amdt. 3897 to S.Amdt. 3899 to S. 1200 (Indian Health Care Improvement Act Amendments of 2007) To modify a provision relating to development of innovative approaches.	Amendment Agreed to (56-38)	Not Voting	Not Voting
32	2	2/26/08	On Passage of the Bill S. 1200 A bill to amend the Indian Health Care Improvement Act to revise and extend the Act.	Bill Passed (83-10)	Not Voting	Not Voting
33	2	2/26/08	On the Cloture Motion S. 2633 A bill to provide for the safe redeployment of United States troops from Iraq.	Cloture Motion Agreed to (70-24, 3/5 majority required)	Not Voting	Not Voting
34	2	2/27/08	On the Cloture Motion S. 2634 A bill to require a report setting forth the global strategy of the United States to combat and defeat al Qaeda and its affiliates.	Cloture Motion Agreed to (89-3, 3/5 majority required)	Not Voting	Not Voting

VOTE No.	SES-SION	DATE	VOTE QUESTION Description	RESULT	OBAMA'S POSTION	McCAIN'S POSTION
35	2	2/28/08	On the Cloture Motion H.R. 3221 Moving the United States toward greater energy independence and security, developing innovative new technologies, reducing carbon emissions, creating green jobs, protecting consumers, increasing clean renewable energy production, and modernizing our energy infrastructure, and to amend the Internal Revenue Code of 1986 to provide tax incentives for the production of renewable energy and energy conservation.	Cloture Motion Rejected (48-46, 3/5 majority required)	Not Voting	Not Voting
36	2	3/03/08	On the Motion (Motion to Invoke Cloture on the Motion to Proceed to Consider S. 2663) A bill to reform the Consumer Product Safety Commission to provide greater protection for children's products, to improve the screening of noncompliant consumer products, to improve the effectiveness of consumer product recall programs, and for other purposes.	Motion Agreed to (86-1, 3/5 majority required)	Not Voting	Not Voting
37	2	3/04/08	On the Motion to Table S.Amdt. 4095 to S. 2663 (No short title on file) In the nature of a substitute.	Motion to Table Agreed to (57-39)	Not Voting	Not Voting
38	2	3/05/08	On the Amendment S.Amdt. 4105 to S. 2663 (No short title on file) To authorize appropriations for necessary or appropriate travel, subsistence, and related expenses, and for other purposes.	Amendment Agreed to (96-0)	Not Voting	Not Voting
39	2	3/05/08	On the Motion to Table S.Amdt. 4094 to S. 2663 (No short title on file) To prohibit State attorneys general from entering into contingency fee agreements for legal or expert witness services in certain civil actions relating to Federal consumer product safety rules, regulations, standards, certification or labeling requirements, or orders.	Motion to Table Agreed to (51-45)	Not Voting	Not Voting

Vote No.	Ses- sion	Date	Vote Question Description	Result	Obama's Postion	McCain's Postion
40	2	3/06/08	**On the Motion to Table S.Amdt. 4097 to S. 2663 (No short title on file)** To allow the prevailing party in certain civil actions related to consumer product safety rules to recover attorney fees.	Motion to Table Agreed to (56-39)	Not Voting	Not Voting
41	2	3/06/08	**On Passage of the Bill H.R. 4040** A bill to establish consumer product safety standards and other safety requirements for children's products and to reauthorize and modernize the Consumer Product Safety Commission.	Bill Passed (79-13)	Not Voting	Not Voting
42	2	3/13/08	**On the Amendment S.Amdt. 4160 to S.Con.Res. 70 (No short title on file)** To provide tax relief to middle-class families and small businesses, property tax relief to homeowners, relief to those whose homes were damaged or destroyed by Hurricanes Katrina and Rita, and tax relief to America's troops and veterans.	Amendment Agreed to (99-1)	Yea	Yea
43	2	3/13/08	**On the Amendment S.Amdt. 4170 to S.Con.Res. 70 (No short title on file)** To protect families, family farms and small businesses by extending the income tax rate structure, raising the death tax exemption to $5 million and reducing the maximum death tax rate to no more than 35%; to keep education affordable by extending the college tuition deduction; and to protect senior citizens from higher taxes on their retirement income, maintain U.S. financial market competitiveness, and promote economic growth by extending the lower tax rates on dividends and capital gains.	Amendment Rejected (47-52)	Nay	Yea

VOTE No.	SES-SION	DATE	VOTE QUESTION *Description*	RESULT	OBAMA'S POSTION	McCAIN'S POSTION
44	2	3/13/08	On the Amendment S.Amdt. 4190 to S.Con.Res. 70 (No short title on file) To add a deficit-neutral reserve fund for repealing the 1993 rate increase for the alternative minimum tax for individuals.	Amendment Agreed to (53-46)	Yea	Nay
45	2	3/13/08	On the Amendment S.Amdt. 4189 to S.Con.Res. 70 (No short title on file) To repeal section 13203 of the Omnibus Budget Reconciliation Act of 1993 by restoring the Alternative Minimum Tax rates that had been in effect prior thereto.	Amendment Rejected (49-50)	Nay	Yea
46	2	3/13/08	On the Motion (Motion to Table Motion to Reconsider) To repeal section 13203 of the Omnibus Budget Reconciliation Act of 1993 by restoring the Alternative Minimum Tax rates that had been in effect prior thereto.	Motion Rejected (49-51)	Yea	Nay
47	2	3/13/08	On the Motion to Reconsider S.Amdt. 4189 to S.Con.Res. 70 (No short title on file) To repeal section 13203 of the Omnibus Budget Reconciliation Act of 1993 by restoring the Alternative Minimum Tax rates that had been in effect prior thereto.	Motion to Reconsider Agreed to (50-50, Vice President voted Yea)	Nay	Yea
48	2	3/13/08	On the Amendment S.Amdt. 4189 to S.Con.Res. 70 (No short title on file) To repeal section 13203 of the Omnibus Budget Reconciliation Act of 1993 by restoring the Alternative Minimum Tax rates that had been in effect prior thereto.	Amendment Rejected (49-51)	Nay	Yea
49	2	3/13/08	On the Amendment S.Amdt. 4196 to S.Con.Res. 70 (No short title on file) To reform the estate tax to avoid subjecting thousands of families, family businesses, and family farms and ranches to the estate tax.	Amendment Rejected (38-62)	Yea	Nay

Vote No.	Ses-sion	Date	Vote Question Description	Result	Obama's Postion	McCain's Postion
50	2	3/13/08	On the Amendment S.Amdt. 4191 to S.Con.Res. 70 (No short title on file) To protect small businesses, family ranches and farms from the Death Tax by providing a $5 million exemption, a low rate for smaller estates and a maximum rate no higher than 35%.	Amendment Rejected (50-50)	Nay	Yea
51	2	3/13/08	On the Amendment S.Amdt. 4204 to S.Con.Res. 70 (No short title on file) To add a deficit-neutral reserve fund for repealing the 1993 increase in the income tax on Social Security benefits.	Amendment Agreed to (53-46)	Yea	Nay
52	2	3/13/08	On the Amendment S.Amdt. 4192 to S.Con.Res. 70 (No short title on file) To repeal the tax increase on Social Security benefits imposed by the Omnibus Budget Reconciliation Act of 1993.	Amendment Rejected (47-53)	Nay	Yea
53	2	3/13/08	On the Amendment S.Amdt. 4203 to S.Con.Res. 70 (No short title on file) To increase funding for the National Institutes of Health and the Low Income Home Energy Assistance Program.	Amendment Agreed to (95-4)	Yea	Yea
54	2	3/13/08	On the Amendment S.Amdt. 4198 to S.Con.Res. 70 (No short title on file) To increase the Indian Health Service by $1 billion in FY 2009.	Amendment Agreed to (69-30)	Yea	Yea
55	2	3/13/08	On the Amendment S.Amdt. 4329 to S.Con.Res. 70 (No short title on file) To establish a deficit-neutral reserve fund to improve energy efficiency and production.	Amendment Agreed to (56-43)	Yea	Not Voting
56	2	3/13/08	On the Amendment S.Amdt. 4207 to S.Con.Res. 70 (No short title on file) To establish a deficit-neutral reserve fund to improve energy efficiency and production.	Amendment Rejected (47-51)	Nay	Not Voting

Vote No.	Session	Date	Vote Question / Description	Result	Obama's Postion	McCain's Postion
57	2	3/13/08	**On the Amendment S.Amdt. 4350 to S.Con.Res. 70 (No short title on file)** To increase funding for the Department of Education's English Literacy-Civics Education State Grant program, with an offset.	Amendment Agreed to (95-2)	Not Voting	Not Voting
58	2	3/13/08	**On the Amendment S.Amdt. 4222 to S.Con.Res. 70 (No short title on file)** To take $670,000 used by the EEOC in bringing actions against employers that require their employees to speak English, and instead use the money to teach English to adults through the Department of Education's English Literacy/Civics Education State Grant program.	Amendment Agreed to (54-44)	Nay	Not Voting
59	2	3/13/08	**On the Amendment S.Amdt. 4259 to S.Con.Res. 70 (No short title on file)** To establish a reserve fund for immigration reform and enforcement.	Amendment Agreed to (53-45)	Yea	Not Voting
60	2	3/13/08	**On the Amendment S.Amdt. 4231 to S.Con.Res. 70 (No short title on file)** To establish a deficit-neutral reserve fund for border security, immigration enforcement, and criminal alien removal programs.	Amendment Agreed to (61-37)	Nay	Not Voting
61	2	3/13/08	**On the Motion (Motion to Waive C.B.A. Cornyn Amdt. No. 4242)** To protect the family budget by providing for a budget point of order against legislation that increases income taxes on taxpayers, including hard-working middle-income families, entrepreneurs, and college students.	Motion Rejected (58-40, 3/5 majority required)	Nay	Not Voting
62	2	3/13/08	**On the Amendment S.Amdt. 4246 to S.Con.Res. 70 (No short title on file)** To raise taxes by an unprecedented $1.4 trillion for the purpose of fully funding 111 new or expanded federal spending programs.	Amendment Rejected (0-97)	Nay	Not Voting

Vote No.	Session	Date	Vote Question / Description	Result	Obama's Position	McCain's Position
63	2	3/13/08	On the Amendment S.Amdt. 4240 to S.Con.Res. 70 (No short title on file) To require wealthy Medicare beneficiaries to pay a greater share of their Medicare Part D premiums.	Amendment Rejected (42-56)	Nay	Not Voting
64	2	3/13/08	On the Amendment S.Amdt. 4218 to S.Con.Res. 70 (No short title on file) To put children ahead of millionaires and billionaires by restoring the pre-2001 top income tax rate for people earning over $1 million, and use this revenue to invest in LIHEAP; IDEA; Head Start; Child Care; nutrition; school construction and deficit reduction.	Amendment Rejected (43-55)	Yea	Not Voting
65	2	3/13/08	On the Amendment S.Amdt. 4328 to S.Con.Res. 70 (No short title on file) To provide for a deficit-neutral reserve fund for Social Security reform.	Amendment Rejected (41-57)	Nay	Not Voting
66	2	3/13/08	On the Amendment S.Amdt. 4232 to S.Con.Res. 70 (No short title on file) To pay down the Federal debt and eliminate government waste by reducing spending 5 percent on programs rated (as mandated under the Government Performance and Results Act (Public Law 103-62)) ineffective by the Office of Management and Budget Program Assessment Rating Tool.	Amendment Rejected (29-68)	Nay	Not Voting
67	2	3/13/08	On the Amendment S.Amdt. 4284 to S.Con.Res. 70 (No short title on file) To provide funds for a Commission on Budgetary Accountability and Review of Federal Agencies.	Amendment Agreed to (49-48)	Nay	Not Voting

VOTE No.	SESSION	DATE	VOTE QUESTION Description	RESULT	OBAMA'S POSTION	McCAIN'S POSTION
68	2	3/13/08	On the Amendment S.Amdt. 4197 to S.Con.Res. 70 (No short title on file) To establish a deficit-neutral reserve fund for a 3-year extension of the pilot program for national and State background checks on direct patient access employees of long-term care facilities or providers.	Amendment Agreed to (89-7)	Yea	Not Voting
69	2	3/13/08	On the Motion to Table S.Amdt. 4309 to S.Con.Res. 70 (No short title on file) To create a reserve fund to ensure that Federal assistance does not go to sanctuary cities that ignore the immigration laws of the United States and create safe havens for illegal aliens and potential terrorists.	Motion to Table Agreed to (58-40)	Yea	Not Voting
70	2	3/13/08	On the Amendment S.Amdt. 4368 to S.Con.Res. 70 (No short title on file) To increase funding for the Department of Justice for the vigorous enforcement of laws protecting children.	Amendment Agreed to (90-5)	Yea	Not Voting
71	2	3/13/08	On the Amendment S.Amdt. 4335 to S.Con.Res. 70 (No short title on file) To increase funding for the Department of Justice for the vigorous enforcement of a prohibition against taking minors across State lines in circumvention of laws requiring the involvement of parents in abortion decisions consistent with the Child Custody Protection Act, which passed the Senate by a bipartisan vote of 65-34, with an offset.	Amendment Rejected (49-49)	Nay	Not Voting
72	2	3/13/08	On the Motion (Motion to Waive C.B.A. DeMint Amdt. No. 4340) To create a point of order against bills that would raise gasoline prices.	Motion Rejected (39-59, 3/5 majority required)	Nay	Not Voting

VOTE No.	SES-SION	DATE	VOTE QUESTION *Description*	RESULT	OBAMA'S POSTION	McCAIN'S POSTION
73	2	3/13/08	On the Motion (Motion to Waive C.B.A. Cornyn Amdt. No. 4313) To protect the family budget from runaway Government spending by increasing the number of Senators necessary to waive the PAYGO Point of Order from 60 to 100.	Motion Rejected (27-71, 3/5 majority required)	Nay	Yea
74	2	3/13/08	On the Amendment (Kyl Amdt. No. 4348) To provide certainty to taxpayers by extending expiring tax provisions such as the R&D Tax Credit that helps US companies innovate, combat pay exclusion for our soldiers in the field, the education deduction to make colleges more affordable and the alternative energy incentives to make the environment cleaner through the end of 2009.	Amendment Rejected (50-49)	Nay	Yea
75	2	3/13/08	On the Motion (Motion to Waive C.B.A. DeMint Amdt No. 4347) To establish an earmark moratorium for fiscal year 2009.	Motion Rejected (29-71, 3/5 majority required)	Yea	Yea
76	2	3/13/08	On the Amendment S.Amdt. 4378 to S.Con.Res. 70 (No short title on file) To protect family businesses and farmers without increasing our nation's debt by providing for an estate tax that sets the exemption at $5 million and the rate at 35 percent, with the benefits of the exemption recaptured for estates over $100 million, paid for by closing tax loopholes that allow offshore deferral of compensation and transactions entered into solely for the purpose of avoiding taxation.	Amendment Rejected (23-77)	Nay	Nay
77	2	3/13/08	On the Amendment S.Amdt. 4372 to S.Con.Res. 70 (No short title on file) To protect small businesses, family ranches and farms from the Death Tax by providing a $5 million exemption, a low rate for smaller estates and a maximum rate no higher than 35%.	Amendment Rejected (48-50)	Nay	Yea

Vote No.	Ses-sion	Date	Vote Question Description	Result	Obama's Postion	McCain's Postion
78	2	3/13/08	On the Amendment S.Amdt. 4276 to S.Con.Res. 70 (No short title on file) To exempt from pay-as-you-go enforcement modifications to the individual alternative minimum tax (AMT) that prevent millions of additional taxpayers from having to pay the AMT.	Amendment Rejected (47-51)	Nay	Yea
79	2	3/13/08	On the Amendment S.Amdt. 4380 to S.Con.Res. 70 (No short title on file) To provide for a deficit-neutral reserve fund for transferring funding for Berkeley, CA earmarks to the Marine Corps.	Amendment Rejected (41-57)	Nay	Yea
80	2	3/14/08	On the Amendment S.Amdt. 4379 to S.Con.Res. 70 (No short title on file) To facilitate coverage of pregnant women in SCHIP.	Amendment Agreed to (70-27)	Yea	Yea
81	2	3/14/08	On the Amendment S.Amdt. 4233 to S.Con.Res. 70 (No short title on file) To require that legislation to reauthorize SCHIP include provisions codifying the unborn child regulation.	Amendment Rejected (46-52)	Nay	Yea
82	2	3/14/08	On the Amendment S.Amdt. 4339 to S.Con.Res. 70 (No short title on file) To provide for a deficit-neutral reserve fund for providing an above the line Federal income tax deduction for individuals purchasing health insurance outside the workplace.	Amendment Rejected (45-51)	Nay	Not Voting
83	2	3/14/08	On the Amendment S.Amdt. 4245 to S.Con.Res. 70 (No short title on file) To restore full funding for the international affairs budget, in support of the reconstruction of Iraq and Afghanistan, nuclear nonproliferation, foreign assistance, fighting global AIDS, promoting sustainable development, and other efforts, with an offset.	Amendment Agreed to (73-23)	Yea	Not Voting

Vote No.	Session	Date	Vote Question *Description*	Result	Obama's Position	McCain's Position
84	2	3/14/08	On the Amendment S.Amdt. 4299 to S.Con.Res. 70 (No short title on file) Expressing the sense of the Senate regarding the need for comprehensive legislation to legalize the importation of prescription drugs from highly industrialized countries with safe pharmaceutical infrastructures.	Amendment Agreed to (73-23)	Yea	Not Voting
85	2	3/14/08	On the Concurrent Resolution S.Con. Res. 70 An original concurrent resolution setting forth the congressional budget for the United States Government for fiscal year 2009 and including the appropriate budgetary levels for fiscal years 2008 and 2010 through 2013.	Concurrent Resolution Agreed to (51-44)	Yea	Not Voting
86	2	4/01/08	On the Cloture Motion H.R. 3221 Moving the United States toward greater energy independence and security, developing innovative new technologies, reducing carbon emissions, creating green jobs, protecting consumers, increasing clean renewable energy production, and modernizing our energy infrastructure, and to amend the Internal Revenue Code of 1986 to provide tax incentives for the production of renewable energy and energy conservation.	Cloture Motion Agreed to (94-1, 3/5 majority required)	Not Voting	Not Voting
87	2	4/03/08	On the Resolution S.Res. 501 A resolution honoring the sacrifice of the members of the United States Armed Forces who have been killed in Iraq and Afghanistan.	Resolution Agreed to (95-0)	Not Voting	Not Voting
88	2	4/03/08	On the Motion to Table S.Amdt. 4388 to S.Amdt. 4387 to H.R. 3221 (Renewable Energy and Energy Conservation Tax Act of 2007) To address the treatment of primary mortgages in bankruptcy, and for other purposes.	Motion to Table Agreed to (58-36)	Not Voting	Not Voting

Vote No.	Session	Date	Vote Question *Description*	Result	Obama's Postion	McCain's Postion
89	2	4/03/08	On the Motion (Motion to Waive CBA Murray Amdt. No. 4397) To increase funding for housing counseling resources.	Motion Rejected (44-40, 3/5 majority required)	Not Voting	Not Voting
90	2	4/03/08	On the Motion (Motion to Waive CBA Kyl Amdt. No. 4407) No Statement of Purpose on File.	Motion Rejected (41-44, 3/5 majority required)	Not Voting	Not Voting
91	2	4/04/08	On the Amendment S.Amdt. 4406 to S.Amdt. 4387 to H.R. 3221 (Renewable Energy and Energy Conservation Tax Act of 2007) To protect families most vulnerable to foreclosure due to a sudden loss of income by extending the depreciation incentive to loss companies that have accumulated alternative minimum tax and research and development tax credits.	Amendment Agreed to (76-2)	Not Voting	Not Voting
92	2	4/04/08	On the Motion (Motion to Waive S. Con. Res. 21, sec. 204. Re: Landrieu Amdt. No. 4389, As Further Modified) To amend the Internal Revenue Code of 1986 to allow use of amended income tax returns to take into account receipt of certain hurricane-related casualty loss grants by disallowing previously taken casualty loss deductions and to waive the deadline on the construction of GO Zone property which is eligible for bonus depreciation.	Motion Agreed to (74-5, 3/5 majority required)	Not Voting	Not Voting
93	2	4/08/08	On the Cloture Motion S.Amdt. 4387 to H.R. 3221 (Renewable Energy and Energy Conservation Tax Act of 2007) In the nature of a substitute.	Cloture Motion Agreed to (92-6, 3/5 majority required)	Yea	Yea

Vote No.	Ses-sion	Date	Vote Question Description	Result	Obama's Postion	McCain's Postion
94	2	4/10/08	On the Amendment S.Amdt. 4429 to S.Amdt. 4419 to S.Amdt. 4387 to H.R. 3221 To provide a longer extension of the renewable energy production tax credit and to encourage all emerging renewable sources of electricity, and for other purposes.	Amendment Rejected (15-79)	Not Voting	Not Voting
95	2	4/10/08	On the Amendment S.Amdt. 4419 to S.Amdt. 4387 to H.R. 3221 (Renewable Energy and Energy Conservation Tax Act of 2007) To amend the Internal Revenue Code of 1986 to provide for the limited continuation of clean energy production incentives and incentives to improve energy efficiency in order to prevent a downturn in these sectors that would result from a lapse in the tax law.	Amendment Agreed to (88-8)	Not Voting	Not Voting
96	2	4/10/08	On Passage of the Bill H.R. 3221 A bill to provide needed housing reform and for other purposes.	Bill Passed (84-12)	Not Voting	Not Voting
97	2	4/10/08	On the Amendment S.Amdt. 4522 to S. 2739 (Consolidated Natural Resources Act of 2008) To require the Director of the Office of Management and Budget to determine on an annual basis the quantity of land that is owned by the Federal Government and the cost to taxpayers of the ownership of the land.	Amendment Rejected (30-63)	Not Voting	Not Voting
98	2	4/10/08	On the Amendment S.Amdt. 4521 to S. 2739 (Consolidated Natural Resources Act of 2008) To require approval prior to the assumption of control by the Federal Government of State property.	Amendment Rejected (19-76)	Not Voting	Not Voting

VOTE No.	SES-SION	DATE	VOTE QUESTION Description	RESULT	OBAMA'S POSTION	MCCAIN'S POSTION
99	2	4/10/08	On the Amendment S.Amdt. 4520 to S. 2739 (Consolidated Natural Resources Act of 2008) To ensure that all individuals who reside, or own property that is located, in a proposed National Heritage Area are informed of the designation of the National Heritage Area.	Amendment Rejected (27-67)	Not Voting	Not Voting
100	2	4/10/08	On the Amendment S.Amdt. 4519 to S. 2739 (Consolidated Natural Resources Act of 2008) To require the transfer of certain funds to be used by the Director of the National Park Service to dispose of assets described in the candidate asset disposition list of the National Park Service.	Amendment Rejected (22-73)	Not Voting	Not Voting
101	2	4/10/08	On Passage of the Bill S. 2739 A bill to authorize certain programs and activities in the Department of the Interior, the Forest Service, and the Department of Energy, to implement further the Act approving the Covenant to Establish a Commonwealth of the Northern Mariana Islands in Political Union with the United States of America, to amend the Compact of Free Association Amendments Act of 2003, and for other purposes.	Bill Passed (91-4)	Not Voting	Not Voting
102	2	4/10/08	On the Nomination PN988 Brian Stacy Miller, of Arkansas, to be United States District Judge for the Eastern District of Arkansas	Nomination Confirmed (88-0)	Not Voting	Not Voting
103	2	4/14/08	On the Cloture Motion H.R. 1195 A bill to amend the Safe, Accountable, Flexible, Efficient Transportation Equity Act: A Legacy for Users to make technical corrections, and for other purposes.	Cloture Motion Agreed to (93-1, 3/5 majority required)	Not Voting	Not Voting

Vote No.	Session	Date	Vote Question / Description	Result	Obama's Postion	McCain's Postion
104	2	4/16/08	On the Motion to Table the Motion to Recommit H.R. 1195 A bill to amend the Safe, Accountable, Flexible, Efficient Transportation Equity Act: A Legacy for Users to make technical corrections, and for other purposes.	Motion to Table Motion to Recommit Agreed to (78-18)	Not Voting	Not Voting
105	2	4/17/08	On the Amendment S.Amdt. 4539 to S.Amdt. 4146 to H.R. 1195 (No short title on file) To call for a review by the Department of Justice of allegations of violations of Federal criminal law.	Amendment Agreed to (64-28, 3/5 majority required)	Not Voting	Not Voting
106	2	4/17/08	On the Amendment S.Amdt. 4538 to S.Amdt. 4146 to H.R. 1195 (No short title on file) To create a bipartisan, bicameral special committee to investigate the improper insertion of an earmark for Coconut Road into the conference report of the 2005 highway bill after both chambers of Congress had approved identical versions of the conference report.	Amendment Rejected (49-43, 3/5 majority required)	Not Voting	Not Voting
107	2	4/17/08	On the Cloture Motion S.Amdt. 4146 to H.R. 1195 (No short title on file) In the nature of a substitute.	Cloture Motion Agreed to (90-2, 3/5 majority required)	Not Voting	Not Voting
108	2	4/17/08	On Passage of the Bill H.R. 1195 A bill to amend the Safe, Accountable, Flexible, Efficient Transportation Equity Act: A Legacy for Users to make technical corrections, and for other purposes.	Bill Passed (88-2)	Not Voting	Not Voting
109	2	4/22/08	On the Cloture Motion S. 1315 A bill to amend title 38, United States Code, to enhance life insurance benefits for disabled veterans, and for other purposes.	Cloture Motion Agreed to (94-0, 3/5 majority required)	Not Voting	Not Voting

Vote No.	Session	Date	Vote Question Description	Result	Obama's Postion	McCain's Postion
110	2	4/23/08	On the Cloture Motion H.R. 2831 A bill to amend title VII of the Civil Rights Act of 1964, the Age Discrimination in Employment Act of 1967, the Americans With Disabilities Act of 1990, and the Rehabilitation Act of 1973 to clarify that adiscriminatory compensation decision or other practice that is unlawful under such Acts occurs each time compensation is paid pursuant tothe discriminatory compensation decision or other practice, and for other purposes.	Cloture Motion Rejected (56-42, 3/5 majority required)	Yea	Not Voting
111	2	4/24/08	On the Amendment S.Amdt. 4572 to S. 1315 (Veterans' Benefits Enhancement Act of 2007) To increase benefits for disabled U.S. veterans and provide a fair benefit to World War II Filipino veterans for their service to the United States.	Amendment Rejected (41-56)	Not Voting	Not Voting
112	2	4/24/08	On Passage of the Bill S. 1315 An act to amend title 38, United States Code, to enhance veterans' insurance and housing benefits, to improve benefits and services for transitioning servicemembers, and for other purposes.	Bill Passed (96-1)	Not Voting	Not Voting
113	2	4/24/08	On Passage of the Bill H.R. 493 A bill to prohibit discrimination on the basis of genetic information with respect to health insurance and employment.	Bill Passed (95-0)	Not Voting	Not Voting
114	2	4/28/08	On the Cloture Motion H.R. 2881 A bill to amend title 49, United States Code, to authorize appropriations for the Federal Aviation Administration for fiscal years 2008 through 2011, to improve aviation safety and capacity, to provide stable funding for the national aviation system, and for other purposes.	Cloture Motion Agreed to (88-0, 3/5 majority required)	Not Voting	Not Voting

VOTE No.	SES- SION	DATE	VOTE QUESTION Description	RESULT	OBAMA'S POSTION	MCCAIN'S POSTION
115	2	5/06/08	On the Cloture Motion S.Amdt. 4627 to H.R. 2881 (FAA Reauthorization Act of 2007) In the nature of a substitute.	Cloture Motion Rejected (49-42, 3/5 majority required)	Not Voting	Not Voting
116	2	5/06/08	On the Cloture Motion S. 2284 An original bill to amend the National Flood Insurance Act of 1968, to restore the financial solvency of the flood insurance fund, and for other purposes.	Cloture Motion Agreed to (90-1, 3/5 majority required)	Not Voting	Not Voting
117	2	5/07/08	On the Amendment S.Amdt. 4719 to S.Amdt. 4707 to S. 2284 (Flood Insurance Reform and Modernization Act of 2007) To provide for the optional purchase of insurance against loss resulting from physical damage to or loss of real property or personal property related thereto located in the United States arising from any flood or windstorm.	Amend- ment Rejected (19-74)	Not Voting	Not Voting
118	2	5/07/08	On the Amendment S.Amdt. 4722 to S.Amdt. 4707 to S. 2284 (Flood Insurance Reform and Modernization Act of 2007) To increase maximum coverage limits.	Amend- ment Rejected (27-66)	Not Voting	Not Voting
119	2	5/07/08	On the Amendment S.Amdt. 4723 to S.Amdt. 4707 to S. 2284 (Flood Insurance Reform and Modernization Act of 2007) To allow for a reasonable 5-year phase-in period for adjusted premiums.	Amend- ment Rejected (23-69)	Not Voting	Not Voting
120	2	5/07/08	On the Amendment S.Amdt. 4705 to S.Amdt. 4707 to S. 2284 (Flood Insurance Reform and Modernization Act of 2007) To require the Comptroller General to conduct a study regarding mandatory purchasing requirements.	Amend- ment Rejected (30-62)	Not Voting	Not Voting

VOTE No.	SES-SION	DATE	VOTE QUESTION *Description*	RESULT	OBAMA'S POSTION	MCCAIN'S POSTION
121	2	5/08/08	On the Motion (Motion to Waive S. Con. Res. 21, 110th, Sect. 201, re: Dodd Amdt. No. 4707) In the nature of a substitute.	Motion Agreed to (70-26, 3/5 majority required)	Not Voting	Not Voting
122	2	5/08/08	On the Amendment S.Amdt. 4715 to S.Amdt. 4707 to S. 2284 (Flood Insurance Reform and Modernization Act of 2007) To provide that no changes in flood insurance status for any areas located in the St. Louis District of the Corps of Engineers can go into effect until the remapping process is completed for that entire District.	Amendment Agreed to (68-24)	Not Voting	Not Voting
123	2	5/13/08	On the Amendment S.Amdt. 4720 to S. 2284 (Flood Insurance Reform and Modernization Act of 2007) Of a perfecting nature.	Amendment Rejected (42-56, 3/5 majority required)	Nay	Not Voting
124	2	5/13/08	On the Amendment S.Amdt. 4737 to S.Amdt. 4707 to S. 2284 (Flood Insurance Reform and Modernization Act of 2007) To increase the supply and lower the cost of petroleum by temporarily suspending the acquisition of petroleum for the Strategic Petroleum Reserve.	Amendment Agreed to (97-1, 3/5 majority required)	Yea	Not Voting
125	2	5/13/08	On Passage of the Bill H.R. 3121 A bill to restore the financial solvency of the national flood insurance program and to provide for such program to make available multiperil coverage for damage resulting from windstorms and floods, and for other purposes.	Bill Passed (92-6)	Yea	Not Voting
126	2	5/13/08	On the Cloture Motion H.R. 980 A bill to provide collective bargaining rights for public safety officers employed by States or their political subdivisions.	Cloture Motion Agreed to (69-29, 3/5 majority required)	Yea	Not Voting

Vote No.	Ses-sion	Date	Vote Question *Description*	Result	Obama's Postion	McCain's Postion
127	2	5/14/08	**On the Motion to Table S.Amdt. 4763 to H.R. 980 (Public Safety Employer-Employee Cooperation Act of 2007)** To improve educational assistance for members of the Armed Forces and veterans in order to enhance recruitment and retention for the Armed Forces.	Motion to Table Agreed to (55-42)	Not Voting	Not Voting
128	2	5/15/08	**On the Motion (Motion to Waive S. Con. Res. 21, 110th Congress, sect. 203 re: Conference Report to accompany H.R. 2419)** A bill to provide for the continuation of agricultural programs through fiscal year 2012, and for other purposes.	Motion Agreed to (74-21, 3/5 majority required)	Not Voting	Not Voting
129	2	5/15/08	**On the Motion (Motion to Waive Rule XLIV, 8(a) re: H.R. 2419 Conference Report)** A bill to provide for the continuation of agricultural programs through fiscal year 2012, and for other purposes.	Motion Agreed to (62-34, 3/5 majority required)	Not Voting	Not Voting
130	2	5/15/08	**On the Conference Report H.R. 2419** A bill to provide for the continuation of agricultural programs through fiscal year 2012, and for other purposes.	Conference Report Agreed to (81-15)	Not Voting	Not Voting
131	2	5/15/08	**On the Motion (Gregg Motion to Instruct Conferees (Tax Increase) re: S. Con. Res. 70)** An original concurrent resolution setting forth the congressional budget for the United States Government for fiscal year 2009 and including the appropriate budgetary levels for fiscal years 2008 and 2010 through 2013.	Motion Rejected (44-51)	Not Voting	Not Voting

VOTE No.	SES-SION	DATE	VOTE QUESTION Description	RESULT	OBAMA'S POSTION	MCCAIN'S POSTION
132	2	5/15/08	On the Motion (Boxer Motion to Instruct Conferees (China - India) re: S. Con. Res. 70) An original concurrent resolution setting forth the congressional budget for the United States Government for fiscal year 2009 and including the appropriate budgetary levels for fiscal years 2008 and 2010 through 2013.	Motion Agreed to (55-40)	Not Voting	Not Voting
133	2	5/15/08	On the Motion (DeMint Motion to Instruct Conferees (China - India) re: S. Con. Res. 70) An original concurrent resolution setting forth the congressional budget for the United States Government for fiscal year 2009 and including the appropriate budgetary levels for fiscal years 2008 and 2010 through 2013.	Motion Rejected (34-61)	Not Voting	Not Voting
134	2	5/15/08	On the Motion (Vitter Motion to Instruct Conferees (OCS) re: S. Con. Res. 70) An original concurrent resolution setting forth the congressional budget for the United States Government for fiscal year 2009 and including the appropriate budgetary levels for fiscal years 2008 and 2010 through 2013.	Motion Rejected (44-51)	Not Voting	Not Voting
135	2	5/15/08	On the Motion (Gregg Motion to Instruct Conferees (Discretionary Spending) re: S. Con. Res. 70) An original concurrent resolution setting forth the congressional budget for the United States Government for fiscal year 2009 and including the appropriate budgetary levels for fiscal years 2008 and 2010 through 2013.	Motion Rejected (47-48)	Not Voting	Not Voting

VOTE No.	SES-SION	DATE	VOTE QUESTION Description	RESULT	OBAMA'S POSTION	McCAIN'S POSTION
136	2	5/20/08	On the Nomination PN1484 G. Steven Agee, of Virginia, to be United States Circuit Judge for the Fourth Circuit	Nomina-tion Confirmed (96-0)	Not Voting	Not Voting
137	2	5/22/08	On the Motion (Motion to Concur in the House Amendment No. 2 with Amdt. No. 4803) In the nature of substitute.	Motion Agreed to (75-22, 3/5 majority required)	Yea	Not Voting
138	2	5/22/08	On the Motion (Motion to Concur in the House Amdt. No. 1 to the Senate Amdt. to HR 2642, with an Amdt. No. 4817) In the nature of a substitute.	Motion Rejected (34-63, 3/5 majority required)	Nay	Not Voting
139	2	5/22/08	On the Motion (Motion to Concur to the House Amendment No. 1 to the Senate Amdt. with Amdt. No. 4818) In the nature of a substitute.	Motion Agreed to (70-26, 3/5 majority required)	Not Voting	Not Voting
140	2	5/22/08	On Overriding the Veto H.R. 2419 A bill to provide for the continuation of agricultural programs through fiscal year 2012, and for other purposes.	Veto Over-ridden (82-13, 2/3 majority required)	Not Voting	Not Voting

SUMMARY STATISTICS (AS A PERCENTAGE OF TOTAL VOTES IN THE RELEVANT SESSION)

	% of Senate Votes Obama Participated in	Obama Voted "Yes"	Obama Voted "No"	% of Senate Votes McCain Participated in	McCain Voted "Yes"	McCain Voted "No"	Obama & McCain Both Voted and Voted the Same	Obama & McCain Both Voted but Voted Differently	Obama & McCain Both Did Not Vote
109th Congress, 1st Session	97.81%	75.14%	22.68%	91.26%	45.90%	45.36%	32.24%	57.38%	0.55%
109th Congress, 2nd Session *	98.92%	67.03%	31.90%	90.32%	53.76%	36.56%	44.44%	45.16%	0.36%
110th Congress 1st Session	62.44%	38.91%	23.53%	43.89%	27.83%	16.06%	13.80%	19.91%	27.38%
110th Congress 2nd Session	44.29%	23.57%	20.71%	25.71%	17.14%	8.57%	5.00%	16.43%	51.43%
Combined *	79.22%	54.36%	24.86%	66.50%	37.90%	28.61%	25.26%	36.43%	15.97%

* Senator McCain's statistics for the second session of the 109th Congress are slightly skewed because we were not able to ascertain his vote for one piece of legislation – the 3rd vote of the session. However, as all the other votes are accounted for, just this one vote will not alter statistics in any meaningful manner.

Printed in the United States
128736LV00002B/34/P

9 781604 502497